C G A^m E^m F

+ a lot g descriptions software + web tools —
could have been shifted to web site +
philosophical + general outcomes
expanded on in the book

→ the web — the natural locus g the
Knowledge Age (p211)

See p136 → for hypertext paper
see kolb my p275

NB
ask Sarah to change email address
on PGCert web form

The Knowledge Web

Learning and Collaborating
on the Net

MARC EISENSTADT & TOM VINCENT
Knowledge Media Institute

kmi.open.ac.uk/knowledgeweb

**KOGAN
PAGE**

To Jacqueline, Amelia, Nathan and Leo (ME)

To Ollie, Bernadette and Christine (TV)

First published in 1998

Reprinted 1999

Apart from any fair dealing for the purposes of research or private study, or criticism or review, as permitted under the Copyright, Designs and Patents Act, 1988, this publication may only be reproduced, stored or transmitted, in any form or by any means, with the prior permission in writing of the publishers, or in the case of reprographic reproduction in accordance with the terms of licences issued by the Copyright Licensing Agency. Enquiries concerning reproduction outside those terms should be sent to the publishers at the undermentioned address:

Kogan Page Limited
120 Pentonville Road
London N1 9JN

© Knowledge Media Institute, 1998

British Library Cataloguing in Publication Data

A CIP record for this book is available from the British Library
ISBN 0 7494 2726 4

Typeset by Simon Keats, Knowledge Media Institute

Printed and bound in Great Britain by
Biddles Ltd, Guildford and King's Lynn

Contents

Acknowledgements

Preparation of the book
We are grateful to the following people who have made significant contributions to producing the electronic version of this book: Simon Keats for compilation, composition, layout and editing; Jon Linney for cover design, and advice on book design, printing and graphics; Jon Linney and Tony Seminara for specific figures throughout the book.

Reprint rights
Much of Chapter 6 was first published in the *Proceedings of the 1997 IEEE Frontiers in Education* conference under the title: 'Innovations in large-scale supported distance teaching: transformation for the Internet, not just translation', and is reused here by kind permission of the IEEE. We are grateful to the following organizations and individuals for permission to reprint figures and/or Web pages: Electronic Text Center, University of Virginia (Figure 2.2), Dan Kaveney, Prentice-Hall (Figure 2.3), Iain Gilmour (Figure 2.5), Marianna Buultjens, Scottish Sensory Centre (Figure 2.12).

Sponsorship
We are grateful to the following organizations that have provided support, sponsorship and funding for research and development projects, the outcomes of which appear within the book. They include:

Andersen Consulting; Apple Computer; BT; Department of Trade and Industry; Department for Education and Employment; European Union (COPERNICUS Programme and ESPRIT IBROW3, PATMAN, and HC-REMA projects); Higher Education Funding Council (England); Gatsby Charitable Foundation; GEC Plessey Telecommunications, Ltd.; Guide Dogs for the Blind Association; IBM; IT World; London Mathematical Society; Macromedia Europe; Nuffield Foundation; RealNetworks, Inc.; Relay Systems Ltd.; Royal National Institute for the Blind; Sun Microsystems Inc.; UK Science and Engineering Research Council; JISC (JTAP programme); UK Science and Engineering Research Council jointly-sponsored CASE Award (with BT); Voxware Inc.; The Open University's Development Fund, INSTILL Programme, Research Committee, Office of Technology Development, IET Research Committee, and Social Sciences Faculty.

People

Many people have been involved in the projects described throughout the book. We would particularly like to acknowledge the following for their contributions:

Rachel Bellamy, Mike Brayshaw, Jenny Bull, Marianna Buultjens, Paula Cole, Chris Denham, Shamus Foster, Adam Freeman, Prue Fuller, Iain Gilmour, Caroline Gray, Jerzy Grzeda, Ann Hanson, Tony Hasemer, Ben Hawkridge, Stephanie Houde, Ralph Keats, Simon Keats, Andrew Law, Ches Lincoln, Fred Lockwood, Mike Lewis, Jon Linney, Ross Mackenzie, Heather Mason, Chris McKillop, Mark Miller, Diane Mole, Philip Odor, Roger Penfound, Barbara Poniatowska, Kevin Quick, Mike Richards, Andy Rix, Neil Robinson, Craig Rodine, Ortenz Rose, Tony Seminara, Malcolm Story, Mary Taylor, Debra Thompson, Chris Valentine, Hannah Walton, Ben Whalley, Matthew Whalley, Dave Williams, Mike Wright.

Affiliations

Most of the authors are members of The Open University's Knowledge Media Institute, located in the Berrill Building at The Open University, Milton Keynes MK7 6AA, UK. The exceptions are as follows (all affiliations are still at The Open University unless otherwise stated):

Sir John Daniel (Vice Chancellor); Josie Taylor and Matthew Stratfold (Institute of Educational Technology); Marian Petre, Linda Carswell, Pete Thomas (Faculty of Mathematics and Computing); Marion Phillips (Open University Oxford Regional Office, Foxcombe Hall, Boars Hill, Oxford OX1 5HR, UK); Alberto Riva (Department of Computer and Systems Science, University of Pavia, Italy).

List of colour plates

Colour plates appear between pages 152 and 153. Figure numbers refer to the black and white figures within the text, where relevant.

Knowledge Media takes off on the Web: introduction and overview of the book

Marc Eisenstadt and Tom Vincent

Knowledge Media is the future of education, and has something to contribute to every facet of the emerging knowledge society. The Web is an important vehicle for the forthcoming changes, and serves not only as a catalyst, but also as a unifying force which brings together disparate strands of research and development. This book is our way of highlighting key aspects of that unifying force, and expounding our own approach, both in the ensuing text and the linked Web site at http://kmi.open.ac.uk/knowledgeweb

Evangelical vs pragmatic views of our work

In the four years we have been working together, we have become fond of confounding our colleagues with the following two apparently contradictory utterances:

- **Utterance one (evangelical):** 'There are three important technologies that all education researchers should come to terms with as a matter of urgency: the Web, the Web, and the Web.'

- **Utterance two (pragmatic):** 'Let's face it, the Web even at its most ideal is a pretty awful medium for studying and undertaking course work... nothing wrong with books and videos!'

The evangelical utterance conveys our sense of enthusiasm and optimism about the rapid pace of developments made possible on that vast portion of the Internet which is the World Wide Web. The Web/Web/Web joke emphasizes the fact that the Web is now all-encompassing, and therefore many new technologies can usually benefit from some manifestation on the Web, regardless of whether they involve advanced multimedia, collaboration, data mining, intelligent agents, or models of learner behaviour. The challenge of creating compelling 'Web-centric content', the scholarly peer community accessible in an instant, and even the vast exposure afforded by the Web are all examples of the resounding benefits of thinking about and working with the Web.

The second rather gloomy-sounding pragmatic utterance makes it clear that this is not a moan about slow connections or poor user interfaces, because it emphatically considers the Web even at its most ideal! This utterance is intended to bring our colleagues down to earth with a thud. Even when the interfaces are stunning, and connections are smooth and ultra-fast, we need to remind ourselves that we are still, after all, only looking at a computer screen. We know (better than most, we hope, and in a way we can demonstrate with numerous examples throughout the book) that there are creative things we can do with those stunning interfaces that put books to shame: we can motivate and empower learners, reach disabled students, simulate existing and as-yet-unimagined worlds, forge new relationships, create communities, and launch whole new endeavours of study. All of this is wonderful, but we mustn't let it go to our heads. 'Studying courses on the Web', in our experience, is a sad misconception. In this book you'll see how Web-related activities can augment course study, but you're unlikely to hear us talk about delivering courses entirely on the Web (unless the Web or a Web-related tool is itself the primary focus of study, in which case it can work beautifully).

Indeed, our pragmatic stance and our appreciation of conventional media help to explain why we've chosen to write a book: you can take this with you, browse it, see what fires you with enthusiasm. But we also know we can do better than a plain old book, particularly given this book's topic! Therefore, the book has an associated Web site, where you can experience the environments that are described in the book, get news about updates and latest research results, and give us critical feedback:

> Book Web site: http://kmi.open.ac.uk/knowledgeweb

The next sections of this overview say some more about our interests and focus. We describe whom the book is for; say something about the aims and scope of the book; define Knowledge Media; describe the Knowledge Media Institute; and preview the structure and contents of the book.

Whom the book is for

This book is aimed at a broad audience of university-level 'practitioners', 'casual observers of new technology developments', corporate trainers, and others who have caught the wave of excitement about developments in learning, organizational memory and knowledge representation on the World Wide Web. We assume that most readers will already be experienced users of the World Wide Web, and interested either in innovative uses of the Web for education and collaboration, or alternatively in cognitive science or knowledge modelling aspects which can benefit from Web usage. You will not need to be a 'Web professional' or 'HTML authoring wizard', although in fact such professionals will find much of interest herein.

The book is suitable for use on university-level courses at both advanced undergraduate and postgraduate (post-BA) level. As a collection of examples, it highlights new and effective uses of the Web in education. As a research document, it opens the door to new avenues of work in multimedia, intelligent agents, collaboration, streaming media, and knowledge modelling.

Aims and scope of the book

Researchers and practitioners concerned with innovative and knowledge-intensive uses of the World Wide Web can usually benefit from seeing case studies and first-hand experiences. Although these are typically available directly via the Web, the surrounding expository material explaining the background, context, justification, experience, and lessons learned may be best presented in written form. Our intention was to have the best of both worlds: develop a book with the expository material, and provide a linked Web site with the actual material we are describing in the book.

This book is the culmination of the first three years of activity in our research lab. It provides a living testimonial to the educational possibilities offered by a carefully-designed research and development programme centred around 'Knowledge Media'. This term, adopted by us and embodied in the research teams of the Knowledge Media Institute at the UK's Open University, reflects the new developments made possible by bringing together researchers in the learning and cognitive sciences, multimedia enabling technologies for disabled learners, and artificial intelligence. The result of this collaboration is described in the 16 following chapters, each of which is linked to a custom-built site on the Web containing up-to-date examples of the work through which readers can explore and engage in on-line experimentation.

Although we use the Web extensively, deliver research results on the Web, and create Web-centric content, our research is not about the Web. The title of the book gives away our interests: the word knowledge is first and foremost, because that is where our interests really reside. The next sections go into more detail about our view of Knowledge Media, which is central to the *raison d'être* of this book, and the Knowledge Media Institute that we launched in 1995 to investigate our joint vision of the future.

Knowledge Media

The best characterization of our work is that it lies firmly within the new discipline that we have chosen to call 'Knowledge Media'. This term was first used by Mark Stefik to describe the profound impact of coupling artificial intelligence technology with the Internet (Stefik, 1986). Our usage of this term is broader: in a sentence, we would argue that Knowledge Media is about the process of generating, understanding and sharing knowledge using several different media, as well as understanding how the use of different media shape these processes. But new disciplines require more than one sentence to define! The subsections below explain in more detail key points concerning our influences and our plans for this new discipline.

Knowledge is power

Consider the landmark cover story that appeared in *Fortune* magazine on 3 October 1994: 'Intellectual Capital'. The magazine article argues that a major challenge facing corporations is how to figure out what their collective knowledge is worth, and how to maximize the earning potential of that knowledge. Unused yet expensive-to-protect patents are but one example, and it is becoming increasingly clear that vast wealth lies within reach of those who understand how to assess and manage knowledge. To pick some salient cases, the wealth of software powerhouses such as Netscape, Macromedia and Microsoft reside in what their teams of wizards know. If those wizards quit their current jobs and started working for you tomorrow, you'd be a lot less concerned if they left their computers behind than if they suddenly suffered from amnesia. Yes, the reams of already-written code would have to be reconstructed or re-derived (and in ways that didn't violate existing copyright), but that's just what knowledgeable people are good at.

Now, in an educational context, consider the school child who can re-derive the formula for determining (say) how fast a particular car needs to be going before it flips over when negotiating a tricky bend. Compare that child with the one who has memorized all the formulae, but can't re-derive them. What's the difference? It's in the knowledge of processes, that rich web of inter-linked operations that enables creative 'workarounds' in the event of a problem-solving impasse. Who'll get higher scores on exams? In reality, it's hard to say – very often, the memorizer will perform better, because many exams favour a certain kind of regurgitation (and we mustn't underestimate what the memorizer knows, because surely such a person picks up a lot more than just the facts). But in the long run, the re-deriver will prevail, because of a richness of understanding. That's knowledge. As Alan Kay, widely acknowledged as the father of personal computing, said in 1972, 'let's not measure number of exams passed per year; let's measure number of Sistine Chapel ceilings created per lifetime' (Kay, 1972).

In principle, we could tediously list what the memorizer knows (eg a long list of formulae, vocabulary items, etc). But in the case of the re-deriver, how on earth could we capture what that person knew? Even if we could capture it and store it, how could we impart that knowledge to someone else? This is surely one of the great challenges of educational theory and practice! Indeed, if we could capture the knowledge, store it, and impart it to others, we would be well on our way towards a theory and practice of knowledge media, because knowledge media is about the capturing, storing, imparting, sharing, accessing, and creating of knowledge.

Yet it would be difficult to point to the knowledge itself: knowledge is an emergent property which transcends the fixed-size-and-space concepts of media and information, just the way it transcends the notion that you can 'impart' it to students by 'filling' them up from the teacher's 'vessel'.

And therein lies the key: the early years of Computer Assisted Learning fell into that very same trap, thinking that 'filling from a vessel' was precisely what you could do, and fruitlessly trying to 'fill up' the poor pupils. The nine-year-long debate about the UK's National Curriculum for schools still hasn't resulted in a clear statement about what it thinks knowledge is. In contrast, decades of work in Developmental Psychology, Cognitive Science and Artificial Intelligence has led to an inescapable conclusion: knowledge is a dynamic process, a vibrant, living thing, resting on shared assumptions, beliefs, complex perceptions, sophisticated yet sometimes crazy logic, and the ability to 'go beyond the information given'. 'Knowledge' is the correct abstraction for describing what people communicate to one another. 'Information' and 'content' are not.

Knowledge capture

Modern specialists in knowledge capture have already developed an impressive array of tools for addressing precisely the problem of how to think more robustly about 'knowledge' rather than 'information'. We now know that it is possible to represent common sense rules that lead children to go through a brief phase of saying 'I gived' instead of 'I gave'. We can equally represent complex chains of reasoning such as the way astronomers discovered the formula describing the motion of the planets, or the way investment bankers hedge their bets in the currency markets. We know that there is a consistent logic present in children who think that 63 - 36 = 30. Even better, we know how this mistake arises, why it persists, how to detect it, and how to fix it. Forever. (Not, incidentally, by saying 'Wrong! Do it again!') What all these examples have in common is a rich symbolic representational language which allows us to describe the innermost thoughts of learners in fine-grained detail. Not that we know 'the truth', just that we know considerably more fine-grained detail than did others in the past.

To illustrate some of these points, you'll be reading later on about ways to capture knowledge using a range of what are called conceptual modelling tools (described in Chapters 13 and 14). These tools enable a knowledge engineer to sketch out in an informal manner the relations, properties and processes involved in the problem solving behaviour of what we call a 'domain expert'. More importantly, however, is that the informal sketching tools are tied to a formal modelling language that enables a rich encoding of knowledge sufficient to capture a vast range of problem solving expertise, and to capture it in a modular way so that relevant portions can be used in different contexts.

In a related vein, but with a more obvious educational focus, Roger Schank's group at the Institute for Learning Sciences at Northwestern University looks at how and why students fail, and what motivates them (Schank and Cleary, 1995). Time and time again, his group comes up with a mismatch between the student's perceptions and the teacher's expectations. He finds that students can be motivated by stories which illustrate key points, because the human mind is geared to pick up analogies between the story and the current real-life situation or problem. The trick is in finding a good story, something which master teachers are quite expert at. Schank's learning 'environments' are dependent upon the students traversing their own pathways, asking questions, finding analogies, listening to stories. These learning environments are delivered by a computer, nicely demonstrating the Knowledge Media mix we are so fond of, and influential in our own work (eg Chapter 16).

The Forthcoming Knowledge Society and Virtual Education (not)
As the new Millennium approaches at the time of writing this book (summer 1998), it's fair to say that we're moving towards what we could call The Knowledge Society. This is characterized by four key changes for educators and trainers.

- Knowing what will be less important than knowing how, in other words process knowledge of the kind illustrated in the 're-deriver' example above.

- What you physically possess in your storeroom will be less important than what you and your employees know, as the Fortune special issue on Intellectual Capital emphasized.

- People will prefer to select for themselves ideas and materials that can be delivered on demand, in other words quickly and at a time appropriate to the learner.

- Presentations and expository articles such as this one may start taking the form of what we could think of as a shared experience.

During this forthcoming period of change, it is tempting to think about the development of 'virtual classrooms', which evoke images of a new era of 'wired users' undertaking multimedia distance learning. But we are convinced that this image is wrong! We have been doing multimedia distance learning for over a quarter of a century at the UK's Open University, and we know that the notion of 'wired users' is seriously misguided, just as the notion of 'TV-watchers' turned out to be a misguided view of a typical Open University student.

The new media are of course important, and we aim to lead the way in creating them and using them effectively, but they are only a small part of the overall picture of open and supported distance learning/training, the success of which depends on a number of key 'quality factors'. The factors are described by Sir John Daniel in Chapter 1, which we urge you take the time to read. In sum, they concern the high-quality content, painstaking student support, slick logistics, and strong research base which have become the hallmarks of The Open University's success. Most Virtual University efforts to date have emphasized content creation and delivery of materials via the Web (ie just part of one key factor), while paying only token attention to the other three factors. The UK's Open University (arguably the mother of all Virtual Universities) has succeeded by understanding how to address and balance all of the key factors.

Yet to provide 'virtual education' in the sense understood by the readers of this book, The Open University and others still need to push hard on the frontiers of all relevant factors, inventing and deploying new technologies as appropriate.

With these changes in mind, we began four years ago to try to convince people to reorient their thinking away from computing and multimedia towards what we prefer to call knowledge media. This is about more than the great convergence of computing, telecommunications, publishing and entertainment that we all know about from the popular press and our own experience. It's about putting knowledge first! The term re-emphasizes the learning and cognitive sciences over the technology, and indeed encourages us to think about knowledgeable media, intelligent software which knows a little something about its users and can therefore respond sensibly.

The Knowledge Media Institute (KMi)

In 1994, our respective research labs, primarily in Human-Computer Interaction, Multimedia Enabling Technologies, and Artificial Intelligence received some timely advice and assistance from Open University Director of Development Kitty Chisholm, Pro-Vice Chancellor for Strategy Geoff Peters, and Vice Chancellor Sir John Daniel, who foresaw the synergies possible from a collaborative research effort. We teamed up as a coalition, and began working together under the 'Knowledge Media' umbrella. By 1995 the OU had provided significant kick-start funding as part of a major £10M initiative launched by the Vice Chancellor to inject new technologies into Distance Learning across the entire University. We acquired a high-tech but tempo-rary hut, attracted some hefty matching funding from industry, and in the summer of 1997 moved into the top floor of a new building (Plate I).

Our remit is to serve as a leading-edge outpost on behalf of the OU, always with an eye towards understanding learning diffi-culties and challenges on the one hand, and delivering experimental new technologies on the other. This gives us access to the world's greatest test-bed, namely our 200,000 currently-enrolled students, and significant freedom to innovate.

We work with a mixture of academic assistant professors, research fellows and assistants, full-time PhD students, and visiting interns, all in roughly equal proportions. Apprenticeships and 'buddy-systems' abound, whereby we work with sponsors and OU colleagues to solve problems of mutual interest. A key aspect is a special 'conduit' though which research prototypes are rolled out and scaled up via the OU's Academic Computing Service.

Our income is derived from a mixture of sources, with UK and European research councils augmenting the Open University's own seed funding, and many industrial household names providing the remainder. We have fixed-price-menu club membership schemes, and à la carte solutions for undertaking specific research programmes at a sponsor's request. Non-exclusive licensing of intellectual property is an important unifying theme.

With funding agencies and Open University course teams alike, the key is to work together with an internal end-user champion, and hand over the mutually-developed prototype in a form that the partner or end user can carry on developing without us.

Our operational view is that Knowledge Media encompasses new learner-centred technologies, including Internet-enhanced collaboration media, multimedia environments for disabled learners, intelligent agents, organizational memories, digital documents, scientific visualization and simulation tools, informal and formal representations of knowledge – in short, innovative approaches to sharing, accessing and understanding knowledge. The practical consequence of this operational view is that KMi creates and studies near-term future technologies for the ultimate benefit of Open University students, staff, industrial sponsors, and a mixture of local and global learning communities. All of our work stems from a strong research base in the areas of Knowledge Systems and Multimedia Enabling Technologies, described next.

Knowledge Systems
Our research addresses fundamental questions at the core of learning, cognition and organizational memory: What do people know? How do they know it? Can we reuse problem solving knowledge in different contexts? Can we capture and re-deploy the tacit knowledge distributed throughout an organization? How can we identify hitherto unrecognized nuggets hidden within vast institutional data banks? Our diverse projects in the arena of Knowledge Systems are key steps on the road to finding out.

Configuration design: One stream of our European-funded project work has uncovered key principles concerning how experts juggle constraints during industrial design. Moreover, the work has yielded practical spin-offs such as an innovative truck cab design previewed at the Hannover Motor Show in spring 1997, and serving as a test-bed for the work described in Chapter 14.

Agents: A UK-funded project is developing software agents which are already helping our students, by picking out key themes from within student-teacher e-mails and online discussion forums, and alerting students so they don't reinvent the wheel (Chapter 16). Another agent called Luigi, described in Chapter 15, will e-mail you on our behalf, if required, to book a meeting... this is such a simple idea that no one else has actually bothered to do it. If you use fancy groupwork diaries, you find they are unusable if just one person involved in a meeting fails to keep the diary up to date, or doesn't use that software. Thus, groupwork diary experts hate our meeting agent, but our own secretaries, who waste a lot of time juggling constraints, love it. When we send Luigi a message to arrange a meeting, it invites others on our behalf (raising many important psychological issues about how we delegate and attribute power and authority to a software agent). Luigi reminds them, handles replies, and generates a custom Web page to show the convenor of the meeting how the participants' time constraints match up as their replies come in (Chapter 15 elaborates on the details).

Knowledge reuse and organizational memory: Mixing formal and informal notations can help organizations reuse valuable knowledge, but only if the context is right and 'ownership' of the knowledge is encouraged. We are building a variety of tools to help foster such contextualized knowledge processing in both academic and industrial settings (see Chapters 8 and 14).

Multimedia Enabling Technologies
All learners have needs – some have special needs. The Multimedia Enabling Technologies Group (METg) undertakes fundamental research to address these needs, developing innovative approaches which benefit a wide variety of learners. METg researchers are developing Active Books and Virtual Science Labs, which aim to present core materials across the curriculum at different levels of granularity as appropriate. Thus, a cartoon simulation for 9-year-olds grows into photo-realistic models with access to underlying equations for 16-year-olds (see Chapters 2 and 3).

The Open University routinely makes available sophisticated laboratory equipment to its students, either at home or at residential schools; some students either can't attend, or have physical disabilities which prevent them from using the facilities; so what METg developed was something better than the real thing, the Virtual Microscope. This was designed from the ground up to be accessible to students with visual impairment and physical disability, and to provide high quality photo-realistic views through very expensive laboratory microscopes, with different filtering and viewing conditions available simultaneously. This work developed a direct-manipulation interface that has led to some innovative new work on tactile multimedia, using media tricks to enable users to feel what's on screen without any special hardware. This is multimedia alright, but with a profound purpose. Examples include: audio-on-demand for the visually impaired; empowering people to do real science, such as designing the Wright Brothers' original plane and then trying to fly it, or building a real robot to navigate a mock-up of Mars and study the rock samples, then perhaps feel them; and hear a spoken version of the relevant textual passage – always driven by a perceived need. Chapter 2 elaborates on these examples.

Other work in the Knowledge Media Institute fits in and around that just described, always looking at ways of either developing new media or harnessing media to explore and understand knowledge. The structure of the book, described next, weaves the rest of the Knowledge Media story.

Structure of the book

We have subdivided the book into three main sections to reflect the diversity of our work in learning media, collaboration and presence, and knowledge systems. The sections are described in turn below.

Part I: Learning media

We take as given the tenet that we are all learners, throughout our lives. Knowledge media take on a particular style and significance when cast in a learning context, because in such cases the goals of the knowledge media creators are fundamentally driven by the needs of the learner. A range of complex issues arise, not least because our research covers many different age groups, many different ability ranges, many different subject domains, and even a range of different goals from supporting students via career advice to helping students help themselves learn about complex mathematical or physical processes.

Chapter 1 is written by Open University Vice Chancellor Sir John Daniel, and provides both a vision of what makes The Open University work so well, and living proof that the OU can put its money where its mouth is. Sir John gave an invited keynote address at IDLCON-97, the 1997 International Distance Learning Conference in Washington DC. Except he wasn't there physically. His speech, captured here in written form, takes a hard-hitting look at the mistake of trying to teach the masses by satellite and videoconferencing, and why he thinks The Open University can do it better. To practise what he preaches, he delivers his presentation to his audience in Washington first by satellite, and then directly via the Internet. An on-demand replay of the presentation is accessible as a 'Webcast' from the book's linked Web-site.

New information technologies have been applied widely in teaching and training during the past two decades. What is not so obvious is the value to learners of many of the applications. In the case of disabled learners, there are examples where information technology has made a profound impact. This includes people studying areas of the curriculum within all levels of education that were previously difficult or impossible to access. The paradox is that many of the applications of the new information technologies that provide enhanced opportunities for learning can, at the same time, create barriers to learning. In **Chapter 2**, Tom Vincent and Peter Whalley consider the role of the Web as an enabling technology. Examples are provided that illustrate how this medium is being used including a shared training environment to support children with communication difficulties, access to library resources for blind people, and a radical new interface for helping learners of all abilities.

In **Chapter 3**, Peter Whalley looks at the ways in which virtual science laboratories can be developed to enhance the learning experience. We know already that such labs have clear benefits when they allow students to work with equipment and materials that would otherwise be too dangerous or expensive, but Whalley looks beyond this: he explores what happens when such environments are used to encourage collaboration among individuals at a distance, and how best to consider these environments in terms of conversational models of learning.

New and rich learning environments of the kind described in this book can potentially frustrate learners if the environments inadvertently become an extra burden and thus get in the way of learning. Tammy Sumner and Josie Taylor, in **Chapter 4**, tackle this problem head on by developing a series of meta-learning environments such as interactive course maps. These environments face a double challenge, because they must self-evidently be even less of a burden than the other tools they are helping students to understand, and they must integrate seamlessly with a rich media mix such as we now find on Open University courses. They must also help maximize the benefits of such a mix, and this is precisely what the Sumner and Taylor meta-learning environments are designed to do.

Learners are people, too, and as such have needs which go beyond the obvious subject-specific content. Among such needs are concerns about careers advice and other matters of a counselling support nature. The Open University takes great pride in the vast (human) support infrastructure it provides for its students, and is harnessing new technologies to increase this support. In **Chapter 5**, Peter Scott and Marion Phillips give some examples of how an advisory system is being migrated from CD-ROM to the Web, and the unique advantages incurred along the way. The advisory system maintains its human face by delivering informative and compelling stories from an archive of many hundreds of student experiences.

Chapter 6, by Marian Petre, Linda Carswell, Blaine Price and Pete Thomas, lays to rest the myth that conventional courses can just be 'migrated' onto the Web. For starters, Open University courses are far from conventional, because they have always deployed a rich student-centred multiple media mix. On top of this, we need to understand that the Web is not just a place where content is deposited! Petre *et al.* have used the Web and other Internet technologies to augment Open University course and tutorial material in a variety of ways: asynchronous and synchronous tutorials, audiographics, electronic assignment handling, role playing, mentoring, and even secure exam delivery. The chapter summarizes their key findings, and drives home the message that transformation is paramount for success.

Part II: Collaboration and presence
One of the most exhilarating and rewarding aspects of the Internet is the way it brings people together. Being able to share and reuse knowledge is a fundamental aspect of the new possibilities made available through creative uses of Knowledge Media. The idea of 'collaboration on the net' is often raised in the concept of joint document preparation or similar workgroup activities. What Knowledge Media adds is a set of novel perspectives, searching for ways to enhance the overall user experience, add tools which have an element of their own intelligence, foster

learned debate, or even provide ways for people at a distance from one another to see 'what is happening' inside a computer program.

Matthew Stratfold provides a bridge between Part I and Part II with his **Chapter 7**, about learner dialogues on the Web. While many chapters in Part I discuss the importance of conversation models and dialogue, Stratfold concentrates on the best way to build upon the added value Web-based environments to deliver a compelling dialogue experience. This requires undertaking a detailed examination of the conference/forum/thread environments that many Internet users now take for granted, and suggesting some significant improvements thereto.

In **Chapter 8**, Simon Buckingham Shum and Tammy Sumner introduce the notion of a tightly-coupled publishing and discussion environment, in which the multimedia artifact under discussion is seamlessly integrated with the discussion itself. Their custom toolkit automates many of the tedious aspects of constructng such environments, and serves as the underpinning of KMi's popular *Journal of Interactive Media in Education*.

The concepts of collaboration and presence go hand in hand, because the more one can enhance the sense of presence or 'being there', the richer the possibilities for collaboration, even at a distance. Peter Scott and Marc Eisenstadt, in **Chapter 9**, look at a new paradigm for telepresence research, based on a collection of tools for hosting tutorials, presentations, master classes and other events on the Internet. These tools have been used for everything from virtual classroom activities to an interactive Pub Quiz aimed at MBA students revising for a final exam at their workplaces in Russia, Norway, Germany, South Africa and Japan.

News reports are a wonderful way of keeping a community of collaborating researchers and interested parties informed, but only if the content is both provided and attended to! KMi Planet, described by John Domingue and Peter Scott in **Chapter 10**, uses software agents to simplify both authoring and delivery of news. The key is a mixture of least-common-denominator environments such as plain text e-mail and the compelling facilities available on the Web, all mediated by agents which try to tie together the best elements of diverse collaboration media.

Joint problem solving is a particularly significant facet of collaboration, because all parties concerned are focused on a common goal. When the subject matter of the problem solving exercise is program debugging, and the parties concerned are Open University students and tutors separated by a significant distance, a unique set of challenges arises. The Knowledge Media approach is to understand the learners' needs, backed by empirical studies, and develop solutions based on a mixture of innovative media, and representations of the relevant knowledge. John Domingue and Paul Mulholland describe just such an approach in **Chapter 11**: students and tutors are provided with the ability to work together on animated visualizations of computer programs in order to help clarify situations which would otherwise be either intractable or, at best, tedious to resolve.

Part III: Knowledge Systems on the Web

Knowledge Systems is the area of work that brings together researchers in Artificial Intelligence (AI) and Cognitive Science, particularly those who have an interest in representations of knowledge and formal methods for manipulating such representations. In years past, we might have distinguished between the typical engineering-oriented approach of AI researchers building intelligent artefacts of one kind or another, and the more empirical approach of Cognitive Scientists (particularly Cognitive Psychologists) studying the nature of human cognitive processing. Today, a unifying theme of Knowledge Systems work is that of representation, which forms the core of our ability to talk concretely about how and what we know; to reason about what we know; to diagnose weaknesses in what we know; to improve ways of knowing. A major tenet of Knowledge Systems research is that without some formal basis, although we can still engage in such discussions, they will always remain just discussions, and rarely lead us to deeper insights about knowledge. Moreover if we can understand how to build representations and reuse similar representations across disparate research and end-user communities, we stand a chance of harnessing and even augmenting knowledge in ways that could be of staggering benefit for humankind. The advent of the Web has brought such opportunities to the fore, and is one of the reasons that the possibilities of Knowledge Systems on the Web are so exciting to us.

The Knowledge Systems community has largely used the Lisp programming language since its inception in the 1960s. In **Chapter 12**, Alberto Riva and Marco Ramoni describe how this language can be used as the basis of a Web server that allows AI applications to be shared worldwide. Their 'LispWeb' offers the best features of local and distributed processing, as appropriate, plus a standardized user interface and the power of advanced symbolic processing. LispWeb itself provides the infrastructure for other activities described in this book, including KMi Planet of

Chapter 10, the Internet Software Visualization Lab of Chapter 11, the World Wide Design Lab of Chapter 14, and the intelligent meeting agent of Chapter 15.

The terminology of the knowledge systems community has become increasingly pervasive in everyday life. For example, we hear about 'knowledge workers' and 'knowledge management' in the business world; it is not unusual to hear about 'smart buildings' and even 'fuzzy logic washing machines'. Arthur Stutt and Enrico Motta, in **Chapter 13**, contend that this pervasive trend indicates an implicit acceptance of knowledge representation as a mainstream human interest. However, they argue, before such a trend can really impact on our lives in a major way, we need to begin coming to terms with the activity of knowledge modelling, ie understanding and representing what people know.

Representations of knowledge permeate the work practices of design teams, too. Disparate teams of engineers working on a challenging design task need to share a common vocabulary and make their implicit assumptions explicit before they can begin to see benefits of working together. In **Chapter 14**, Zdenek Zdrahal and John Domingue show that it is more than just a vocabulary that such teams need: formal representations are needed to enable one team to work with another, or even to reuse ideas at a later date on a similar project. They have been developing the World Wide Design Lab precisely in order to facilitate the co-development and sharing of such representations.

Design teams are not the only parties at the Knowledge Systems table! Software agents can participate in the sharing of knowledge representations, and indeed must rely on sophisticated representations to function properly. But 'functioning code' alone does not account entirely for the behaviour of an agent, whether human or artificial. In **Chapter 15**, Stuart Watt investigates what it is about the behaviour of an agent that enables us to attribute 'intelligence' to it, or indeed to entrust it with a delegated task. This dilemma is as much about psychology as it is about Artificial Intelligence.

One kind of software agent that can take advantage of activity on the Internet is one which monitors online discussion forums and chimes in with helpful comments. As Simon Masterton shows in **Chapter 16**, this is particularly useful when the discussion forums involve Open University students and the software agent is his Virtual Participant that can identify common elements of disparate discussions and thereby help tutors avoid re-inventing the wheel.

Your journey begins here

Knowledge Media looks to us as if it will be the key not only to education in the next Millennium, but also to many facets of society. As we said at the beginning, we are pragmatists as well as evangelists. We have no illusions, but we are enthused and excited by the developments ahead. This book is a beginning, and we are particularly pleased that the book itself is not a 'closed unit': by visiting the associated Web site at http://kmi.open.ac.uk /knowledgeweb you will be able to experience the latest developments as they happen, and join us on this exciting journey.

Part I
Learning media

Chapter 1

Can you get my hard nose in focus? Universities, mass education and appropriate technology

Sir John Daniel

Group teaching in front of remote TV screens? This is not only an awful way to undertake distance learning, but flies in the face of everything that we have learned while conducting successful open and supported learning on a massive scale for the past 27 years. Our lessons are the key to addressing the triple crises of access, cost and flexibility now facing higher education world-wide.

Introduction: background context *[by the editors]*

In March 1997, Open University Vice Chancellor Sir John Daniel presented the keynote address at the International Distance Learning Conference (IDLCON-97) taking place in Washington, DC. Sir John was unable to be in Washington at the time of the conference, and had been asked to deliver his address live by satellite using the facilities of the BBC Open University Production Centre in Milton Keynes, UK. At the suggestion of IBM's Mel Bynum, who had been tracking and partially sponsoring our own work on virtual classrooms (see Chapter 9), we decided to use the very technology we had been developing to help make a key point – live during Sir John's presentation.

Since the conference was heavily dominated by satellite and videoconference vendors and users, of which the Vice Chancellor was highly critical, a three-pronged approach was adopted:

- the content itself would remain unchanged and hard-hitting;

- we would use a satellite broadcast to convey the Vice Chancellor's presentation live from the UK for the opening ten minutes, parenthetically demonstrating by example that we could still do this better than anyone else;

- in mid-presentation, we would switch over in full view of the 1,000-strong audience to an Internet-based presentation, using a live RealAudio feed plus an arsenal of graphical 'avatar' tricks (described in Chapter 9), all received on a

Figure 1.1 (Plate II). What the audience of one thousand IDLCON-97 conference-goers saw on their giant display screen after the Internet feed began. A moving avatar depicting Sir John Daniel appears on our left, and an artificial audience can be seen in the foreground. The 'slide content' area was expanded to fill the screen during the main part of the talk (Chapter 9, Figure 9.4).

notebook computer running over a 28.8Kbps dialup modem which was connected to an Internet Service Provider in Washington DC.

A central mixing deck was used to fade from the satellite feed to the Internet feed, and the output of the mixing deck was relayed to a giant screen in the auditorium (Figure 1.1). The next section of this chapter is the verbatim contents of Sir John's keynote speech. The references to the Russian Embassy reflect the fact that they were hosting an open evening during the IDLCON-97 conference. The Web replay of the talk, with the original look and feel experienced by the audience at the time, is available on the Web site which accompanies this book.

The keynote speech

Good afternoon. It is a pleasure to join this IDLCON conference. Thank you for allowing me to participate at a distance like this. I was in Washington DC last week to speak at the American

Association for Higher Education conference, but I had to return to London for a meeting of the Open University trustees. It simply wasn't possible for me to come back again so soon. I ask your forgiveness – but I also ask, if the IDLCON conference can't handle a speaker at a distance, who can? I shall try to turn that distance to advantage – for we are all believers in distance learning.

I address you from The Open University in Milton Keynes – Britain's newest and nicest city – about fifty miles north of London. My title for this short keynote is 'Can you get my hard nose in focus?' There is a sub-title: 'Universities, mass education and appropriate technology'. Let me unpack the title for starters.

Can you get my hard nose in focus? First, take that literally. Can you see my angular features and, more importantly, can you hear my funny accent. Ad hoc videoconferences are not always reliable. However, with the combined technical horsepower of the BBC and IDLCON I hope we'll be OK.

Second, what about the metaphorical meaning of my title? Why do I have a hard nose? Webster defines hard-nosed two ways. First, hard-bitten or stubborn. I'm not hard-bitten because I've had a wonderfully fulfilling career as a university educator in five political jurisdictions – six if I dare include the USA. But I am stubborn in the defence of important ideas, because I'm an academic. Webster's second definition of hard-nosed is hard-headed, especially with regard to budgeting. I am hard-headed about getting value for money in education – and I shall accuse you of not being hard-headed enough. Be warned.

The blurb in your [IDLCON-97] programme about this session is flattering about The Open University. It says we are the 'origin of much of The Open University and distance learning in the world' and that 'we are the international leader in distance learning'. Thank you for those accolades. I myself can take little credit for The Open University's remarkable achievements because, for most of its 28 year history, I worked in Canada. But I gratefully accept your plaudits on behalf of my colleagues.

Let's look at The Open University for a minute – I'll call it the OU. Why do you acclaim it as the pioneer of distance learning and still the world leader? Several reasons.

First, like any genuine educational innovation, it was rooted in idealism. At the OU's inaugural ceremony, held in the week that the Apollo astronauts returned from the first moon landing in 1969, our first Chancellor declared an inspiring mission: to be open as to people, open as to places, open as to ideas and open as to methods. In the last quarter century the OU has achieved those noble ideals more fully than any university in the world.

Open as to people: The OU has 150,000 degree credit students this year: 1,500 at PhD level; 10,000 masters; over 100,000 baccalaureate. And this is not just access. It is access to success. Open access – yet overall degree completion rates equalling those of your campus universities in the USA. A university placed in the top 20 per cent of national quality rankings. Acclaimed for the excellence of its teaching in subjects like music, earth sciences, chemistry and initial teacher training, where even enthusiasts like yourselves would not claim that distance education had a natural advantage.

Open as to places: 20,000 students outside the UK. Sadly, this satellite link doesn't allow me to drink vodka with you this evening at the Russian embassy. Distance teaching does have some drawbacks! But please raise a glass to the 5,000 Russian students of The Open University. They are to be found all the way from the Urals to the Kurile Islands. They are taking our business courses – in Russian – and I doubt that any other university outside Russia has had such a massive impact on helping ordinary Russians prepare themselves for the new world order.

Open as to ideas: The central mission of all universities – yet too often forgotten by the promoters of distance learning. The aim of distance learning is not to get instructional designers to package old academic orthodoxy in fancy new technology. It has a greater responsibility than other forms of university to move the intellectual paradigms forward. That is the most striking success of the OU's course team approach. The Open University is an academic pacesetter. Our course materials are used massively in other universities because they are intellectually exciting.

Open as to methods: This is where my hard nose starts to show. The Open University has led a succession of revolutions in the methods of distance learning. First we integrated the mass media of TV and radio broadcasting with the older medium of print. So today a drop-in audience of millions enjoys our TV programmes. Next we integrated the personal media, your VCR, the computer in your den, the tape deck in your car. So today the OU is a family show. Right now we're integrating the knowledge media in another revolution. Knowledge Media is a term coined by Marc Eisenstadt – who is at your conference – for the technologies now emerging from the convergence of computing, telecommunications and the cognitive sciences [see Eisenstadt and Vincent overview for the origins of the term Knowledge Media, particularly Mark Stefik's usage in 1986 – Eds].

But there is a deeper openness to methods and that, I fear, is where my hard nose starts to intrude into this cosy chat. There are really only two approaches to distance education. There is a great divide between them – and therefore a great divide – other than the Atlantic Ocean – between me and you. What is this fault line I am talking about? I summarize it in three points.

Point 1: The first approach to distance education targets individual learning; the second focuses on group teaching. Whatever terms people invent, distributed learning, correspondence study, flexible learning, home-study, remote-classroom teaching, tele-education, guided study, or whatever, distance education still boils down to these two traditions, individual learning or group teaching – and they are very different.

Point 2: The most important difference is that the group teaching approach is based on synchronous communication. Teachers and students must communicate in real time. The individual learning approach is based on asynchronous communication. You re-create the campus in the student's home or on their desk at work so they can study where and when it suits them.

Point 3: Another important consequence follows. In the group teaching scenario the teacher communicates with students in a network of classrooms in real time. It is a teacher-centred form of education. That's not meant pejoratively. It's simply a fact that if you try to set up a system for a teacher to address a number of remote groups you must design it from the teacher's point of view. Under the individual learning scenario you re-create the campus in thousands of homes and workplaces – so it has to be a student-centred approach. You must figure out what constitutes an effective home learning environment for the student.

No prizes for guessing which tradition of distance education this IDLCON conference is about. Every picture on the conference program [sic] shows students in remote classrooms looking at TV screens. We're talking about teaching to groups. This session is a perfect example of everything I've said. Number 1, this is a synchronous session – you're paying to hear me live. Number 2, all the folk involved in running the session are focused on my activity as a teacher. As the speaker I do worry a bit about your learning, although mostly about not upsetting you too much. Are you able to focus on my core message, which is that you are missing the big opportunities in distance learning through your obsession with video-conferencing? But that's my worry – everyone else is simply keeping their fingers crossed that the transatlantic satellite link doesn't die on us.

My fundamental point is that this focus on group teaching not only has a high cost but, more importantly, a high opportunity cost. By focusing on remote group teaching you are passing up the opportunity to use distance education to respond to the great educational and training crises of our time. They are a triple crisis: of access, cost and flexibility. The real challenge is to reach many more people, to reach them inexpensively, and to make it convenient for them. Remote-group teaching fails those tests. The individual learning tradition of distance education has much more to offer: mass access, low cost and personal flexibility. Let me explain briefly. I do so at more length, and with great lucidity and persuasiveness, in my recent book: *Mega-universities and Knowledge Media: Technology Strategies for Higher Education* (Daniel, 1997). Read it if you can handle a personal intellectual paradigm shift.

Mega-university is my term for a distance teaching university that enrols over 100,000 students. There are now 11 of them with nearly three million students between them. All of them, except the Chinese TV University system, focus on individual learning – not group teaching. That is the secret of their success. I've already given The Open University as an example because it has had a huge global impact. It operates on a large scale: that's the answer to the crisis of access. It operates inexpensively – half the cost per student of other British universities. That's the answer to the crisis of cost. It operates conveniently: 130,000 students in Britain, 20,000 in a hundred other countries. That's the answer to the crisis of flexibility.

How has this been achieved? There are four keys to the national and international success of the Open University formula for distance learning. One: very high quality multi-media learning materials produced by multi-skilled academic teams. Study materials must be excellent and varied to make the campus in the home or workplace a congenial experience. Two: dedicated personal academic support. Each Open University student has their own tutor for each course, one of OU's 7000 adjunct faculty. They comment on and mark the student's assignments, hold group meetings and give support by phone, e-mail and computer conference. Three: slick logistics. Each individual student must receive the right materials and information at the right time. With over

150,000 students around the world that requires careful attention to detail. Four: a strong research base. When thousands of students use the materials for each course and millions of people view each TV programme the content must be academically up to date. Thanks to economies of scale The Open University has the resources to move the academic paradigms steadily forward.

In summary, focusing on individual learning offers more than remote-group teaching. Take flexibility. The focus on the individual gives students flexibility over where and when they study. It may be the home, the workplace, the commuter train or the airport lounge. Because it is convenient and flexible you can reach large numbers – so access improves. And because you reach large numbers you get economies of scale, so study costs less for all concerned. You also get higher academic quality, because the scale allows you to make a bigger academic investment. What I don't understand, because it is all so clear to me, is why you don't see it that way too. After all, the great contribution of the United States to the advancement of humankind has been to stress the importance of the individual. Why, in distance education, are you so fixated on the collectivity in the classroom?

My tentative hypothesis is that American higher education values teaching more than learning. You may have other hypotheses. Perhaps it's the pressure from the big telecoms operators who want to sell you lots of bandwidth for your videoconferences and for events like this. You can't expect them to vote for targeting individuals at home, just as you can't expect landlords who rent apartments to students near the campus to vote for any kind of distance education. Turkeys don't vote for Thanksgiving either. But I'm sure you will come round in time. As your lively Ambassador in Britain, Admiral Crowe, said to me recently, 'The United States will always do the right thing – after having exhausted all other possibilities'.

By this stage if you're still listening to me, rather than enjoying other mental fantasies, you'll be either depressed or annoyed. None of these are good frames of mind for individual learning, so I ought to give you hope for the future. Here goes. Let me show you a corner of the future for the last few minutes of my address.

So far, my hard nose has been coming to you exclusively, expensively, and inflexibly by a broadband satellite link. I shall switch over and come to you via the Net using technology that has been developed here at The Open University by our Knowledge Media Institute, the KMi, under Marc Eisenstadt's leadership. We call it the KMi Stadium, the development of telepresence on a large scale.

[At this point the presentation was switched in real time from the satellite video feed to a streaming audio/graphic presentation, connected via dialup modem. – Eds]

Now I'm coming to you on the Internet via an ordinary dial-up modem. I may be delayed a few more seconds than the satellite link, and you may even hear some of this twice as a result, but the implications are profound: suddenly, there is world-wide access to my concluding words. Now the distinction between synchronous and asynchronous learning begins to blur. In fact, my address to you has been going out on KMi Stadium from the start. So if you were asleep for the last 20 minutes you can find it on the Net when you get home and view it again. Furthermore, because it is a Net-based technology it is easy to follow up the session with questions, discussion and verbal blows to my hard nose even if you viewed it asynchronously. J.S.Daniel@open.ac.uk will find me.

I've been somewhat rude today about the approach to distance learning that involves teaching to groups in remote classrooms through videoconferencing. I apologize to the oxen that were gored. But don't get me wrong. I believe that other forms of teleconferencing represent the great breakthrough that the knowledge media are bringing to distance learning. Specifically we find that computer conferencing is highly popular with students and enhances their performance in courses. In this application the key to success is Metcalfe's Law, or the Law of the Telecosm. It says the value of a network is proportional to the square of the number of users. That means that if we only had 350 students taking our freshman course in technology from home each student would find the network and the computer conferences one hundred times less valuable than it is with 3,500 students who can be linked from home. The Law of the Telecosm creates a real breakthrough in distance learning. Hitherto, with so-called interactive media – like video-conferencing – the interactive value went down sharply as student numbers went up. Suddenly we have a medium where that is not true. More students means better education. We have found the Holy Grail that educators have sought since the beginning of time.

That's why we are investing so much effort in scaling up these interactive Internet technologies. We are able to enrich and extend distance learning by creating a Web of student-to-student communication and by giving guided access to academic resources that we could not otherwise use.

What we have done, in effect, is to add the essence of video-conferencing to the toolkit of the individual learner. But we've eliminated the main drawbacks of videoconferencing, which is the need to assemble students in groups and therefore the impossibility of scaling it up. But please don't misunderstand. We are not saying that this is the total answer to distance learning.

In the last 25 years over two million people have studied with The Open University. If we have learned one thing from all those students, that rich tapestry of humanity, it is that there is no magic single medium. People are different and the mix of media they like to learn from is different. What the Net does, helped by technologies such as KMi Stadium is to provide a communicative glue that increases the synergy between the other media.

Which is a good moment to let my hard nose go out of focus and to wish you well with your conference. And please remember to drink a toast in vodka to the 5,000 Russian students of The Open University when you go the Russian Embassy this evening.

Chapter 2

The Web: enabler or disabler

Tom Vincent and Peter Whalley

New developments in information and communication technologies have opened up some of the most promising possibilities yet available for overcoming barriers to learning experienced by disabled people. Paradoxically, the technology which offers this potential can also become a barrier and limit access to the World Wide Web.

From CD-ROM to the Web

In many respects the Web can be considered as an enormous CD-ROM. At any instant a snapshot of the Web appears as an extensive and rich resource of information. This analogy has been exploited by developers who produce CD-ROM/Web applications using the same browser for each medium. The concept can be extended further by linking these media and having dynamic data transmitted via the Web and relatively static data made available on the CD-ROM. This integrated approach offers many interesting possibilities as well as overcoming limitations imposed by the bandwidth of networks.

The integration of CD-ROM and the Web is illustrated by a development at The Open University which has resulted in disabled students being able to receive print-based teaching materials in alternative media that offer greater accessibility. There are nearly 7,000 who declare a disability. Of these students, there are approximately 1,000 who would prefer to study in an alternative medium to print. Although there is a significant proportion of these students who have a visual impairment, there are other impairments and factors that govern this preference. A student indicates some of his difficulties:

> I have no central vision in either eye, but I do retain some peripheral vision. Essentially, I do most of my seeing out of the left side of my left eye. With this restricted vision I am able to read text magnified to a sufficient size at a rate of about 40 words per minute.

An Electronic Environment for Learning (EEL) has been developed at The Open University (Vincent, 1994) which integrates digital media (text, audio, images) versions of print-based course materials on CD-ROM (Figure 2.1). Access is provided via an interface that is compatible with a range of enabling technologies (synthetic speech, magnification, Braille).

Enabling technologies (also known as access technologies). These include, for example, screenreaders for blind users that provide, in a pre-determined way, access to text displayed on a computer screen via a speech synthesizer; and alternatives to a keyboard and mouse that allow someone with limited dexterity to operate a computer with a switch and software keyboard emulator.

The functionality of the interface called ReadOut (Vincent and Taylor, 1995) includes navigation, searching, indexing, bookmarking and note-taking.

A key feature of EEL is the auto-tracking between the electronic text and the digital audio. In practice, for example, this enables a blind student to navigate (using an appropriate enabling technology) through teaching materials as appropriate to learning needs using text to synthetic speech translation. When required, an almost instant transition can be made to the digital

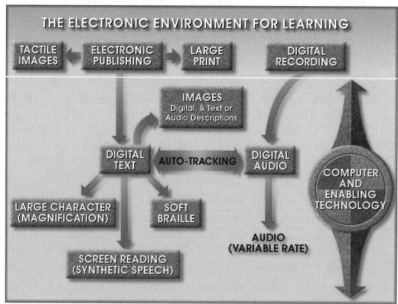

Figure 2.1. Electronic Environment for Learning (EEL)

audio (human recording) version of the course material at exactly the same place in the material. This is in marked contrast to the use of conventional audio tapes where courses may require over 100 hours of analogue tape (more than 60 C90 cassettes) which may mean a student taking several minutes to find a section of text. This latter method puts students in a passive, linear learning environment which is time-consuming and very limiting.

Access to pictures and diagrams in alternative media to print poses many challenges. A key issue is the importance and value of these images in educational course materials. This can vary considerably from 'providing a break' in a long sequence of text to images that convey a concept that is fundamental to the understanding of a topic or a course. It is essential that descriptions or translations of images into alternative media truly reflect an author's intent, and an indication is made of their relative importance in course materials. For example, an author might include in a text a graph to illustrate exponential growth (such as a population increase). This may only need to be described by a simple qualitative expression, in which case a detailed description of the axes of the graph and other quantitative features would be of little value. More complex diagrams need to be carefully analysed in terms of descriptions (normally by the author) to ensure that redundant information is not included. This also applies to tactile representations where a one-to-one transcription is not normally appropriate (Wild and Hinton, 1992).

Print-based course materials transferred into alternative media and delivered by CD-ROM offer disabled students a more individualized learning environment. However, there are still several limitations. For example, all students receive printed updates for teaching materials throughout an academic year. Increasingly these changes are being distributed by electronic mail rather than by post. In response to this, EEL/ReadOut has been enhanced so that components of the transformed media (such as audio files) can be accessed as appropriate via the Web rather than from the CD-ROM. This integration is an important development as updates often contain crucial, short notice information.

Another dimension is access to complementary print-based materials such as books and journals which are referenced within teaching materials, ie the equivalent of the library. This aspect has been helped significantly by the increasing number of publications which are being made available via the Internet. For example, the University of Virginia has created a World Wide Web

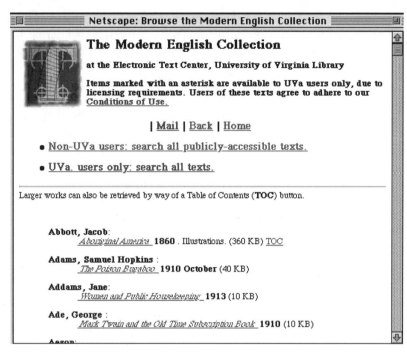

Figure 2.2. University of Virginia — Electronic Texts Web page
(http://etext.lib.virginia.edu/)

site (Figure 2.2) of English books. The copyright issue has been addressed by identifying which books can only be accessed by local students where restrictive agreements have been reached, and out of copyright books made accessible to everyone. Downloading these texts to a student's computer which has an appropriate enabling technology allows someone to read the text in another medium.

Publishers are experimenting with different methods of making books accessible via the Web. An interesting approach is taken by McKnight at the University of Wisconsin-Madison with a Prentice-Hall publication, *Physical Geography* (Figure 2.3). In this case the Web version plays a complementary role to the printed book. The structure of the book is retained on the Web page and numerous links are made to other sites where there are resources (information, animations, simulations, etc) that have a direct relevance to the student using the printed book. Other features of the Internet are exploited including the introduction of

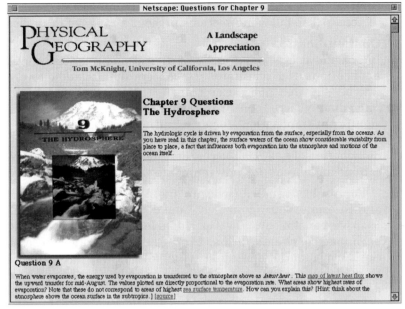

Figure 2.3. Beyond a book on the Web
(http://www.prenhall.com/mcknight/)

questions which can be answered and sent electronically to a grader.

Overall, CD-ROM and the Web offer new possibilities for providing access to teaching materials. However, a key issue is the accessibility of these resources to disabled people who cannot use conventional computers. It is no advantage, for example, when a book is made available electronically on the Web if the interface to it is not compatible with enabling technologies. This issue is addressed in a later section when accessibility of the Web is considered.

Web for Access

Barriers to learning for disabled people can take many different forms. In a science course, for example, a laboratory or field study trip may be inaccessible to students who have restricted mobility. A solution to this might be an emulation of an experiment or a virtual representation of a physical environment. In either case the use of multimedia, delivered by CD-ROM or the Web could be used to create appropriate applications. There is increasing evidence as to how such applications can provide access to the curriculum in areas that were previously difficult or impossible to access. The following sections present a range of examples.

Communication

Increasing use is being made of digital audio for Internet/Web applications. It is an interesting concept that an audio recording can be digitized and, after transfer to a server, can be made immediately accessible world-wide via a Web page. This has significant implications for distributing talking. Also, real-time audio presentations and discussions are possible. The real-time distribution of audio is the cornerstone of a range of Web presentations and discussion environments (see Chapter 8 and 9).

For disabled students who are unable to travel to study centres and tutorials, setting up electronic discussion groups has many positive benefits. At The Open University widespread use has been made of clients such as First Class which offer these facilities. One potential limitation is that 'discussions' are undertaken through typing messages. This aspect can be a barrier when such discussions take place in real-time for someone with limited manual dexterity. Hence the value of using audio as the communication medium. It also has the advantage of being closer to what happens in conventional tutorials. However, it is recognized that

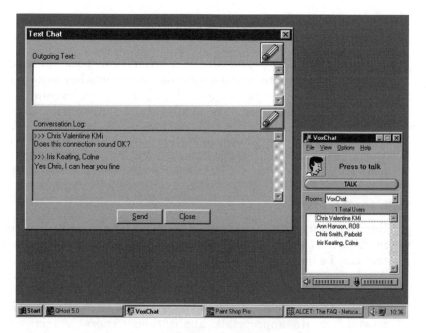

Figure 2.4. Voxchat audio discussion environment

this would not be appropriate for students with a hearing impairment where communication via a keyboard is preferable.

Voxware's Voxchat (Figure 2.4) is one example of a simple interface that provides effective audio communication facilities for a group of people. One important feature is the icon which shows who is speaking – a feature that is difficult to have with telephone conferencing. Another advantage is that other applications, such as a whiteboard or Web browser, can be run simultaneously.

Environment

For anyone who is unable to visit a geographical location, the Web can provide virtual equivalents. Two applications that help achieve this are QuickTime VR and Web cameras such as SiteCam.

In the study of earth sciences, field study trips are undertaken to places of geological interest – often very inaccessible. QuickTime VR can be used to capture multiple images of rock formations. Panoramic views can then be created to provide students with a visual tour that includes the key points of interest. Two advantages of this approach that go beyond physical access are that it provides a permanent record for later reference, and comparisons can be readily made between different

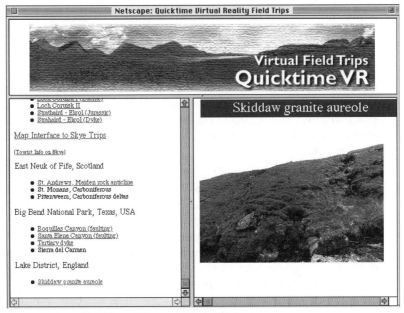

Figure 2.5. Skiddaw Virtual Field Trip
(http://earth2.open.ac.uk)

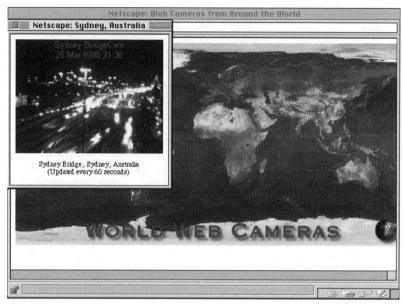

Figure 2.6 (Plate III). World map interface to Webcams
(http://met.open.ac.uk/oiler/worldcam)

geographical locations, ie the equivalent of multiple field trips which may not be possible for all students because of time and distance constraints. The example in Figure 2.5 illustrates the use of this technique in an Open University earth sciences course.

Another possibility where there is growing interest is the use of Webcams. This technology allows views of any location to be transmitted over the Web at refresh rates appropriate to a scene. For example, this could bring a world map to life by comparing views from different latitudes which illustrate time differences (Figure 2.6).

Virtual experiments

The Virtual Microscope (Whalley, 1995) is an emulation of an Open University Science Summer School experiment (Figure 2.7). This was introduced into the course in 1994 to meet the needs of a significant number of students who, because of a physical impairment, could not use a conventional microscope. The success of this multimedia application is very clear. Students who could not participate in this experimental work before can now have a significant involvement through the use of this emulation. Subsequently the Virtual Microscope was adopted for all students. This is not to replace the microscope but to enhance and accelerate

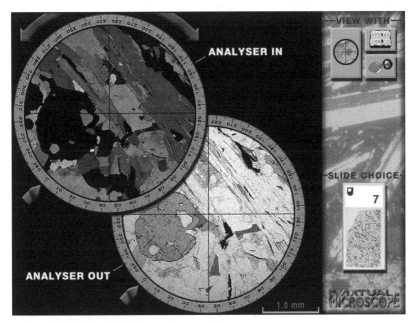

Figure 2.7 (Plate IV). The Virtual Microscope
(http://met.open.ac.uk)

the learning and understanding associated with its use. A Web version has also been developed.

The Virtual Science Laboratory (VSL), described by Whalley in Chapter 3, provides a broader context for emulations such as the Virtual Microscope. The VSL opens up opportunities for collaborative learning which go beyond the individual use of a single emulation.

The Mars Buggy (Figure 2.8) goes a step further by setting up 'real' experiments via a Web interface (Whalley, 1998). This approach has been successfully introduced into the control technology curriculum (UK National Curriculum) in several schools. A physical model of the Marscape together with a controllable buggy that is linked to a Web site, allows direct analogue control or the use of a control programming language (Whalley, 1994). Experiments have been conducted with an interface that is accessible to partially sighted students. Control technology is an aspect of their curriculum that is often neglected. A secondary benefit is that it involves mobility and orientation which is important to experience and experiment with for many physically and visually impaired people.

Figure 2.8. The Mars Buggy
(http://mars-buggy.open.ac.uk/buggy)

Figure 2.9 (Plate V). First Flight — Wright Brothers plane simulation
(http://met.open.ac.uk)

Another related example is First Flight (Whalley, 1998) which, through emulations of early experiments in flight, helps in the understanding of the associated physics. A facility to experiment with the design, and flight, of classic planes (Figure 2.9) has educational benefits and, for people unable to build a physical model, it offers an experience that could not otherwise be achieved.

Information

The Web provides a vast and rich resource of information. However, the quality and relevance of the information varies considerably. There is a range of search engines available together with indexes but these often fall short of identifying a narrow enough selection of sites and specific pages. This is a factor for disabled people using enabling technologies because the techniques associated with them are less efficient than conventional means of accessing a computer.

One example of improving the efficiency of access is the Topic Focus Resources (TFR) (Figure 2.10) interface (Whalley, 1998). TFR has been used in a school context. After the selection of a curriculum topic, appropriate key words are searched for using a conventional search engine which generally results in thousands of possible locations. By applying general selection criteria, the sites are reduced to less than 100. At this point, teachers involved in this aspect of the curriculum advise on a further reduction to

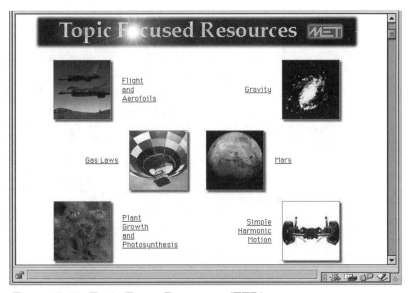

Figure 2.10. Topic Focus Resources (TFR)

about ten sites. The next, and crucial, stage is to obtain 'thumb-nail' extracts from the sites which are located on a local server. If the sites contain animations or simulations the 'dynamic thumb-nails' are captured. The TFR interface is designed so that a teacher or pupil can subsequently quickly browse a topic and, if any of the thumb-nails are of interest they select the URL to a specific Web page. The TFR is built progressively as more topics are added.

The Topic Access Video (TAV) interface (Whalley, 1995) provides a topic structure for images, video fragments and audio. It has been applied to a training requirement at the ACE Centre, Oxford, which assesses children with communication difficulties. The first topic was switches. This involved bringing together a wide range of information about these devices and capturing images and video fragments illustrating how they are used with individuals who have communication difficulties. Initially the training resource was delivered using CD-ROM with a TAV interface. Subsequently, this resource has been used on the Web (Figure 2.11). In this way, distance training can be supported. Also, a dynamic link can be established via the Web so that alternative access structures can be used within a Web page that, in turn, access the media resources on the CD-ROM.

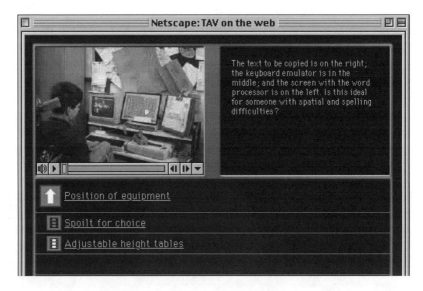

Figure 2.11. Topic Focus Resources interface on the Web

Web Accessibility

The previous section described a number of examples of how the Web is used for access for communication and learning. These all involve Web sites. In order for them to be fully utilized they must themselves be made as accessible as possible. There are two approaches to accessibility. First, well designed pages (clear layout, contrasting colours, simple structures, etc) can make a considerable difference to many users. A high standard of design should be a target to all users – good design benefits everyone. Second, by following certain guidelines, compatibility with enabling technologies can be considerably enhanced. There are several Web sites that offer information and guidelines concerning accessibility (for example, see http://trace.wisc.edu).

The optimization of access without the use of enabling technologies is a crucial objective because, in most circumstances, enabling technologies are less effective than conventional means of access. Often this is because there is a significant increase in the time required by a user to perform an action associated with the courseware. For example, the use of small point sizes for screen fonts (9, 10 or 12) can prove difficult for partially sighted students. Screen magnification software can overcome this difficulty but this is likely to require additional keyboard actions which is inevitably slower than not being required to use the keyboard at all if the text can be read. Hence an important target for accessibility is the avoidance, where possible, of the need for enabling technologies. This cannot be achieved for all users. For example, a blind student will always need some form of enabling technology as will someone unable to use a conventional keyboard. But the principle remains that accessibility should be first optimized in order that the minimum number of users will be required to use enabling technologies.

Accessibility to courseware is an issue for all learners. For example, consider interface design where factors such as screen layout, navigation methods and typography all have important parts to play. With the advent of graphical user interfaces (GUIs), user interactions have moved away from typing in lengthy commands towards direct manipulation that involves clicking on or moving graphical objects which is usually performed with a mouse. This requires courseware designers to take into consideration the size, shape, colour and positioning of objects. Accessibility can be improved by keystroke alternatives to actions performed by pointing devices. This is just one facet of design which can be drawn from a detailed consideration of accessibility issues. These issues have implications for all learners. Indeed it can be claimed that by taking into account the needs of disabled learners in designing courseware, everyone can benefit.

In the UK, the Disability Discrimination Act 1995 addresses issues of discrimination in employment and the provision of goods, facilities and services. Although education as a service is excluded from the provisions of the Act, training – including that provided by higher education institutions – is not. As employers, institutions are required to ensure that disabled people are not treated less favourably than non-disabled people and are required to make reasonable adjustments to working conditions or the workplace to enable a disabled person to do a job. The implications of the Act are currently being teased out but clearly, courseware and other curricular materials should be accessible to students and to staff. At an international level, legislation such as the Americans with Disabilities Act (US Department of Justice, 1990) and various European Directives already require minimum standards to be observed in the provision of education (Kemppainen *et al.*, 1995).

Complementary to the availability of guidelines on making sites accessible are software tools that can be used to assess the accessibility of Web sites. One example is Bobby (http://www.cast.org/

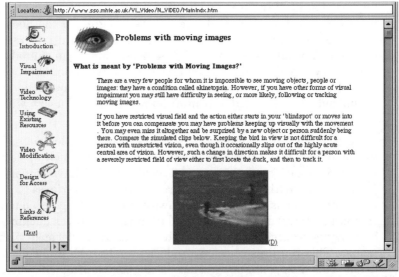

Figure 2.12. Improving Accessibility of Educational Video Material for Students with a Visual Impairment (http://www.ssc.mhie.ac.uk)

bobby) which is an on-line service provided by the Center for Applied Special Technology. Bobby analyses single Web pages for their accessibility to disabled people. Another option is to check out what a Web page would look like when using a text browser such as Lynx (http://lynx.browser.org). Lynx has a high degree of compatibility with enabling technologies.

The Scottish Sensory Centre and the University of Birmingham have researched and identified problems of access to video and multimedia materials by visually impaired learners. The outcome is a CD-ROM and Web site. The topics covered include: range of conditions and effects of visual impairment; good practice strategies for teaching and learning; ideas for adapting existing materials, and how to embed access strategies in new material (Figure 2.12). It is also an interesting example of using HTML authoring so that hot links within the CD-ROM material lead directly to useful Web sites.

Conclusion

There is no doubt that the World Wide Web offers opportunities for disabled learners to access aspects of the curriculum that are difficult or impossible to achieve otherwise. There are an increasing number of examples of how the Web can make a significant contribution. These include: new methods of communication to overcome remoteness; virtual experiments and environments to overcome physical barriers; and the availability to information from worldwide sources to overcome barriers to traditional means of accessing information.

However, in order to fully exploit these developments on the Web there is an important factor to take into account – the general accessibility of Web sites for the disabled learner. This has wider implications in that our experience has shown that consideration of the needs of the disabled learner in the crucial early design stages leads to a greatly improved Web site. This aspect has wider implications. By addressing the needs of disabled people everyone benefits.

Chapter 3

Collaborative learning in networked simulation environments

Peter Whalley

Best-practice science teaching often involves highly motivating hands-on experiences for learners. Simulations can provide equally profound experiences, especially when learners can collaborate and communicate with one another. Users of such simulation environments can be located anywhere on the Internet, and gain a richer understanding through their shared dialogues.

Introduction

The focus of this chapter is the potential development of Virtual Science Labs (VSLs), and the collaborative learning environments that might be built around them in the classroom, and between classrooms. For VSLs to work it will be necessary to bring together ideas concerning virtual science simulation environments, the potential for collaborative dialogue and resource sharing provided by computer mediated communication (CMC), and the lab or classroom based teaching of scientific experimentation within which they must be integrated (see Figure 3.1). Very large research literatures exist for each of these individual topic areas, but this chapter will focus on projects whose purpose has been to cross the boundaries between them. A key criterion of the success of networked VSLs will be the extent to which teachers want to embed them in their whole-class teaching of science, rather than simply view them as add-on computing tasks.

It is the 'process' aspects of science education, children discussing 'why we did this', 'measured that', etc, that are most likely to be facilitated by collaborative VSL environments, and which are valued sufficiently as a UK National Curriculum requirement to justify any extra organizational or resource costs. Simulation interfaces are generally designed to provide information or experiences for the individual learner, and it will be important to design-in the additional role of acting as a 'conversation piece' from the beginning, rather than simply adding a technical layer of communications to existing simulation software. This chapter will first review work which had such integration as a design goal and then detail the Virtual Spring

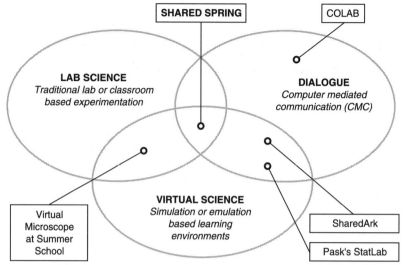

Figure 3.1. Relating CMC and Virtual Science to traditional class-room practice

Collaborative Microworld (VSCM), developed as an exemplar of how a VSL microworld could be designed to fit the needs of the classroom environment.

Simulation based learning

Pask's conversational model of learning

Amongst the first uses made of electronic computers was to provide simulation engines for calculating projectile flights. Similarly, the notion of providing learners with direct interactive modelling environments dates back to the earliest uses of computers in education. Gordan Pask's work is fundamental to any discussion of dialogue and simulation environments in that he pioneered the thoughtful use of computers in education. He was unfortunately at least 20 years ahead of his time in terms of the technology that he had at his disposal, which can make his work appear rather quaint, and he was prone to using fairly impenetrable formalisms for representing knowledge change. However his work has influenced much research into the use of simulation environments for teaching, even if often at second or third remove. A key aspect of Pask's work for our purposes is that his simulation microworlds were created primarily for the purpose of bringing about an engaged dialogue between student and teacher, and also between students. His model of learning focused on this use of the microworld as a 'conversation piece' by

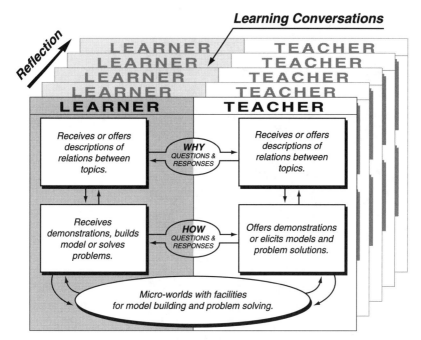

Figure 3.2. Pask's conversational model of learning

the teacher and learner; they were simulations designed to create conversations (Figure 3.2).

The heart of Pask's best known teaching system was the modelling environment provide by the 'STATLAB', a computing device on which the teacher could overlay problems and then give the student 'permission for discovery' (Figure 3.3). An analysis of the transactions in Pask's conversational model of learning shows how at the top level the teacher describes relations between the topics being taught, and the student asks 'WHY?' questions in response. The roles can also be reversed in that the teacher can ask 'WHY?' questions and receive a response from the student. On a parallel level, the teacher offers and requests demonstrations. 'HOW?' questions are asked, within a microworld that has been set up to model the most important features of the topic being taught. The model represents the key topic in the 'entailment structure' around which the teacher plans to hold the 'conversation'.

An added complexity of Pask's model is that all this represents only a single 'time-slice' of the learning conversation, in that over time both learner and teacher are encouraged to reflect on what is going on and thus to improve their learning and their teaching.

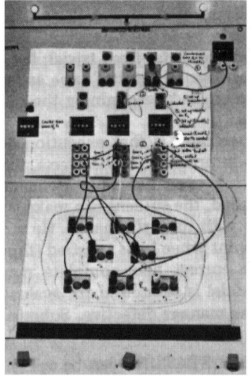

Part of Pask's STATLAB system (1973)

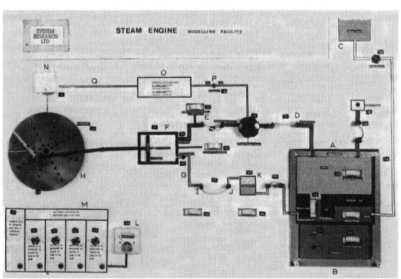

Pask's modelling facility for heat engines (1976)

Figure 3.3. Early attempts to create virtual science environments

Because of the difficulties mentioned earlier, his work has probably had a greater direct influence on the area of research concerned with 'learning to learn' than any other. An important part of the role of VSLs in the classroom could be to similarly externalize what is being learnt about the processes of scientific experimentation for group or whole-class discussion.

Animation works, sometimes

Animated graphical displays have always played a key part in representing the functioning of simulations, and the role of animation must therefore be considered in any development of virtual experimentation. Studies of the use of animations in computer based teaching have generally found that when used appropriately they improve learning, particularly in terms of knowledge of procedural processes (eg, Large *et al.*, 1995). This is not surprising given the additional time-based information that can be provided by the medium. However in an article reviewing the use of animations in computer based teaching Rieber writes, 'Unfortunately, animation is often used with the intention to impress rather than to teach. Sound and graphics have always been seductive features of new technologies, but the needs of the learner and the demands of the learning task should determine when and where animation is necessary' (Rieber, 1990, p77). A significant problem for the use of animation in teaching is that many important scientific models involve counter-intuitive effects, and again not surprisingly studies have shown that students are prone to develop scientific misconceptions from badly constructed animations (eg, Rieber, 1991). But there are still many situations where an animation can make clear ideas or relationships that are difficult to 'see' in a static diagram.

Scaife and Rogers (1996) view the issue of 'interactivity' in the use of animation as being critical. Only shallow cognitive processing is allowed for by what they refer to as 'passive' animations, and these may even provide less benefit to the learner than static diagrams. They point out that the claims made for computer-based graphical representations 'are often underpinned by assumptions which have little empirical support' (p209). They argue against the uncritical acceptance of the superiority of the new graphical technologies for promoting learning, and suggest an approach that analyses how the different representations work in terms of the cognitive processes that they bring about. It will be important in the design of VSLs not to become carried away with the use of graphic technologies for their own sake, as have others. Keeping a balance between what is attempted on the screen, as against what is best carried out with conventional equipment, requires that development work be firmly grounded within the context of classroom trials.

Mission-control and simulation exercises

NASA and other space related organizations are developing systems that nominally allow classes to link up to and control shuttle missions, telescopes, buggies, etc. Such mission-control exercises can easily achieve a high profile, a lot of funding and encourage much interest in science based activities in the classroom. They are also likely to bring about a great deal of communication and collaboration between schools. It will be important that the promise of real control is not oversold, because it would be unfortunate if the children ended up feeling that they were simply being allowed to watch adults having fun. Much of the children's real activity on these topics is likely to involve running simulations, eg shuttle mission launches.

Skills-based training

Skills-based training environments represent another important, and very well funded, simulation topic. BBN's well known intelligent tutoring system SOPHIE was developed in the mid 1970s. Attempts to build in adaptive/intelligent guidance to simulation systems have continued since then. Because of its military significance, many excellent simulation environments have been developed around the topic of 'electronic troubleshooting', and these are now being extended as 3-D virtual worlds with tactile force-feedback sensors. However collaboration in these simulation environments tends to be viewed as a matter of efficiency (how many trainees can work on the same simulator before individual performance levels drop) rather than as a possible source of enhanced learning.

Tait (1994) describes the latest reincarnation of this line of work, a large scale DELTA project into developing tools for the production of multimedia simulation environments. These were intended to have 'educational layers' added to provide learner support, although as Tait points out the nature of such a layer has 'still to be resolved' (p113). This study references others which question the effectiveness of simulation environments, and details how their own failed to overcome many of the students' misconceptions. However this perhaps says more about a premature attempt to replace the instructor with canned expertise than simulation environments per se.

Network-based simulations

Real-time games played over the Internet are starting to take off, although many have to rely on text windows for participant

Figure 3.4. Fighting Sail, a realtime Internet game built on Microsoft's DirectX multimedia platform

communication unless played over fast networks (Figure 3.4). The major software developers are creating tools to aid games developers, and even high-level authoring packages like Director and mTropolis now allow direct network linking between cast members. It could reasonably be expected that the developers of educational simulation environments would begin to build in collaborative 'sharing' facilities, once it was shown to be an educationally valued feature. The ability to have a parallel voice channel, without great cost or complexity, is obviously important and may be the key to the popularity of shared games.

Gaming environments that require 'twitch' reaction speeds, such as car and plane simulators, are being facilitated by direct linking networks, and potentially these might be employed for shared real-time educational simulations. However Internet connection may have operational advantages, and a pilot project suggests that even a simulation as sensitive to response time as one providing a sense of tactile 'feel' can be built into a shared environment using ordinary modem connection to the Internet. This shared dynamic simulation, shown in Figure 3.5, had to use 'client-side prediction' techniques to accommodate missing time-critical information, but the reduced latency of ISDN connection

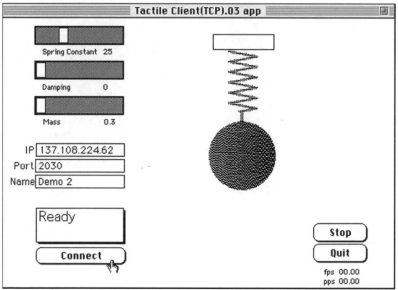

Figure 3.5. A prototype shared modelling environment with parallel voice link

is likely to make such software much easier to develop as it would then not have to adapt to so much missing data.

Computer mediated communication

An important part of CMC has been the development of tools for collaboration in the work place, eg COLAB (Stefik *et al.*, 1987). The organization of ideas and meetings can be supported and augmented by shared whiteboards, adaptive databases, etc. It is interesting to note how, as the shared tasks have become more conceptual and less task orientated, the 'cooperative work' of CSCW has evolved into the 'collaborative learning' of CSCL. Cooperation implies that the task has been worked out or pre-specified for the group, and that all they have to do is to simply 'work together', eg changing settings and recording results in synchrony in the simulation domain. Collaboration involves working through and understanding a problem with others. The implication is that the presence of partners, bringing their own contextual knowledge and conceptualization of the problem, will aid in its resolution. Recent reviews of the CSCL domain describe its most recent evolution as 'computer supported collective learning'. This primarily reflects the concerns of researchers using simple e-mail and conferencing facilities to study the effects of computer based communication on group interactions and purpose.

One of the best examples of collaborative communication is the SharedArk system of Smith (1987) which in one instantiation had a simulation of a factory sequencing process built into it. This work is probably the closest existing realization of what a VSL might achieve, although the SharedArk project and its derivatives expend most of their technical and conceptual effort in attempting to simulate the affective aspects of communication using a methodology, and at a cost, that is difficult to justify for the results achieved. For immediate practical purposes, and particularly in the classroom environment, VSLs will have to assume little more than the parallel facilities of telephone, or perhaps the simplest video-phone, level of conferencing communication. The provision of an information-rich link between the participants' simulation environments should be the key to success.

Virtual Science in the classroom

Most of the literature concerned with the use of animations and simulations to teach science in the classroom is concerned with small scale studies of a short duration. Research studies involving the children collaborating whilst working in shared-simulation environments have also tended to involve fairly contrived situations, where each child has deliberately been set up with a different perspective on the problem to start with (eg, Joiner *et al.*, 1995 and 1996). They have been created primarily to investigate learning processes and peer interactions in the classroom, but are still likely to be useful for analysing the dialogues between children with naturally occurring differences in perception of an experimental problem or scientific procedure. Figure 3.6 shows a hierarchy of possible relationships involving simulation models in a conversational classroom context.

Madinach and Cline (1996) describe one of the few large scale projects in this area. The study involved several schools where the system modelling environment STELLA was introduced across whole areas of the curriculum, with some success. This project involved collaboration between students within each school, but unfortunately only involved teachers in the link between schools. A high level of collaborative discussion between students was found to be the norm, with the unforeseen consequence of some teachers finding it difficult to adjust their classroom management to be able to share control of the technology with their students.

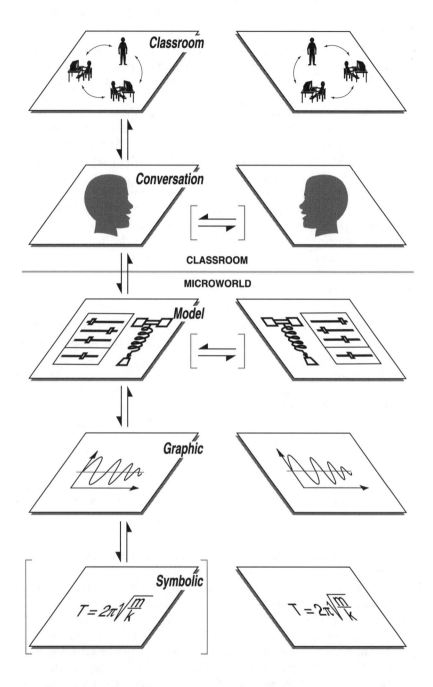

Figure 3.6. A layered view of simulation environments and their teaching context

The Virtual Spring Collaborative Microworld

Design goals

The Virtual Spring Collaborative Microworld (VSCM) was developed as an exemplar of how a VSL microworld could be designed to fit the needs of the classroom environment. Much of the literature relating to collaborative systems involves high-end workstations and fast networks; however the VSCM was designed around the level of computer performance and networking resource likely to be available in the classroom over the next few years. The topic of spring extension was chosen because it is frequently used as an example in UK National Curriculum documents to introduce the procedural ideas underlying data collection and representation. Springs and weights are fairly low cost items and fairly easy to manage in the classroom environment, so why create an emulation of them? The microworld was not designed to teach the scientific concepts underlying spring extension required by the National Curriculum. These would be gained through the direct practical experience of adding masses to different springs and observing the effect, which would precede any use of the VSCM. Our aim was simply to create an environment in which the procedural aspects of the transformation of observation to data, and data to symbolic representation could be brought out clearly, and allow

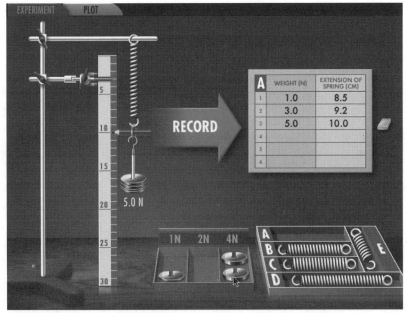

Figure 3.7. The experiment mode of the Virtual Spring

them to be enriched by collaborative discussion of what appears to be happening and the children's predictions of what will happen next. This version of the VSCM was expressly not designed to aid understanding of the problems of error in data collection, another important process aspect of science teaching, nor was it intended to introduce the scientific concepts underlying nonlinear spring extension.

The VSCM

The experiment mode of the VSCM, Figure 3.7, allows the children to create a table of observations by choosing a spring, adding different masses to it, and recording the extension. The teacher can set the mode of the extension measurement to be either 'absolute' or 'relative'. In the first case no calculation is needed, but the plots for springs of different lengths do not have the same origin. In the second, the extension re-calculation is played out as each data cell is recorded. The plot mode, Figure 3.8, dynamically illustrates how each pair of data points combine to make a single plot point, and is designed to extend conceptually the 'what if' thinking that children may already carry out with spreadsheet packages. Within the plot mode, users share a set of coloured markers which they can use to predict data values. Lines are only plotted between acquired data values or where the appropriate prediction has been made. All users share the same model space, and if in the same mode are locked together and see

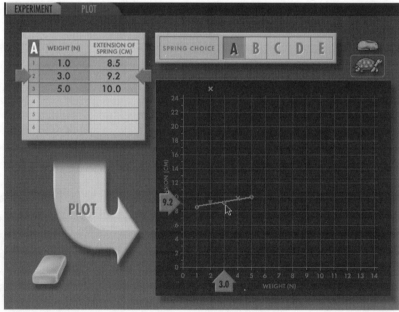

Figure 3.8. The plot mode of the Virtual Spring

the result of each other's actions. However the system permits loosely-coupled collaboration to the extent that users can operate independently if they are in different modes. This means that one child can return to the experiment mode to collect more data for a particular spring whilst the other is making further predictions or even plotting the data being acquired, but not that they can simultaneously collect or plot data from different springs.

The weigh mode, Figure 3.9, turns the plotted function that they have developed for each spring into a virtual spring balance. The graph that they have created becomes a newton-meter which the children can now use to measure the force exerted by known and unknown objects. In conceptual terms, this represents the use of the scientific method to develop and calibrate a practical tool. It is often difficult for teachers to convey the wider significance of scientific investigations to children and examples such as this can help.

Implementation and trials

The VSCM has been developed in Macromedia Director using XTRAs that add TCP/IP communications functionality. Versions have been created that work as an application under the Mac OS (running in 6 MB of memory) or as a ShockWave download to Netscape under the Mac OS and Windows 95 (needing about 15 MB). Both versions work well in parallel with the voice-link

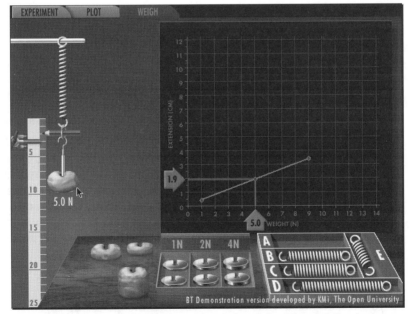

Figure 3.9 (Plate VI). The weigh mode of the Virtual Spring

capabilities of Netscape Communicator using ISDN connections. The system can be configured to work as a client/server that can accept a link from a single client or as a server that can link to two or three clients, logging the transactions. The first mode is likely to be the most common use of VSLs of this form, the 'full server' mode being most appropriate for educational research use or in a distance tutoring scenario as it requires a substantially more powerful processor.

One of the most important findings in our early trials has been that the performance limiting factor of the VSCM is client processor power rather than communication bandwidth. Unfortunately one of the most important design criteria, rapid reflection of referential pointing gestures made with the other user's mouse, requires the most processor intensive operations and can interfere with the proper maintenance of a dynamic multimedia interface. The importance of gesture in the human computer interface is of obvious importance to the 'immersion worlds' of VRML systems, but has also been recognized as a possible constraint to the natural flow of human communication in video conferencing environments, eg Machin and Sheppard (1997). If a VSL topic were to benefit from the presence of more than three or four simultaneous users, it seems likely that gesture communication would have to be allocated a separate channel from that needed by the normal command clicks made to the multimedia interface if it were not to become a frustrating experience.

Conclusion

Modelling and simulation microworlds have become a common feature in the use of computers for education. It is the quality of the representation that they provide and the ease with which they can be manipulated, that are usually taken to determine the usefulness of particular microworlds. Is it an adequate model of the general topic? How easy it is to understand? Does it engage the learner in a significant direct experience? However, important though these aspects of simulation are, the key to the successful adoption of VSLs in the classroom is more likely to be bound up with their ability to bring about true learning conversations between children who are discovering the processes of science at first hand in easily manipulable environments.

It is clear that the role of the teacher will be crucial to the successful acceptance of VSLs in the classroom. They will have to be convinced that a positive outcome in terms of National Curriculum requirements will result, eg in terms of the process aspects of science education. Also they will have to learn to judge from the 'public' outcomes of the shared interactions and conversations when and how to intervene, as they normally would by keeping an eye on the development of the children's workbooks. To aid this it will be important to design-in to VSLs logging facilities to help teachers monitor the extent and order of the learning taking place, and also to build in control features which allow them to tailor these conversational simulation environments to the needs of their particular class.

descriptive
dialogue? collaboration?

Chapter 4

Media integration through meta-learning environments

Tamara Sumner and Josie Taylor

While mixtures of new media can offer significant opportunities for Open University students, they can also be a daunting hurdle for newcomers. A collection of tools such as interactive course maps, deployed in the context of a new computer course for over 5,000 students, points the way towards helping students successfully manage the media mix.

Introduction

In recent years, there has been a realization of the importance of learning, particularly lifelong learning, to the envisioned knowledge-based economies of the next century (Dearing, 1997). With this realization, there has been an explosion of interest in new forms of teaching and learning made possible by new technology – particularly on-line distance education and multimedia learning environments. These two areas are perceived as offering the potential to promote lifelong learning by supporting flexible learning, fostering learner control, and stimulating learner engagement.

Given these perceptions, it is not surprising that many educational institutions have started or announced plans to 'put their courses on-line' and make 'significant use of new media'. In these institutions, students will be working with a wide array of computer-based tools – ranging from standard office productivity tools, to various kinds of communication software, to Web-based hypermedia, to specialized learning environments tailored to particular curricular needs. Thus, courses will consist of a diverse collection of learning resources distributed across numerous media and technologies.

A challenge for learners in such a situation is effectively 'managing the media mix' to achieve their educational objectives (Laurillard, 1995). Learners are not only trying to master the subject or domain content, they must also now cope with: (1) mastering a potentially complex assortment of software tools, and (2) developing new study habits to make effective use of these tools. Recent empirical studies indicate that many learners, particularly those who are inexperienced with computer technologies, feel overwhelmed when faced with this new way of learning.

We are investigating how interactive course maps and study guides can help beginning students successfully manage potentially complex mixes of new technologies to enhance their learning process. In effect, we are trying to create meta-learning environments; ie, environments to help beginning scholars 'learn how to learn' with new media. This research is currently being conducted in the context of a new introductory course on object-oriented computing. This chapter describes the interactive Course Map and Study Calendar created for this course and discusses future developments in this ongoing project.

Requirements for meta-learning environments

Wherever students are learning, whether at a distance or face-to-face, they need support. This means they must always be able to answer questions such as 'what should I be doing?', 'why am I doing it?', and 'when is it due?'. This entails an explicit understanding of the relationship between the various components of the course, and their uses, as well as a means of 'appropriating' that material, of stamping their mark upon it and recording progress through it. In other areas of education, it has been found that telling students the 'whys' and 'whats' beforehand improves their performance (see Conway and Kahney, 1987, and Stasko *et al.*, 1993)). Meta-learning environments can fulfil this role at the beginning of a course and as a course progresses.

Study guides have traditionally been the mechanism used to provide study advice in existing Open University (OU) paper-based courses. However, in courses that make significant use of new media, something more is often needed. Like traditional study guides, meta-learning environments provide students with information on the structure of the course and pacing information. They differ from traditional study guides in that they: (1) focus on how to use new media to achieve learning objectives, and (2) provide active support for new learning processes. We have identified several key areas that meta-learning environments need to support.

Orientation
Specifically, environments should lay bare the structure of the course so that students always know what they should be doing, what needs to be done next. This information is commonly found in study guides. However, we need to provide more support than

study guides typically do on what resources they should be using at particular points in the course.

Understanding the relationship between tasks and resources
This relationship needs to be clarified at two different levels: a 'global' level and a 'bridging' level. At the global level, students need to have a general understanding of the overall role of different learning resources in the course in order to be willing and able to use them effectively. At the bridging level, students need more explicit support in bridging between general task-oriented goals and specific activities in various resources. This level of task semantic support is commonly missing from many virtual learning environments, but is usually provided in traditional classroom situations by teachers and other students (Taylor, *et al.*, 1997) . Given our distance learning situation, it needs to be provided in some other form; we can not rely (at least initially) on electronic communication tools since these are the very resources that students are having difficulty with.

Establishing and maintaining new study habits and ways of working
There have always been large variations in the study habits of different students. Indeed, studies have identified important differences between 'good' and 'poor' students (Chi *et al.*, 1989) . These differences can be accentuated by technology since academically disadvantaged students have traditionally been those that are also technologically disadvantaged. Thus, if we are to design courses for these populations that use new technologies, we must take explicit actions to address these differences. Specifically, many students need explicit advice about how to work and study using the course resources.

Confidence building
Ideally, a meta-learning environment should be easy to understand, easy to use, and even fun. It should help alleviate students' lack of confidence, and not contribute to it further by introducing yet another mysterious or difficult bit of technology.

Integration
Ideally, a meta-learning environment could help relieve students of some of the burden of tool management by integrating different resources and media. Such an environment would act like a 'course-specific launcher' enabling students to access their learning resources easily and in a contextualized manner.

Enrichable and annotatable
To assist students to appropriate learning materials and make them their own, and to help foster methodical study habits, a

Project Title	Requirements being Investigated	Project Description
The Interactive Course Map	• Orientation • Global Support • Bridging Support • New Study Habits • Confidence	Course-related multi-media CD-ROM for use by large distance learning population (N = 5,000).
The Study Calendar	• Integration • Updateable	Web-based time-line which indicates which resources are relevant at different points in the course. Has direct links to other web materials and provides students with a single, integrated, task-based interface to a diverse collection of web resources. Easily updateable during course presentation.
The Progress Advisor (See McKillop, 1997 for more details.)	• Feedback and Progress	Exploratory study using intelligent agents to provide students with feedback on study planning. A simple agent was embedded into a version of the course map that used two forms of knowledge – information from students on their previous study activities and information about the structure of the course – to provide students with advice about what sections they should review and how long upcoming acitvities may take.
The Personal Learning Manager	• Updateable • Annotatable	This project builds on the Course Map and looks at how to extend the Map in two ways: 1) supporting dynamic updates during presentation and 2) supporting aspects of the Map to be 'authorable' or reusable in other courses and institutional contexts.

Table 4.1. Meta-learning environment projects

meta-learning environment should be enrichable and annotatable by the students themselves.

Tracking and feedback
Students need easy mechanisms to keep track of their progress through the course, thus motivating themselves when things get tough. Feedback on one's actions is also an important element in effective learning processes (Rowntree, 1992). In traditional class-room situations, feedback usually takes the form of two-way communication between teachers and learners. In distance education, where communication occurs through other media such as print, e-mail, or computer conferencing, there is a lack of immediacy in the feedback provided. Computational meta-learning environments can be used to provide some forms of immediate feedback to learners.

Table 4.1 provides an overview of the projects we are conducting to investigate these different requirements for meta-learning environments. In the remainder of this chapter, we'll focus on two of these projects – the Interactive Course Map and its related Study Calendar.

Setting: An introductory computing course

Let's step back for a moment first, and look at a particular course that has provided the context for this research. The setting for this work was the design and development of a new undergraduate introductory computing course called 'Computing: An Object-oriented Approach' (M206) developed in the Maths and Computing Faculty here at the OU. Such courses often have 3000 to 5000 students enrolled during a given presentation. Here, we'll give a brief overview of the design goals and the resources created for this course; a more detailed discussion can be found in Woodman and Holland (1996).

A key design goal was to achieve the educational aims of the course team; that is, the team had certain expectations about what students should learn and experience by participating in the course. The straightforward educational aims were for students to get a solid understanding of object-oriented design and programming, networked computing, and software design. However, the course team also wanted students to have 'big thoughts' about more philosophical aspects of software design and to perceive both the software they used and the software they created as designed artifacts, embodying trade-off decisions between competing goals and objectives.

Course Resources	Function in Course
Printed Texts	Provide the conceptual and theoretical learning materials in the course; designed to give the students a 'good read' without requiring being on-line; also used to integrate the other course materials by setting up the larger context and directing students to other resources.
Smalltalk LearningBooks Programming Environment	Provides the practical learning materials supporting the learning-by-doing activities related to programming, object-oriented concepts and software design.
Set Book: Parsons & Oja (Second Edition, 1996)	Provides much practical information on computer hardware, software and networked computing and relates many general ideas in these areas to existing real-world applications.
Eleven Television Programmes	Contextualise the students' activities in the course to larger trends in the world and real-world problems and applications. Many programmes feature interviews with designers, users, engineers and clients; thus enabling students to view the technology from the different perspectives of all these participants.
Two Multimedia Titles – The Object Shop and Grumble's Grommets	Provide two experiential, learning-by-doing environments in object-oriented concepts (Shop) and networked computing (Grommets).
Electronic Glossary	Supports linking of key terms and ideas into larger related concepts and, by integration with the Smalltalk environment, linking of practical actions with general concepts.
World Wide Web Site	Acts as the course library containing complementary course materials and materials of a timely nature, such as those that change from year-to-year, new updates to course resources, and pointers to further background materials.
Computer Conferencing	Supports general communication among course participants and the necessary discourse between group members during collaborative design and group working.
E-mail	Supports student-tutor communication and electronic assignment submission.

Personal Productivity Tools; eg, word processors and drawing packages	Students use word processors for written work and drawing packages for diagrams for their marked assignments in order to submit them electronically.

Table 4.2. Course resources and their different functions

A second set of design goals were based on The Open University charter of supporting 'open learning'; that is, allowing for and designing for students with diverse backgrounds who need to study in their own time and place. We know that students in this course will have extremely diverse backgrounds in key areas such as academic study, programming, and computing in general. For many, this may be their first experience with higher education. In terms of computing, the course could attract people with a range of skills – from those using computers daily in the workplace to other first-time users who bought their computer especially for this course.

Table 4.2 shows the resources that were created by the course team with these different design objectives in mind. What is striking about this table is the multitude and diversity of learning environments used to support a rich, year-long course. The materials are both complementary and overlapping, with each resource playing an important role in the overall course. While some media may support overlapping objectives (eg, the printed texts, the set book, and Grumble's Grommets all deal with networked computing), each does so in a different way. These different ways include supporting a different learning style (ie, experiential versus reflective cognition (Norman, 1993)) or providing a different perspective on the same material (ie, the printed texts take a theoretical look at networks and communication protocols whereas when using Grumble's Grommets, students design a network using today's existing technologies). This is consistent with the use of diverse media in other OU courses, as described in Chapters 6 and 7.

Preliminary experiences with the new course
As with any new course developed at the OU, the resources underwent developmental testing. We conducted two forms of evaluation (Sumner and Taylor, 1998) with learners: longitudinal surveys and in-depth interviews. The longitudinal testing looked at whether people were able to use and learn with the resources. During the testing, a group of 14 people were paid to act as students and 'take' the course using the preliminary materials.

As these 'students' worked through each chapter, they filled in a survey about the resources and the subject matter. These surveys were followed up by telephone interviews with each tester at regular intervals.

We also conducted in-depth, one-on-one interviews with eight of the testers. These interviews focused on trying to understand their experiences working and learning with the computer-based resources. We asked them in detail about how they studied, how they organized their on-line work, and how they organized their study time. Where possible, we asked the students to show us their notes, filing system, diaries, etc and explain them to us.

Analyses of the survey data showed that overall things were going fairly well. About half of the participants were able to do the practical programming activities and seemed to grasp the various object-oriented concepts with no significant problems. Unfortunately, other participants were having difficulties and seemed to be frustrated, particularly those with little prior experience with new technologies. Despite their initial enthusiasm for going on-line and being interactive, many participants were not really making effective use of their computer-based course resources and instead were relying heavily on the paper-based materials. The interview data also identified several related areas of concern: lack of confidence, lack of clarity, and prolonged suboptimal use.

Lack of confidence
Some testers had little confidence in their ability to work and learn with the computer-based resources. What emerged from the interviews was that confidence was very fragile and took a lot of time and effort to cultivate and minutes to destroy. Several had long-standing fear and anxiety about computers prior to the course and this was slow to change. Others had experienced setbacks, eg, a difficult installation or 'Web' session, that had shattered their confidence.

Lack of clarity
Nearly all the participants suffered from some lack of clarity about the role of the various resources in the course and how they should be using them to support their learning. While most could use the resources to carry out specific activities, they often had difficulties making the connections between different practical activities and larger conceptual issues. As a result, they tended to develop isolated and piecemeal views of their computer-based resources.

Prolonged suboptimal use

Many testers were falling back on their lifetime of experiences learning with paper-based materials and relying heavily on reading texts. Some did not even try other resources unless they were explicitly directed to and it was essential to task completion. For others, lack of confidence with technology was clearly a contributing factor, leading to suboptimal use patterns (eg, always starting from scratch rather than editing and saving an existing LearningBook) and reducing people's willingness to experiment with new ways of working.

In retrospect, these results are not particularly surprising. We had a collection of 'just plain folks', ie, many people with little computational experience, thrown into a new way of working and learning with technology. They assembled and plugged in their hardware, opened and installed a diverse collection of software, and had expectations that they should become productive users virtually overnight. Instead, some felt overwhelmed by it all, lost

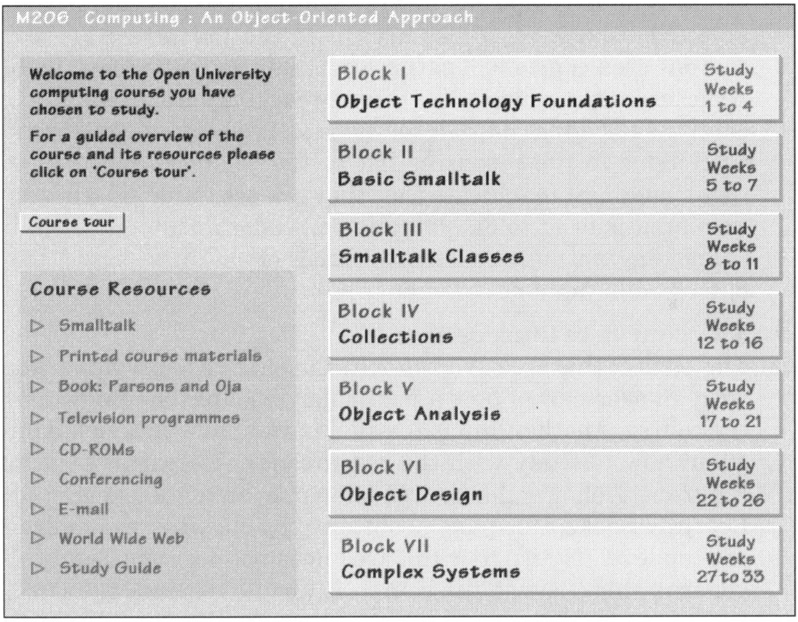

Figure 4.1 (Plate VII). The interactive course map

The course content area (right half of picture) reflects the block structure of the course and provides information about what students need to do each study week. The course resources area (bottom left) provides a high-level overview of how each resource is used in the course. The tour area (top left) is used to provide students with advice about how to study and how to use the Map.

confidence, and focused on trying to master isolated bits of technology and lost track of the larger goals for the course.

The Interactive Course Map

Clearly, our testers needed more assistance to appropriate their learning materials, take control of their own learning process, and feel comfortable and confident about what they were doing – it was not just going to happen on its own. To help this appropriation process, we created an Interactive Course Map (see Figure 4.1) that meets some of the requirements for meta-learning environments. The colours and fonts were chosen to match those used in the course printed text and in the course Web site. Thus, where possible, resources used in the course have a familiar and consistent 'M206 look', regardless of the medium. By using a familiar look and following a simple and straightforward layout, we hoped to make the Map seem friendly, fun and relatively intuitive to use.

The Map is composed of three main areas: the course content area, the course resources area, and the tour area. The course content area consists of seven large buttons, reflecting the block structure of the course. The course resources area is simply a list of all the resources used in the course. As the mouse cursor moves over items in the resources list or the big block buttons, these items highlight to indicate that they are pressable. The box in the tour area is used to display an 'explicador' head with headlines supporting an audio narrative. Each of the three areas will be described in more detail below.

The course resources area

The aims of this area are two-fold. One aim is to provide students with an overview of how a particular resource should be used in the course. Another aim is to provide students with global advice about how to study with the resource for this particular course. Figure 4.2 shows the course resource area for the Smalltalk LearningBooks; this pane is obtained by clicking on Smalltalk at the top level. Notice how the area does not describe Smalltalk in general: this is what the course is about! Instead, it focuses on describing the LearningBook structure and how one might study using this structure.

Likewise, the area on the World Wide Web does not describe it in general terms but focuses on how it will be used in the course. Specifically, it describes the supplementary learning materials available at the M206 Web site and how the students will be instructed to download updates of materials from the site

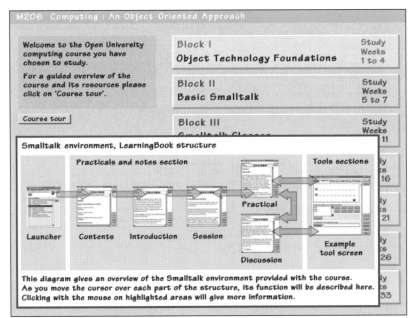

Figure 4.2. The Smalltalk pane in the course resources area

This pane describes the structure of the Smalltalk LearningBooks used in the course. As the mouse cursor rolls over each of the pages shown, an overview of its purpose appears at the bottom of the pane. The arrows illustrate one idealized workflow using the LearningBooks. An annotated picture showing the key parts of each page can be obtained by clicking on the small page icons.

periodically. Even the area on television programmes contains advice on how to watch TV! Previous experience has shown that while everyone knows how to watch television for entertainment purposes, most people do not know how to watch it for educational purposes.

The course content area

This area has been designed to meet several of our objectives for meta-learning environments. First, it is designed to support orientation by laying the structure of the course bare. Pressing the Block 1 button at the top level brings up the two panes shown in Figure 4.3. Each block area is structured into two panes – the block overview pane (on right) and the weekly resource pane (lower left). The block overview pane shows how each study week is composed of one or more chapters. Clicking on any chapter title will bring up a third level pane containing a chapter description.

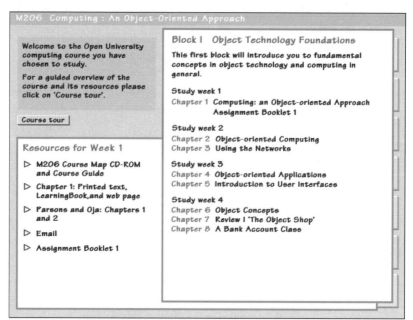

Figure 4.3. The contents of Block 1

Each block area is structured into two panes – the block overview pane (on right) and the weekly resource pane (lower left). The block overview pane shows how each study week is composed of one or more chapters. The left side of the weekly resource pane shows what learning resources are used in any given study week.

The weekly resource pane shows what learning resources are used in any given study week and what resources comprise each chapter. As you can see below, chapter 1 consists of a printed text, a Smalltalk LearningBook, and an associated Web page. As the mouse cursor rolls over the study weeks shown in the block overview pane, the weekly resource pane changes to show the resources used for week being rolled over. This mechanism enables students to get a quick overview of the amount and types of work they'll need to do for any given week.

The colours used for the pane borders match the colours used to identify the different blocks (eg, the light blue is always used for Block 1 and the deep red for Block 7). Thus, the colours are not only pleasant, they reinforce a sense of orientation.

Our second objective was to provide bridging support to help students make connections between general tasks or learning goals and more detailed activities in specific resources. This objective is supported by the interplay between the block pane and the weekly resources pane. These two panes are layered; clicking on one brings it to the front and overlays part of the other pane. The chapter descriptions available from the block pane focus on learning goals and high-level tasks. The left side of the resources pane shows what tools and resources are used to achieve the learning goals or complete the tasks. Clicking on the resource pane brings it to the front and makes the right side visible. For each item in the weekly resource pane, the right side of the pane discusses how the resources will be used to meet specific learning objectives. If the resource being discussed is a television programme or an interactive multimedia title, then previews or demonstrations are available on the right hand side.

The tour area
We have outlined the structure of the map and the ways in which it can be navigated. At this point we return to the goal of bridging between resources and course content. We wanted not only to help link different media with different learning experiences, but to also provide a guided experience which would take learners through the map, and show how to use it through a process of self disclosure (DiGiano and Eisenberg, 1995). We combined this notion of self-disclosure with Plowman's notion of narrative guidance and the use of an 'explicador' (Plowman, 1996).

Plowman describes Buñuel's account of people called explicadors who, at the turn of the century, used to stand in front of the cinema screen interpreting for the audience the revolutionary new form of the moving picture (Buñuel, 1985). This was necessary because audiences had not yet built up a grammar of interpretation to allow them to understand filmic devices indicating passage of time, change of location, intensity of focus and so on. Plowman adapts this role to multimedia, arguing that users have similar difficulties in acquiring an appropriate grammar, or literacy, in the new media, so explicadors are needed to help in the process (see Laurel *et al.*, 1990) for related work using guides and agents).

In the map, the explicador(s) take learners on tours of the map. There is a general Course Tour and a Block 1 Tour. Students can obtain transcripts of the audio track if they wish (this is essential for supporting hearing impaired students consistent with the goals of Chapter 2). The Course Tour introduces the overall structure of the course, but most importantly, students are shown each of the various media and given advice about how to use that medium to maximum benefit. The Block 1 Tour steps through the different activities in each of the first four study weeks, discussing how the computer-based learning tools will be used in the different activities. The Block 1 Tour also emphasizes the need to get organized and get the software installed.

The explicador in the Map is not a full-screen full-motion 'talking head' video. Not only would such a representation be a drain on the computational resources available, thereby slowing the tour down, but we also felt it was unnecessary. The particular form of the explicador is adapted from KMi Stadium (see Chapter 9) and is a low bandwidth format which conveys a small amount of information when attention is focused on the explicador, but otherwise stays very much in the background. We used members of the course team as explicadors (as opposed to famous celebrities or cartoons) since, from our experiences with television, we know that students enjoy seeing programmes which feature course team members because they like putting faces to names.

We have completed the formative testing using six volunteers representative of people who would typically register for such a course – see (Sumner *et al.*, 1997) for more information. To summarize our results, all participants were very enthusiastic and positive about the overall look and feel of the map, and had very few problems navigating, seeming easily to find the things we set them to look for. We were most anxious about the tours however, because there was a strong chance that people might find them simply irritating, and of no use whatsoever. Our testing results alleviated our concerns. All six participants described the tours as 'helpful' in the following specific ways: for taking them through the structure of the course phase by phase, for introducing the media and for showing them how to use the map itself. All participants said they would probably listen to all, or parts, of the tours several times.

The Study Calendar

In this course, we needed to represent a very diverse collection of media resources from video clips and overviews of Smalltalk, to television broadcast times and assignment submission dates. These resources can be categorized along two different dimensions: (1) rich versus lean, and (2) stable versus dynamic. For instance, a video clip is a rich resource in that video clips consume large amounts of storage space when compared with lean, text-only resources. Additionally, video clips of television programmes produced for the course are a relatively stable resource in that it is highly unlikely that the show will be modified during the life of the course. Conversely, some resources, such as television broadcast times and assignment submission dates are dynamic in that they change from year to year.

In our case, the course resources fell into two categories: rich/stable and lean/dynamic. Early in our design process, we decided to acknowledge these two types of resources and create a lean, Web-based Study Calendar to complement the media-rich, CD-ROM-based Course Map. The Calendar is a Web-based resource whose contents and design are easily updatable by the course team.

The Study Calendar's design performs two integrating functions: one is time-based and the other is task-based (Figure 4.4). It provides a simple time line of key events and activities in every block. More importantly, it provides a task-based way for students to interact with a diverse collection of Web-based resources – when studying M206 Chapter 3, there is a single point of entry to all the Web resources related to that chapter.

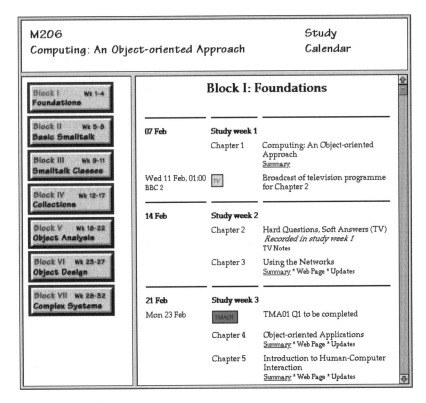

Figure 4.4. The Study Calendar

Conclusions

In summary, many students can feel overwhelmed when facing a new way of working and learning. We hypothesized that meta-learning environments could alleviate this problem by helping students take control of their learning process, making clear the relationships between resources and learning goals, and helping students stay oriented as the course proceeds. We have built an initial version of such an environment: The M206 Interactive Course Map and our experiences with the map so far are very promising. Besides benefitting students, constructing the Map seemed to positively influence some course team activities in that it helped a diverse group of designers focus on and articulate key course design issues that needed to be represented in the Map.

So what next? Are the phenomena we described simply transitional? Do meta-learning environments only fulfil a short-term need? With increased exposure to tools, environments and media, will students develop the kinds of skills and literacies that eliminate the need for meta-learning environments? We don't think so. In both the short and longterm, the need for meta-learning environments will not disappear. We accept, as a fundamental principle, that learners also need support from their teachers, no matter how sophisticated their materials are, nor how elaborate the learning environment is. This support may be provided in a variety of ways, and need not always be from the human teacher to the learner on a one-to-one, face-to-face basis. But we can – and do – confidently assert that students will always need help!

Chapter 5

Developing Web-based student support systems: telling student stories on the Internet

Peter Scott and Marion Phillips

Students need advice of many kinds both before and during their academic careers. CD-ROM based databases and automated advisory programs can be enhanced in numerous ways when Web-enabled, particularly if emphasis is placed on the personal/affective side of the student experience.

Introduction: What guidance do students need?

Guidance and support are needed at every stage in a student's career: at entry; during study; between courses; and at the end of a study programme. In an ideal educational environment the student should be seen as a whole person whose learning takes place in the context of past experiences, present circumstances and future hopes and aspirations. Educational guidance and support are at the heart of this view (Bailey *et al.*, 1997). This means providing support which is both responsive and developmental. Responsive guidance and support involve providing effective responses to enquiries and student needs and problems as they arise. Developmental guidance and support are concerned with the student's overall progress, across all courses and study programmes; and with their educational, vocational and personal development. In most universities the support services tend to be responsive, but not developmental.

So what are the needs of students? In addition to course specific academic support, students may need all these things:

- *pre-entry educational and vocational guidance.* To help students make informed decisions about appropriate courses, qualifications and vocational options including advice and information on educational, financial and practical issues.

- *orientation into learning methods.* To enable students to gain the maximum from the variety of learning resources available.

- *preparation and development in learning skills.* The ultimate aim is to enable students to become independent (autonomous) learners – support may cover such areas as learning how to learn (see Chapter 4), time management, writing skills (essay writing, report writing, note-taking), numeracy, IT skills, examination skills, etc.

- *confidence.* In adult education confidence in study is vital. Returners to education have a great need to review their skills in the appropriate context – so that they are realistic about what they can achieve but do not undervalue themselves.

- *personal support throughout study.* To clarify possible ways forward and make progress – to help them to deal with the inevitable problems that will arise.

- *study planning.* To ensure that students' course choice and longer term planning are to meet their often complex (and changing) requirements eg, advice on credit transfer, vocational qualifications, professional recognition. There may be a need to access specialist services (eg, careers advice) and guidance on further study.

- *support for students with special requirements.* For disabled students, as well as those with other special needs such as exam anxiety, support should be based on the objective of enabling all students to lead a full student life and to meet the university's academic requirements.

- *monitoring and support of student progress.* Close monitoring of the student's progress should enable the tutor to intervene quickly with support where students are not making progress and allow the university to plan and target its services more appropriately.

- *personal counselling.* Higher education can be very stressful. When students experience anxiety and depression there are a number of sources of help that they will turn to. Formal academic related support systems can be one such source.

In this chapter, we will focus on the first of these issues, pre-entry educational and vocational guidance.

What happens in higher education now?

There is a growing awareness that higher education needs to be more supportive and that students should have greater access to advice and guidance, but still many student support services tend to be (reactively) responsive rather than (proactively) developmental. A reactive response system can only deal with problems when they become acute: for example, counselling for exam anxiety during the exam period, or offering vocational advice immediately before graduation!

In distance education there are particular challenges associated with supporting students. In the UK's Open University, the principles of educational guidance and support (academic counselling) are at the root of all its teaching. The OU was founded on a multimedia approach combining initially print, television, radio and audio cassettes, face-to-face tuition and academic counselling, telephone communications and correspondence tuition to teach and support students. These 'traditional' media have been joined by video, and more recently by computer media such as CD-ROM, computer mediated conferencing, electronic mail, and now the Internet.

Supporting students with new media

The new computer based media provide a particularly interesting addition to student support systems, since in addition to facilitating tuition and making information available, they have considerable potential to support advisory and guidance activities, to overcome potential student isolation, and to build links between students and the university. What is rare however is any attempt to integrate the diverse services and packages in this field into a coherent whole.

Computer based support packages can be conveniently divided into two main categories: the stand-alone, and the networked. Stand-alone packages can provide easy access to large databases from personal computers. There are numerous examples of such programs currently in use, such as 'FORMSCORE', a computer-mediated vocational guidance system (JIIG-CAL, 1997) and 'ECCTIS+' a database of Higher Education establishments and courses available in the UK (ECCTIS, 1998). Stand-alone systems can also be used to present services to users as interactive multimedia (eg, Scott *et al.*, 1996).

In contrast, network services are much more recent developments, but increasing in sophistication. With the growth of networking, and in particular the growing penetration of the Internet into even the domestic world, students can now access remote, dynamic and rapidly updated electronic resources with ease. This medium also offers an opportunity for communication through the use of conferencing and e-mail. Thus, even very remote students can have access not just to information but also to expert advice and guidance and to the ability to network (in the social sense!) with peers.

Below we present two multimedia systems that can be used as Internet network services. The first is a stand-alone CD multimedia package that has been re-cast in a Web form. This re-casting of the stand-alone multimedia system is compelling because the potential to integrate discrete systems into greater and seamless student experiences is very powerful. The second is a new prototype system – designed from scratch as Internet multimedia.

Moving a student support package to the Internet

A view of system 1 : OU Support Services for Students

The Support Services for Students system was produced by Regional Senior Counsellors at the Open University using Macromedia's Director. It aims to inform current and prospective students about the facilities offered by the University across the world and to provide a perspective on studying with the OU from a variety of different angles. At the core of the system are stories told by OU students about how the issues affect them. The stories themselves are assembled from real student experiences – but each individual story was carefully constructed by the counsellors to cover a number of key issues that are problematic for OU students.

The system has three major parts: map based views of the University's regional centres; personal stories of students; and detailed topics on getting started and studying with the University.

The key to the usability of the system is that the simple messages are delivered though the voices of students and advisors. The on screen text and images are simply support for the voices that are telling the stories. The work of Schank and Cleary (1995) highlights the profound benefits that accrue from compelling multimedia story presentations particularly when intelligently and sensitively matched with students' needs.

Internet delivery of this project

Simple multimedia systems of this sort can move relatively transparently to the Internet. Although the most tempting solution is to deliver them as is, a better solution is to re-cast them for the new medium. This system was implemented in Macromedia Director which provides a very transparent and free Web browser plug-in called Shockwave. Director projects must be first compressed, using the free Macromedia utility called Afterburner (now integrated into the developer package itself) and can then be viewed plugged in to a recent version of a browser such as Netscape's Navigator or Microsoft's Internet Explorer. Unfortunately, this project was not ideally suited to this form of Internet delivery. The project used a number of separate and interdependent sections that would have needed to be merged together, and a very great deal of audio. Besides, even when compressed for Shockwave the project still amounted to megabytes of software which would take a very long time to download over an average modem. A more satisfying solution was to rework the system as an Internet product. The use of the RealNetworks RealMedia browser plug-in made the delivery of the audio, streamed from a server, a realistic possibility.

In Figure 5.1, from the experimental Web version of the Support Services for Students project, the student is invited to

Figure 5.1. An OU Support Services for Students Web page

hear the personal stories of a number of OU students. Each story raises a number of issues which are then explored further within the system.

Each individual screen consists of text and graphics with appropriate links to other pages – as in any hypertext. The more graphics intensive screens can take some while to arrive over a slow domestic modem connection – but they are a small load compared to even a well compressed 'all-in-one' Shockwave version. For projects such as these – where it is the quality of the information, its relevance and ease of use that are the key – this sort of conversion is clearly viable. The heavy reliance of the Support Services for Students project on quality audio was a problem until the release of excellent streaming audio tools like RealAudio. The original Director CD contained many megabytes of AIF sound files.

In Figure 5.2 we see a student 'Dave' raising some of the issues related to studying as a blind student, by telling his story. The sound-track of Dave's story is here synchronized via the RealNetwork's RealAudio Netscape plug-in to a cartoon depiction of his story – seen here in the top right frame.

The audio in the network version is delivered streamed as required, a few bytes at a time – with the quality negotiated in

Figure 5.2. A Support Services for Students Story: Dave talks about his experiences as a blind student

Learning media

software between the server and client. It is also seamlessly synchronized to simple screen based events using a combination of RealAudio and Javascript. The story is supported by the use of simple cartoons that illustrate sequences in the story.

A view of system 2 : a prototype Course Choice Advisor
The interactive course choice guidance program is currently running as an experimental prototype intended to demonstrate the potential of a multimedia student advisory system. The goal of the prototype is to show how we could provide pathways to enable users to ask and answer important questions about themselves. These questions relate to such issues and areas as personal requirements, type of study, career plans, professional recognition, qualification routes, credit accumulation and transfer. The emphasis of the program is two-fold: primarily to offer students a process through which they might be guided in their course and qualification choices; and thereby also to improve their understanding of the decision-making process itself and increase their ability to become more independent learners in terms of their own educational choices.

The central feature of the system design is around the student making notes as they proceed which they should be able to print out as part of an ongoing personal and learning development portfolio.

The system begins by helping to focus on the questions that the student brings to the course choice advisor. We frame these questions in a notepad – into which the student may also write – and from which they can proceed to an animated discussion with advisors and a variety of students who may be able to help them to think about the issues.

Constant in the environment (and in Figures 5.3 to 5.8 at the bottom pane of each screen shot) are the following: links to the University, a link to their own notes, links back to the home area for the advisor system, volume and status controls, and controls for moving back, forward and to the start of each segment. Extra audio and video controls are available as pop-ups, as is the main notetaking environment and its associated save and print features.

The notetaking model used by the students to make notes for their development portfolio is here seen with one page 'ripped out' to help them focus on key questions. The ripped pages provide key starting point menus.

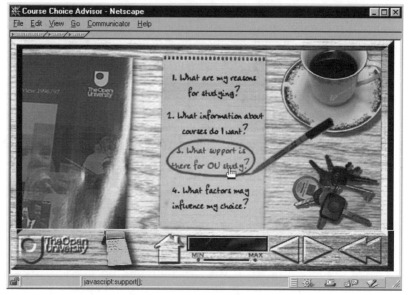

Figure 5.3. The notepad interface to the Advisor prototype

Figure 5.4 shows one result of a student selecting to explore a particular question from her notes. In this case the student has entered an office-setting advisory environment.

A series of advisors sit at the desk to the left hand side of this environment and a series of helpful students appear through the door to the right. Support information (graphic and text) appears on the flip chart in the middle.

Here the student may begin to explore the first of the issues from the menu above – reasons for study. The advisor talks the student through a number of the issues on this topic – inviting them to consider each one further.

In this case, in Figure 5.5, she should consider what is her main reason for interest in study – either to start/change/enhance a career; for a specific qualification; or simply for her own personal interest.

There are a number of different advisors, for different topics and issues, and a number of linked students who present a complementary perspective to the issues raised.

A student, seen in Figure 5.6, enters when he or she has a helpful story to present regarding an issue of concern. Student stories are intended to be a constant over all of the issues covered

Figure 5.4. Entering the Office in the Advisor prototype

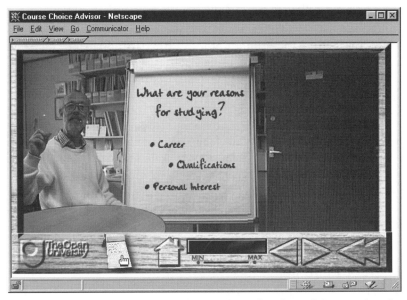

Figure 5.5. An advisor speaks to the whiteboard issues in the Advisor prototype

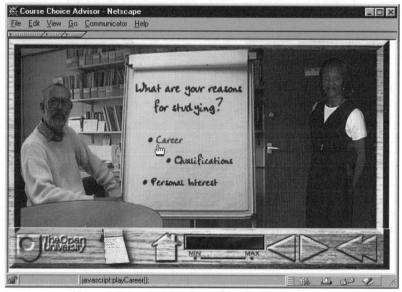

Figure 5.6. A helpful student in the Advisor prototype

because, as in the previous prototype discussed, one story can raise a number of important points relevant to the enquirer and their portfolio notes.

In general the student story is illustrated with more sketches and cartoons than the bullet points which tend to support the advisors (Figure 5.7). The design aims are to present fellow students that the enquirer can identify and find common cause with, and to give their focus on the issues a lighter and more informal feel than the advisors. It should be noted that the students and advisors all focus as much on problems as on their solutions – so that the student is able to think them through in his or her own context.

The advisor may also draw upon a sequence of video segments that helpfully illustrate issues that the student needs to consider (Figure 5.8). Further discussion of this prototype is given by Phillips *et al.* (1988).

Internet Multimedia to support students

There are many issues that could be raised in the comparison between network delivered services and stand-alone services. Here we discuss just a few that are particularly striking in this student support context, starting with disadvantages of network

Figure 5.7. The student can also speak to the whiteboard

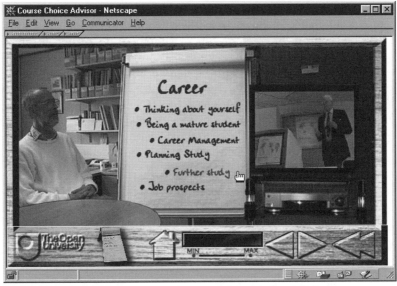

Figure 5.8 (Plate VIII). A video segment in the Advisor prototype

student support context, starting with disadvantages of network delivery.

Disadvantages

- The visual quality of the final product is invariably poorer as one makes design compromises to suit students with slower connections. This is particularly true in an open learning context where adults are learning in their own homes, and in the UK, paying their own telephone/connection charges. It is still very difficult to deliver projects that require good quality video due to limitations in bandwidth and compression.

Advantages

- The project is instantly accessible from anywhere with network access. Anyone with a suitable PC and modem can now access these systems. They do not have to find out about the availability of the system and wait for the CD to come to them – as soon as they know about the system they can come to it!

- It is very easy to monitor the use of the system. Whilst one can count the number of CDs that are put in the post to students it is much harder to determine the use that is made of them after they enter the postal system. Similarly, feedback is hard to collect from stand-alone systems, as students have to go out of their way to return a questionnaire. However, every access to every page of the server of the Web versions can be logged, and feedback is so easy for the student to give via e-mail links on pages, that it is hard to stop users telling you what they think about the system, even before it is properly released! At the moment these systems are still experimental and we have no formal usage data but we hope in due course to report on the network evaluation of the systems.

- Integration with other major network resources. From the students' point of view the distinction between the various related projects becomes significantly less.

In the next section we give two examples of how we see this proceeding.

Integrating network student support systems

Apart from multimedia information systems, two other types of system should be very naturally integrated into the Internet support of students. The first is database access, the second is conferencing systems.

All universities maintain databases that could be used by students. For some institutions, the appropriate information is being laboriously re-cast directly and by hand as HTML Web pages. However, most such databases are already in an electronic form that could be used, via an appropriate interface, directly by students. The most obvious common database, that some universities have made available for many years, is that of courses and their selection.

The Sibyl system is a student database system developed by the Academic Administration Office of the OU. It provides core and automatically updated information about OU courses and qualifications and was designed to inform staff who deal regularly with queries from students. The system is available via a Windows PC interface on the OU intranet and is in regular use by staff. As a network service it extracts and presents the course information from the University's CIRCE central student records system. The OU Sibyl office is currently developing a student-accessible version of this information system which will be available on the World Wide Web. From prospective students thinking about enrolling in a course to continuing students making choices through their academic life: the need to find out about courses, be advised on the issues involved for them in study, and the ability to discuss their needs with others could all be addressed by a common and seamlessly integrated experience.

In Figure 5.9 we see a query page from the experimental Web version of the Sibyl system. The student has asked the system which courses use the keyword 'psychology' in their database descriptions. At the time of this query, there were 18 OU courses which satisfied this criterion. The student may then move to each course description and find further information such as prerequisites, current fees, contact information, etc.

With respect to conferencing systems, we can see that the students can use their on-line exploration to do more than seek out information and help from systems: they can also use the context to communicate with other students. In the OU, conferencing systems like CoSy and FirstClass are used extensively for the support of academic work (Mason, 1994). However in a student support context the SoftArc FirstClass system has recently been used to support the OU Technology Foundation course (called T102). Here it was used for staff-student and

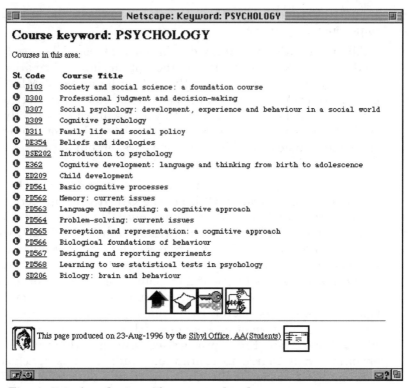

Figure 5.9. A web view of a course database

student-student conferencing and e-mail. In an academic counselling role for this course counselling staff could support students and encourage them to support each other in, for example, periodic progress check up sessions, and to address specific concerns such as exam preparation (Phillips and Harrington, 1998).

The FirstClass Course Choice Fair is divided into subject areas. By clicking on an icon, the student enters a conference (Figure 5.10) where they can ask questions about any course they are considering for the future, learn the opinions and experiences of students who have already taken that course, and seek expert help from advisors.

The integration of these electronic systems presents quite a challenge, yet from the student's point of view any move among the different systems cited should no longer be a perceived barrier. Students should be able to leap between advice on a welfare issue to a story related by a student who has some shared

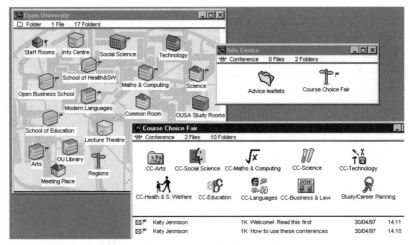

Figure 5.10. A FirstClass course choice conference

circumstances; to an information system that tells them about course specific constraints; then back to a system which guides them through some of the points to consider in selecting a new course.

In Figure 5.11 we show one view of how some of these systems could be organized together. (We should stress that the systems discussed here are far from seamlessly integrated and that this architecture shows only one view of how they may be!) In this case

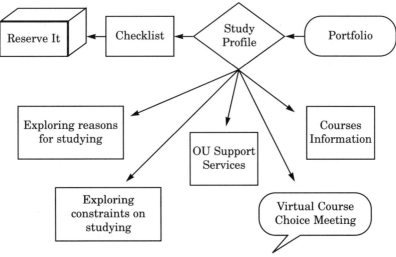

Figure 5.11. One view of integrating web based support systems around the student study profile

we show the centrality of the student study profile (informed by the portfolio – discussed in the course choice advisor). This is only one view of the architecture of the system because there are many interlinks among the subsystems involved. The portfolio is the student's own evolving record – and is relevant to all of the other subsystems. The Web courses information and reservation systems are shown here where the students look into the courses databases; as is the conferencing section in which the students can talk to real students and tutors about their own needs and experiences.

Conclusion

In this chapter we have aimed to show some snapshots from our ongoing work in student support systems. The examples we have given should have illustrated three key things:

- *Student support systems are essential.* Whilst it is easy to focus on the delivery and management of academic content, the support of students is an essential feature of any educational system. In any university, the services for students will be distributed amongst a number of different groups and systems – a common Web infrastructure will make the sensible cross linking of these services easier, but shouldn't be at the expense of innovation.

- *Internet Multimedia is compelling and not that hard to do.* By far the hardest part of multimedia development is deciding what it is that you should be doing and how you should start going about it. Once you have delivered a concept in one system it is actually very much easier to deliver it in another – even if it involves remaking it from scratch to follow a similar story-line. Web multimedia producers tend to sacrifice sophisticated animations for simplicity and ease of updating. The quality assurance standards you need for the production of CD multimedia are much higher than the standards you need for Web multimedia because Web errors can be much more easily fixed, late in the day; material can be kept very much more up-to-date; and the delivery can be much more (people) interactive – even if it is just sending an e-mail at a certain point in your exploration!

- *The Web can greatly facilitate talk.* In this book there are many chapters which present different views of how we can communicate more effectively using the Internet: we can talk to real people and even to software agents. The systems that we have discussed here show how we can even use talking to 'canned' people to effectively (and affectively) communicate. The goal of this set of student support projects is not so much the information itself as the guidance of students through a process of thinking about what that information means for them! They need to be guided to ask questions of themselves so we have provided them with some prerecorded stories to listen to that will help them through these questions. This design decision changes not just the visual design of the prototypes but also their structure and function. The stories we present provide a personal contact with 'canned' people whose experiences could find an echo in the students' own experiences.

Chapter 6

Innovations in large-scale supported distance teaching: transformation for the Internet, not just translation

Marian Petre, Linda Carswell, Blaine Price and Pete Thomas

In a carefully controlled series of trials, students on Open University Computing courses were introduced to innovations in teaching and learning. Asynchronous and synchronous tutorials, electronic assignment handling and a variety of other approaches were meshed with a range of personal styles. The key to success lies in appropriate transformations that build upon the unique opportunities afforded by the new media.

Introduction: transformation, not translation

The use of technology, and more specifically the Internet, has been an important advance for distance education. The Internet has the potential to meet students' changing social and educational needs – in particular the need to choose their own time, place and style of study. Universities respond to societal trends, and it is natural that they should follow the trend to use technology (Adamson-Macedo, 1996). 'Universities, like other organizations, are having to re-examine their ways of working, stimulated by developments towards "an information superhighway" and the ease of accessibility to non-discursive global information resources' (Steeples *et al.*, 1996). Educators are looking to technology to solve many of their problems – including increasing student:staff ratios and diminishing funding – while at the same time seeking to improve their teaching to provide a better student experience (See Sir John Daniel's comments in Chapter 1, and also Reinhardt, 1995; Skillicorn, 1996; Thomas *et al.*, 1996).

Yet innovation comes at some cost, and knock-on effects may include increased demands on staff time, complication of the supporting administrative system, and additional overheads for students (Laurillard, 1993). Many institutions are converting lecture notes or other paper-based materials to HTML for the World Wide Web, but, with little support provided for the student, the gains are minimal. Simply translating material from familiar media into electronic form is rarely productive – and is certainly inadequate for supported distance education, which aims to engage the student in a 'community of learning'. If we hope to improve rather than translate, we must understand the whole teaching and support process through a critical examination of its functions. What the popular enthusiasm for the Internet and the superficial translation exercises tend to overlook are the fundamental questions:

- whether technology's effect on the learning it is meant to support is constructive, rather than obstructive; and

- whether the benefits offered outweigh the costs involved.

For two years, we have been developing a learning environment to support the whole instruction process, encompassing students, instructors (known as 'tutors'), staff support, and administration. The thrust of the work is the integration of support systems to improve the teaching process holistically. We have investigated mechanisms for:

- interactions among students and tutors;

- assignment marking using an electronic marking tool;

- electronic assignment handling;

- synchronous and asynchronous Internet-based problem sessions;

- automatic student registration; and

- examination.

The systems have been tried on an entry-level and an upper-level Computing course, involving approximately 350 students and 23 experienced tutors in 1996, and involving some 500 students in 1997.

The chapter begins by considering how instruction and support functions can be served and potentially enhanced by an Internet-based structure. The chapter summarizes selected findings of an extensive evaluation involving several hundred students over three courses and considering learning, student experience, assignment marking, problem sessions, scalability, and integration into existing administrative structures. It considers which changes in culture help to preserve or improve teaching quality while adapting to screen-based and often asynchronous interactions. It highlights both costs and gains of using the Internet to transform the distance learning environment for those associated with it: students, tutors, administrators and the institution.

Supported distance education at the Open University

The Open University (OU), which teaches around 150,000 students at a distance, has developed (over more than 25 years) a well-tuned machine for providing high-quality university education for part-time students studying at a distance. 'Quality' in this context means:

- *relevant and of high academic standard* in its content;
- *effective* in conveying the desired information;
- *suitable* for a diverse student population;
- *supportive* of largely independent study;
- *engaging* for students;
- *consistent* in its delivery and assessment; and
- *cost-effective* in its use of resources.

The teaching and support network for students manifests itself in five distinct aspects: teaching materials; tutorial support and assessment; counselling support; examinations and enquiry services. Each student studies at home using teaching materials delivered primarily by post but using a variety of media. For each course, the student is allocated a local tutor who teaches via correspondence and helps with queries related to the academic materials. The tutor is normally contacted by telephone or post. Students may also attend local, face-to-face tutorials run by their tutors, and they may choose to form 'self-help groups' with other students.

The mainstay of teaching is the tutor-marked assignment (TMA; hereafter 'assignment'). Throughout the course, the student is required to submit written assignments, which the tutor grades and which the tutor annotates freely, providing essential feedback. The assignment has two roles: summative and formative, for assessing student progress and as a teaching tool for taking remedial action. Tutor notes, including a marking scheme, are provided to the tutor in order to ensure assessment quality, and marked assignments are monitored regularly for consistency and marking quality.

The pre-eminent commitments for the OU are to access and quality:

Access: The OU has no barriers to entry; the ethos of the university is to be 'open and equal'. Admission is on a first-come-first-served basis, and all entry-level courses are designed to allow students with little formal background to reach university entrance level quickly. Yet students can still be disadvantaged: personal, local, or geographical constraints may restrict individual students' access to face-to-face sessions or telephone contact with the tutor. As a result, many students rely solely on the printed material and assignment correspondence with their tutors.

Quality control: Courses are designed by a multi-disciplinary team producing custom text, software, audio cassettes, video for broadcast, and CD-ROMs. All materials must be completed and evaluated in advance; courses undergo rigorous developmental testing with a student cohort before presentation. Quality must also be maintained in presentation. On a course with 5,000 students (eg, an introductory Computing course like the one described in Chapter 4), some 200 part-time tutors' work must be co-ordinated and sustained at uniform standard.

The key challenges for a large, distance teaching university are scale and rapid feedback to a dispersed student population.

Scale: In some courses in The Open University, there are as many as 8,000 students, and the total number of students per year exceeds 150,000.

Rapid feedback: Even though 40,000 assignments are processed per week, the efficiency of the UK postal service means that the students usually receive their marked assignments within a week (often within days) of the tutor submitting them. Retaining and motivating students hinges on rapid feedback, which makes communication (paper-based or otherwise) a key issue. This has been one of the barriers to the OU teaching outside the UK, where communication systems are often less reliable.

Electronic communication is hoped to have significant impact in each of these four areas: overcoming access barriers, providing flexibility and responsiveness in accommodating various student circumstances, providing automatic records and checks against minor errors, and providing efficient tools for administrators and over-stretched tutors. But an electronic system must prove itself secure, robust, scalable and affordable.

Internet presentation trials: mechanisms

Our solutions must observe the OU ethos of being 'open and equal' with respect to technology access, both in the UK and abroad. Hence a key foundation of the technology described in this chapter is plain-text Internet e-mail, which can cater for almost any student, regardless of the speed of the network connection or software available. A number of inter-related mechanisms have been developed:

- a Web-based, automatic registration system (see http://mzx.open.ac.uk);

- electronic examination using encrypted examination papers downloaded via the Web at strictly supervised examination centres at appointed times;

- an electronic assignment handling system, including electronic assignment submission, a marking tool (with a component for monitoring), and automatic verification and record-keeping; and

- conferences and Web resources.

Only the latter two will be discussed in this chapter.

Electronic assignment handling

The university has well-established procedures for grading paper assignments which must be interpreted for electronic assignments. Assignments are marked in conformance to a scheme specified by the Examination and Assessment Board which also sets the assignments and provides 'post-mortem' discussions of them. The tutor then sends the assignment to the central Assignment Handling Office which enters all the information into a database, verifies details, and returns the assignment to the student. The paper system requires the assignment to be posted three times and potentially to be photocopied at more than one stage. If any of the details is incorrect, the tutor is contacted for corrections; this happens in about 5 per cent of the OU's annual throughput of approximately half a million assignments.

The current electronic system (Figure 6.1) is Unix-based, involving a central collection of databases, and with supporting software written in Perl and Java. It accommodates:

- student assignment submission;

- tutor assignment marking and handling;

- automatic data logging, verification and acknowledgement at all stages of handling (ie, automatic administration);

- monitor access and commenting.

Since the administrative tasks (form filling and arithmetic) are performed automatically, administrative errors of the type cited above do not occur.

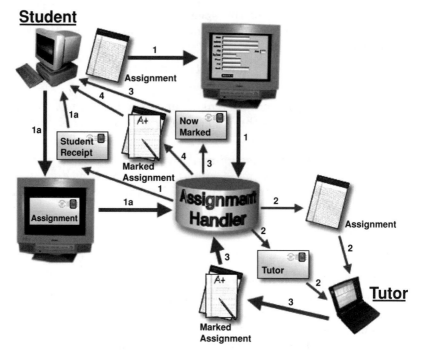

Figure 6.1. Diagram of assignment handling system. Key: [1] Students can fill in a Web form, attach their assignment and receive an instant receipt number on screen and via e-mail; [1a] (alternative) Students can submit an assignment by e-mail to a special handler. A receipt is issued by e-mail; [2] Tutor notified by e-mail that an assignment is waiting, downloads assignment from Web page; [3] After marking assignment electronically, tutor returns it through a Web page, where the handler logs it, and notifies student that marked assignment is waiting; [4] Student downloads marked assignment from Web page or requests that it be e-mailed.

Electronic assignment marking

The tutor uses a forms-based WWW interface to download assignments. An assignment-marking template for use in conjunction with Microsoft Word 6/7 has been developed for the course. When the student document is opened, the application automatically converts it from its original format to the native format. The template uses a data file to provide the student's and tutor's administrative details automatically, except the grades and the tutor's comments. The template has a number of built-in tools to aid marking (Figure 6.2 shows a marking sample). The tutor can

Question 3
Did the Re-Design Work

- **Conceptual Issues** – these include -automatic opening of the Address Box when the Create button is pressed, the possible inclusion of a drag and drop ~~method~~ technique for assembling the 'To' and 'Copy To' lists in the Address list, automatic opening of the Priority and Save To dialog boxes when pressing the Send button, automatic query if there is no text in the Subject or Message fields, ~~and less control over deletion of mail.~~

LOGICAL FLOW FOR MESSAGE CREATION

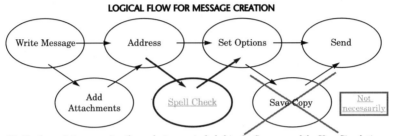

50. Further points concerning the re-design are included in the Summary of the User Simulation at Annex C.
Basically a good answer—see detailed hypertext comment below.

Figure 6.2 (Plate IX). Example of marked assignment

delete or insert text in any font or format anywhere in the document; inserted text appears underlined in blue, and deleted text is displayed with a red strike-through. Check marks and crosses can be inserted with a keystroke. Annotations can be added which provide a kind of hypertext comment (which appears in a separate frame on screen or as end-notes if the document is printed). Marks for questions are entered using a dialog box which automatically verifies that the grade is in the correct range for that question, copies the number into the data file, and adds up the marks. The drawing tools included in the word processor are available, so that freehand drawings are possible.

The marking tool includes a comparable template for the monitor (a senior member of staff who reviews tutors' performance) which allows the monitor to add typographically distinct comments or corrections to the marked assignment.

Conferences and Web resources
Our conferencing system allows one-to-many and many-to-many communication. Its interface is a forms-based WWW system simular to that described in Chapters 7 and 8 which supports membership access control, sub-grouping, user-selected e-mail notification of any posting, and embedded HTML with images and 'hot links' which mean that, when a posting refers to another point on the WWW containing additional teaching material or software

to be downloaded, the student need only click on the link to go directly there. As course material is moved onto the WWW, tutors are able to provide answers or present tutorials which refer to course material with live hyper links, rather than static references. The notification facility supports a 'stop press' conference to which all members of the course are automatically subscribed, giving them (a) an automatically-sent e-mail copy of every posting, and (b) read-only access to a reference copy of the announcement. Thus, those students whose access is through a slow Internet connection or simple e-mail are not disadvantaged. Other conferences are available for both social and work-related discussions; most are for 20 to 50 students to keep discussions manageable. Students with e-mail only access can treat these conferences as mailing lists and remain full participants. Tutors have Web access to a database of tutorial material, examples and frequently-asked-question sets.

Internet presentation trials: tutorials

Distance students often report a feeling of isolation when studying because of their lack of contact with an instructor or other students. Problem and discussion sessions, known as 'tutorials', are crucial in establishing student networks and self-help groups. The emphasis on electronic tutorials arises from previous experiences of electronic presentation, as well as from earlier analyses of what students derive from face-to-face tutorials (Coats et al., 1992; Fung et al., 1994).

Reported student benefits
The benefit to students is only partly academic; the tutorial is an important social focus that allows students to build relationships with their instructors and other students. Students report that tutorials provide:

- demonstrations of expert behaviour; worked examples;
- alternative perspectives and explanations; unexpected issues; extended scope of discussion;
- clarification and reinforcement of concepts;
- structure; milestones; incentives; pointers to what's important;
- pointers about the kind of problems they will face in assignments;
- learning from other students' questions, mistakes, insights;

- reassurance that progress is appropriate, and that the student's progress is comparable to that of other students; sharing problems;

- social contact with other students; a sense of belonging to a community.

OU statistics over years indicate that students who attend tutorials tend to perform better than those who don't.

What is a typical face-to-face tutorial?

Instructors are given a 'free hand' in running their tutorials, but the 'typical' tutorials they report fall into three general formats.

- Open question and discussion sessions which are student-centred.

- Lecture-type sessions which provide an augmented view of the course material, either through additional explanation or worked examples.

- Workshop-type, problem-solving or practical sessions in which students work individually or in small groups on problems of varying difficulty. Interaction and discussion are emphasized.

Electronic tutorial models attempted

At the start of the 1996 term, several electronic tutorials were suggested to the tutors, based on an analysis of existing practice. The suggested models tried to accommodate both the constraints and the opportunities inherent in electronic communication in order to provide valuable tutorial functions within the simplest effective technology – and hence emphasized structured, asynchronous tutorials. Those models were woefully inadequate; trying to run electronic problem sessions to mimic face-to-face sessions produced disappointing results. Fortunately, the tutors adapted and invented; identifying new, appropriate structures for electronic sessions proved effective and engaging. A distillation of those experiences is presented below, grouped by mode (asynchronous, mixed and synchronous).

Asynchronous models

There were nine different styles, and several additional variations, employed. Where a chronological sequence is involved, we number these, whereas a collection of tasks or activities is presented using bullet points.

Asynchronous problem-solving and discussion

1. Timetable is announced (typically either 2–3 days or 7–10 days);

2. problems are set, often in stages; these may be programming problems, questions about program fragments, design questions, etc;

3. students submit solutions (either directly or anonymized), discuss each other's responses, and ask questions (either on conference or via e-mail);

4. instructor contributes to the discussion, guiding the work;

5. instructor reviews important points and sends 'model' answers, sometimes only by request.

The following variations occurred:

Asynchronous topic discussion: Students discuss issues or topics, sometimes responding to notes or worked examples posted by the tutor, often responding to provocative statements, rather than solving aspects of programming problems.

Fetch-and-respond: Students are expected to read material or collect information or examples off-line which they report and discuss via e-mail or conference.

Cumulative asynchronous problem solving: eg 'Asked for volunteers... persuaded students to circulate efforts... shared later tasks... to combine for a big solution to a modularized problem'.

Revision tutorial: Former examination questions are given, discussed, and solved collectively; a post-mortem is provided by the instructor.

Asynchronous group work

1. Problems are set; these are usually based on a scenario about developing a piece of 'real world' software;

2. groups are set, either by subscription or by problem choice (students must declare themselves in advance);

3. groups collaborate and agree on the solution which is submitted for general discussion;

4. instructor keeps tabs on groups and comments or guides as necessary;

5. instructor reviews important points and sends 'model' answers, sometimes only by request.

A variation on this model was 'cumulative asynchronous group work' with staged weekly sub-tasks contributing to a longer-term solution.

Role play for collective programming

1. Students subscribe;

2. students bid for or are given tasks which contribute to a modularized group project or at least to group discussion;

3. instructor summarizes.

A variation on the role play model was 'cumulative role play', with stages occurring over a month.

Q&A repository
Instructor presents on the Web a collection of:

- questions, discussion and answers from e-mail with students;

- 'thought points' to get the students thinking beyond the course material;

- questions followed by worked examples.

Stand-alone tutorial
Structured hypertext is presented on the Web: sequences of discussion, problems, answers covering a series of topics.

'Open mentoring'
A question-asking service, student-driven, with answers broadcast to all students.

The individual tutorial

1. Problems are announced (either on conference or via e-mail); these may be programming problems, questions about program fragments, open-ended questions, etc;

2. students reply and ask questions via e-mail to instructor;

3. instructor makes individual replies; no general discussion.

The continuous tutorial

1. The tutorial is instructor-driven: problems are set on a regular basis, with discussion and then post-mortem;

2. new problems are set when students provide answers to the current ones;

3. programming problems are inter-mixed with discussions on programming topics or conundrums.

(One example had 14 rounds.)

The Web treasure hunt
Students are expected to solve one step in order to get the instructions for the next step; steps are distributed in different Web locations.

Mixed-mode tutorials

Only one mixed-mode style was used, involving the following sequence.

1. Timetable, introductory material and problems posted by instructor;

2. time for asynchronous e-mail discussion;

3. Q&A accumulating during tutorial are assembled on Web;

4. Internet Relay Chat (IRC) is staged on a specified date;

5. IRC log is distributed to all participating students via e-mail.

Synchronous tutorials

Two kinds of synchronous tutorial were used: IRC and audio-graphic.

IRC tutorial

- 'Interactive Relay Chat': synchronous text-based interaction via the Internet;

- instructor-led discussion, typically about an hour;

- problem solving, discussion of topics, or informal lecture;

- a text file of the discussion can be saved.

Audio-graphic tutorial (Figure 6.3)

1. Tutorial materials distributed in advance by instructor;

2. quasi-real-time audio and video from instructor; pre-prepared materials (both text and graphics) plus synchronous annotation displayed in workspace shared with students;

3. shared 'chat' space for textual submissions from students.

Evaluation and lessons

Considerable data, both qualitative and quantitative, have been collected to support well-founded comparisons of conventional and electronic delivery: the project has access to all examination results, about 3,000 marked assignments, some 1,000 questionnaires from both students and tutors, all conferences and most

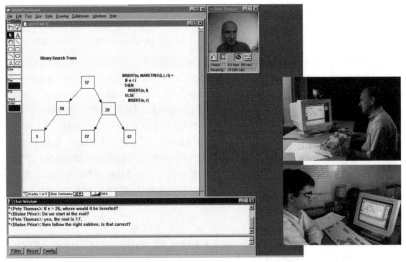

Figure 6.3 (Plate X). Audiographic tutorial student screen dump with inset photos of student and tutor

electronic mail, tutor records of their interactions with students, and records of de-briefing meetings with tutors. Some participating tutors have combined electronic and conventional tutorial groups; others have all-electronic or all-conventional groups. This has allowed us to make comparisons among delivery methods and to examine the impact which individual differences in tutor style have on resource usage and on learning effects.

Detailed reports of specific analyses are presented elsewhere (Carswell, 1997; Petre and Price, 1997; Price and Petre, 1997; Thomas *et al.*, 1996). Presented here are some of the main observations, including some examples illustrating the fundamental lesson of the trials: that it isn't enough merely to translate existing practice; the underlying function must be served through strategies that exploit the strengths of the medium.

Learning and the students' experience

Performance indicators (assignments and examination results) for all of the students, both conventional and Internet, were compared statistically. Questionnaire responses, assignments and examination results were analysed for 75 students (45 conventional; 30 Internet) on the entry-level Computing course in 1996. The aim was primarily to assess the impact of the delivery medium and secondarily to identify factors related to learning: indicators of attitudes, learning styles, and performance for each group of students were compared statistically (Carswell, 1997).

The nature of the detailed assignment marking and quality-controlled examination mechanisms used in the OU arguably make it reasonable to use grades as indicators of learning.

Performance is comparable
There was no significant difference in final grades between the Internet and conventional student cohorts. Moreover, learning style was found to predispose students to better or worse performance using a particular communication medium. There was however, a significant correlation of attributes such as the student's perception of his or her ability, confidence, and previous experience to performance. It appears that the student's self-image and expectations have the greater influence on learning outcomes.

Interaction
Students reported that their rapport with their tutor developed, and many reported that contact was freer via e-mail than it would have been by telephone. Some tutors reported that they had more interaction with their electronic students, especially the weaker ones, who find electronic communication less inhibiting. The diagnostic function of face-to-face sessions shifted away from the electronic tutorials to individual e-mail interaction. On the other hand, more Internet than conventional students were disappointed in their fellow students, and most felt that there had been insufficient interaction.

Prompt response to problems is crucial
Students' and tutors' background and end-of-term questionnaires from both conventional and Internet cohorts were examined in order to assess the students' experience of the courses. The 1996 presentation faced a number of 'teething' problems (eg, faulty communications software, tools under revision, materials not ready), but these subsided after the start of the course, and both students and tutors appear to have been remarkably resilient and tolerant. Tolerance is conditional on the speed of response to technical problems; fast, reliable response reduces students' perception of problems and increases their tolerance for any subsequent difficulties. Students reported that problems solved quickly and sympathetically were quickly forgotten, but problems left unanswered escalated.

Importance of expectations
Questionnaire responses indicated that many of the Internet students would or could not attend face-to-face tutorials, even if available; the electronic presentation attracted a different contingent of students from the conventional course. Those students

have different expectations about level and kind of interaction. Starting with appropriate expectations is crucial to a positive experience; tutors and students both emphasized the need to set 'ground rules' for communication. Inexperienced students perceive electronic mail as 'instantaneous' but adjust quickly when told what response time to expect.

The tutors' experience

Opportunities for collaboration

Geographically separated tutors were able to collaborate on tutorials, and team-tutoring was easy to implement and advantageous for both tutors and students. Tutors enjoyed the opportunity to share experiences, jokes and complaints: their peer community was brought to life when the tutors' own conference evolved into an 'electronic staff room'. The synergy among tutors contributed significantly to their development of new techniques and strategies.

Greater control

Although many tutors spent longer on e-mail queries than they did on telephone queries, in the main they preferred handling student enquiries by e-mail, because they had greater control over the time and manner of the interaction. They could choose when to reply (eg, no answering the telephone during dinner), they could take longer to consider their replies and word them carefully, and they could sometimes re-use a response.

Adapting skills and strategies

Internet presentation demanded more adaptation from tutors than from students. Practice had to be adjusted for all aspects of teaching: handling student enquiries, diagnosing of student status and difficulties, assignment marking, tutorials. Many well-honed skills had to be renovated for electronic tuition, and new strategies had to be developed to support efficient practice. But tutors willingly made the start-up investment; they felt the effort was rewarded by greater control over the interaction (for them) and higher quality response (for the students). For example, the opportunities to re-use material off-set the investment in careful wording demanded by re-playable interactions.

Assignment marking

Student and tutor questionnaire data, and a substantial corpus of assignments (n = 184: 97 paper; 87 electronic) were scrutinized thoroughly, giving particular attention to the comparison of electronic and paper treatments by five instructors with combined groups (Petre, 1997 gives an interim analysis). A secondary aim was to begin to unpick how individual instructor differences affect adaptation to electronic marking in terms of their strategies, their tool use, and the feedback they provide.

Tutors provide feedback in proportion to the points lost on both paper and electronic assignments. Quantitative and qualitative evidence (including the monitor's report) shows that the nature and quality of feedback are maintained or improved in electronic marking; if anything, electronic marking improves expression. The greatest gains from electronic handling are in legibility and faster turnaround time. Tutors report that their turnaround for electronic assignments is usually 2–3 days, whereas turnaround for paper assignments is usually 5–7 days. Students report that the total turnaround time for electronic assignments is usually 5–7 days, two weeks for paper.

Although quality is maintained, the tutors' experience of marking depends largely on how well their marking strategies and skills match the medium. Tutors' facility in using non-text marks, and the coherence and sophistication of their marking strategies increased during the trials. Speed of marking is largely dependent on typing speed, equipment specification (CPU speed, size of screen), and marking strategy. For example, strategies that involve swapping among different students' assignments carry higher overheads, especially on low-specification machines. On the other hand, electronic marking facilitates re-use of materials, so tutors benefit from strategies that plan for re-use, eg, amassing a corpus of high-quality re-usable commentary from which selections can be made appropriately for individual work. Electronic marking of assignments on Computing courses also facilitates execution of students' code and enables some automated marking. Students, too, can run substitute code or test input provided by tutors, and so electronic handling can lend 'relevance'.

Electronic problem sessions
Face-to-face problem and discussion sessions (tutorials) are a focal point in teaching, where concepts become immediate and personal through students' interactions with both their tutors and each other. In translating the tutorial for Internet presentation, the priority is to preserve the immediacy of the face-to-face tutorial, despite the problems of cost, compatibility and synchronization. In order to assess the efficacy of electronic tutorials, we scrutinized all conferences, electronic mail between tutors and students, tutors' logs of tutorials, records of tutor de-briefings, and tutor and student questionnaires (Price, 1997).

Electronic problem sessions require different models and mechanisms
Although the problem session models we proposed were based on our own and others' analyses of conventional practice, they didn't transfer effectively into electronic communication. Fortunately, the tutors were resourceful in finding new models, eg,

- week-long, asynchronous, role-play scenarios using problems built up in stages to effect a cumulative, collaborative solution;
- mixed-mode tutorials incorporating both asynchronous e-mail discussion and synchronous Internet Relay Chat discussion, backed up by logs and question-and-answer digests;
- the 'continuous tutorial', in which problems, issues and conundrums are set, discussed and reviewed on a regular basis, with one rolling into the next.

Devices such as fortnightly diagnostic queries (usually single, open-ended questions) and registration for tutorials were found to help draw students into effective interaction.

New patterns of participation; lurkers
In 1996, the number of 'active' participants in electronic tutorials tended to be low, from 1–8 students (usually 2–5). Nevertheless, many of those tutorials were successful, involving effective, instructive discussion. Tutors who checked with non-participants found that most, if not all, of the remaining students 'lurked' and found doing so beneficial, which students corroborated in their questionnaire responses. Many cited the ability of students to 'lurk' as an advantage of electronic tutorials, even though the lack of direct interaction is frustrating to tutors.

Bringing the social interaction alive
The key seems to lie in bringing the social interaction alive. Some tutors and students achieve this though asynchronous text, whereas others need a 'social starter': a face-to-face tutorial, a synchronous text session, video or audio delivered through the Internet – some way of conveying personalities within the group. All of the groups reporting successful tutorial interaction used plenty of humour, including witty problems and lightly-phrased coaching. Structure also matters: most of the successful tutorials were presented in stages, with clear tasks and milestones, and a clear review of the key points in the material covered.

Summary: costs and gains

The value Internet technology brings to distance education lies not in direct translation from other media but in transformation of support mechanisms to exploit its potential range.

Taking care over the integration of the electronic tools into the existing administrative infrastructure paid off. Administration is faster and more efficient with electronic assignments. Turnaround time is reduced; less paper is consumed; access to assignments and records is facilitated; and automatic logging increases accountability. But, on the scale of 150,000 students, there is still real concern about managing demands on communications and about consequences of system breakdowns.

Supported Internet presentation is not a cheap option, but it may be one that can provide greater flexibility and can shift effort from mundane tasks (administrative details) to teaching. We summarize with lists of observed costs and gains.

Costs

More technical support: Supported Internet presentation demands suitable technical support from a dedicated resource; in addition to existing computing support services, our trials had a full-time project officer to handle queries. Effective electronic administration requires an unwavering commitment to technical support to maintain key systems continuously.

Tutor expense: The highest costs in the initial year were borne by the tutors, who had to master new tools and new skills, evolve a new culture, devise new strategies, prepare new tutorial materials, and adjust to new types of impoverished feedback (ie no body language, no eye contact) from students.

Student expense: Internet presentation also requires new skills, new strategies, and greater responsibility from students. Some of the presentation costs (eg, connect time, printing) are off-loaded onto students.

Equipment upgrades for tutors: When the quality of equipment the tutors use has such an impact on the time required to do their work, then upgrading equipment must be a priority.

Loss of social interaction for some: Except for those who did not seek interaction or for whom conventional face-to-face sessions were never an option, most students were disappointed in their interactions with other students; with limited resources, this is a difficult medium in which to establish a 'community of learning'.

Less satisfactory tutorials: At this level of technology, electronic tutorials are no substitute for face-to-face inter-action, although they clearly have value and tremendous potential. And yet the potential must be realized at this sort of level – where technology is inexpensive and available – so that technology makes education accessible rather than exclusive.

Gains

More rapid feedback for students: Feedback on assignments is a crucial part of teaching; the faster the feedback, the more likely it is to assist learning.

Increased tutor collaboration and communication: Re-use and sharing are two crucial means for improving produc-tivity, exploiting expertise, and reducing the load on any one tutor. The increased loads experienced in the early years may well be off-set in subsequent years by the advantages gained in materials collections, re-distributed loads, and so on. Semi-automated tools, such as those described in Chapter 16, can be beneficial in this respect.

Greater access for students: The potential exists for global access.

Increased administrative efficiency: The electronic assign-ment handling, with its automatic checks and record keeping, can substantially reduce the costs of mundane administration, including photocopying costs, while poten-tially improving the retention and handling of student data.

Reduction in administrative errors: The electronic assign-ment handling system is shown to substantially reduce (if not eliminate) minor administrative errors (currently affecting the total throughput of half a million assignments per year).

Potential for flexibility: Students potentially have access to more tutors, more problem sessions, and more different supporting materials as archives and dialogues accumulate on the Web. Tutors can use the breadth of material to address individual needs.

Reduction of time and place constraints: Just as students have access to tutors outside their regions, tutors are able to collaborate with remote colleagues and have more control over the time and manner of their interaction with students. Tutorial structures no longer need to be organized geographically; they can be structured to take advantage of tutors' interests and expertise.

Conclusion

Making the shift to Internet presentation effective requires cultural change by both students and tutors. Students must take responsibility for their own learning and take initiative in bringing problems to the notice of tutors. Tutors must adapt their expectations and practices to accommodate a remote, often invisible student body. Our tutors took up the expanded opportunity for communication as an opportunity for collaboration; Internet presentation may further require culture change from the university, for example by re-organizing the tutor network away from the current regional structure.

But the real key to successful application of technology is good teaching: using technology only when it is a cost-effective servant of pedagogy. Experience has shown that it is easy to propose an electronic solution that is more expensive and time-consuming than the paper-based system it is supposed to improve upon (Pilgrim and Leung, 1996). We must analyse our existing processes deeply and critically in order to provide fully- and appropriately-realized Internet teaching that serves learning well, using the medium to augment the learning process in a compelling and cost-effective manner.

Part II
Collaboration and presence

Chapter 7

Promoting learner dialogues on the Web

Matthew Stratfold

Asynchronous on-line discussion forums known as 'conferencing systems' are widely used, but take on new characteristics when integrated with the Web. Sensitivity to learners' needs pays big dividends and suggests new styles for conferencing interfaces.

Introduction: conferencing via the Web

Asynchronous computer mediated conferencing has now reached a state of maturity (see Mason, 1998, and examples in Chapters 6, 8 and 16). Yet opportunities still exist for innovative ways to integrate conferencing and the Web. Indeed, Web conferencing has some distinct advantages over traditional text based conferencing systems, as we argue next.

Easy access and easy maintenance

For many people the Internet and the World Wide Web are synonymous. It is true that almost everyone who accesses the Internet does so through a Web browser. Therefore if conferencing facilities are provided via a Web browser then it is no longer necessary to provide users with specialist software that they don't already have. Non-Web based conferencing systems often require dedicated client software to be installed on user's machines.

The advantages of using a Web browser for conferencing are that the software:

- is familiar to the user; users are likely to have used a Web browser before and already understand the principles;
- is installed on the user's machine; if learners already have an Internet connection from home or work then they will already have a browser installed;
- is available widely; the Web conference is available from any Internet connected system. Nothing is stored locally on a machine so a user may work from different computers. One student observed of the system described below 'During the course I worked in Geneva, San Francisco, UK and offline at 35,000 feet!';

- does not have to be installed by the conference provider; the learner will normally obtain the browser from their Internet service provider (ISP). No extra software needs to be sent for them to use the conference;

- does not need to be maintained or updated by the conference provider; as above this is handled by the ISP;

- is cross platform; there are browsers available for most computer systems. Mac, PC, Unix, Amiga, even palmtop computers such as the Psion have Web browsers – a Web conference should work on all of them;

- integrates into the Web; the conference becomes part of the Web, and may draw upon the Web. This point is expanded below.

These advantages must be of great benefit to both users and conference provider. In short, Web conferencing can be made available to anyone who has access to the Internet with no extra set-up or installation for the learner.

The Web as part of a message (the Web into messages)
Providing conferencing over the Web has other advantages over existing conferencing systems. Web conferences are able to draw upon the features that the browsers and HTML offer at little or no extra cost. Not only is it possible to use HTML to format the text of a message (browsers are now coming equipped with tools to make this easy) but a Web conferencing system also provides routes into other kinds of services. Images, video sound and interactive content via Java or Shockwave can become part of a message, as illustrated in Chapters 5 and 9.

The most important benefit of locating a conference on the Web is the ability to include links to other Internet sites as part of a message. A message may make a link directly to supporting evidence, bring in examples elsewhere or provide starting points for Web exploration.

Messages as part of the Web (messages into the Web)
There are a number of mechanisms by which messages left within Web conferences can become more general Web content. Web pages that form a focus for a particular interest group will often have a Web conference or bulletin board attached. These areas are different in use from a Web conference for a course. They often comprise questions and responses, news items, reviews, advice and criticism. These message areas become a valuable Web resource for other people; a particular question may already have

been answered, or views on a new product posted. The Web Mastery site (LaLiberte and Stegall, 1998) provides examples. Some Web sites go further. I recently discovered that some scripting advice I had left in an online discussion had become part of a help site for the topic (Stratfold, 1997). This filtering and collecting process is the means by which many Web FAQ (frequently asked questions) pages are developed.

Disadvantages

The main disadvantage for the use of Web conferencing software is that it is limited to what a browser can do. If the browser is not able to do it then it cannot be part of the Web conference. For instance current Web browsers use a page based system – if part of the information within a page needs updating then the whole page needs to be resent. The use of frames, separate windows and layers can reduce this problem but using these advanced HTML features can alienate uses who have simpler browsers. This raises the other main problem with Web based systems, that despite the agreed standards, page layout and presentation always differ slightly between browsers. Normally this is not a problem but it is important to check that a particular Web conferencing system is usable with the most popular browsers.

Interacting with others on the Web

So, the Web has great potential for interacting and collaborating with other people. The form this interaction takes is determined by the activity that is desired for the course being taught. The options fall broadly into these three areas.

- *Unstructured / guest book*. New comments are added to the bottom of a linear list of comments, the text and titles of all the messages being displayed in one page. Structural cues such as 're:' can be added to the titles of messages. This type of use is more informal and is suited for occasional visitors.

- *Real time and near real-time / Chat Boards*. These are often similar in look to the guest books. The pages are designed to automatically reload at regular intervals. Each reload shows new messages added. This enables the time between posting a message and reading a reply to be very short, short enough for a conversation to be synchronous rather than asynchronous. Comments that are added are often not archived and may only be available for a short while.

- *Conferencing*. A conferencing system has more structure than a guest book. It provides mechanisms to see how messages interrelate. The messages are usually viewed by selecting their subject heading from a structured list of message headings. This provides a better mechanism for linking in longer messages and supporting an asynchronous discussion.

This chapter is concerned with educational uses of Web-based dialogue. The three broad categories above all have their places within learning online. As always it is important to select the right tool for the required job. In education the starting point is normally with questions such as 'what do the students need?' or 'how can we help them to study more efficiently?'

These kinds of questions are context dependent and we shall examine a particular context later in the chapter.

An educational use of a Web discussion system is likely to be different in nature to other uses. Typically, educational uses of the Web for learner dialogues will have the following characteristics.

- *Limited number of users.* A conference system as part of an educational course is likely to be of interest to a particular group of learners, a class or tutor group for example.

- *Frequent visits.* Learners will want to make frequent visits to the system to find and add new messages.

- *Closed environment.* The system is able to shut out access from people who are not part of the course

- *Focused discussion.* Discussions are likely to be guided or focused around particular issues.

- *Use of tutors.* There is likely to be a formal or authoritative role in the conference for either a moderator or tutor.

- *Reference to other material.* The system should be able to integrate or link to reference material such as course guides or online academic papers.

- *Course management.* The system ought to provide some mechanism for guiding the learners through a course, such as tying up a particular discussion and opening up new activities or topics.

- *Review of messages.* Some mechanism to allow learners to search and review messages may be important in assisting revision or putting together a message that draws on other contributions.

- *Extended interaction and collaboration with other people.* As the conference is used over a period of time and for complex interactions the system should support clear ways of viewing and working with dialogues that take place.

These kinds of characteristics best describe the conferencing category from our earlier list. There is an ever increasing number of Web conferencing systems (Woolley, 1998). Each of these systems has particular properties, some being more suitable for educational uses than others, as defined by the above requirements. It is inevitable that whatever system chosen for a course will impact on the design of the course and on the learner's experience.

In the next section we will look at how the design of a particular Web conferencing system attempts to meet these needs.

The Extended Bulletin Board System

The Extended Bulletin Board System (EBBS) is a Web conferencing system adapted from BBS, a much simpler system created by Winer (1998). The system has been re-developed to provide the features that are necessary for use in online teaching. The updating of the system has taken place within the Institute of Educational Technology at The Open University where it is used for short courses and for tutoring the MA programme for two years.

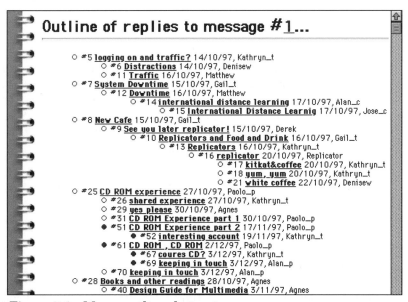

Figure 7.1. Message thread structure

System introduction

The EBBS uses a hierarchical tree structure to store the message/reply structure (Figure 7.1). This kind of structure allows the development of a conversation where the relationship between messages and responses can be seen clearly. A subsection of the tree where a series of interchanges takes place is referred to as a thread. The various threads come together at the root of the tree that is the starting point for the whole conference.

There are two ways to visualize this structure in the EBBS. The outline (Figure 7.1) gives an overview of the conference (or thread) by showing a hierarchical list of headings. If a heading is indented in relation to the heading above then it is a reply to that message.

The message reader (Figure 7.2) shows the second way to view the structure: the message at the top (Figure 7.2, C) and a list of the immediate replies beneath (Figure 7.2, D). The strip above the title of the message displays the messages ancestry in the tree (Figure 7.2, A). The links beneath open up the responses to the message.

The button bar along the bottom of the page provides the functions necessary to navigate and respond to the messages. This kind of message structure is not unique to the EBBS; in fact this kind of structure can be found in most conferencing systems.

Design to support learning

Generating and supporting dialogue within an online course, or using a conferencing system as a supplement to face-to-face teaching, is a serious challenge if the Web is to serve as an educational medium.

A distance learning course where the learners have never met and their only means of contact with each other and the tutors is the conference system, must be the most challenging situation of all. The rest of this chapter will look at the use of the conferencing system in courses taught at a distance from the Institute of Educational Technology at The Open University.

Structure

The hierarchical structure (Figures 7.1 and 7.2) contains important information that is an essential part of following and contributing to a dialogue. There are three pieces of information that must be available: attribution (who said what), sequence (in what order) and relationship (to whom). This much seems common sense and most systems (not all) have this information. Because an interchange in a Web conference may well take place over a period of weeks it is important that this information is

---

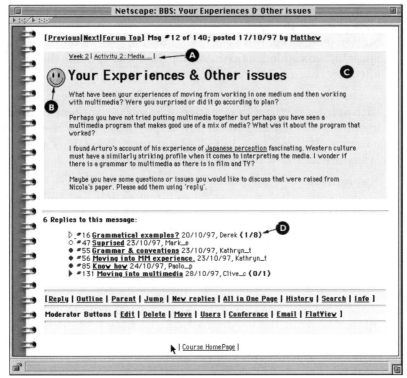

Figure 7.2. A message from the EBBS

KEY to Figure 7.2.

A: Ancestry, showing the context of the current comment by its position in the hierarchy of 'discussion threads' in the system

B: Icon, one of a set of ten from which students can choose to indicate the spirit in which a comment is to be taken

C: Body, is the main text of the message

D: Replies, lists the responses to the message. Listed are the subject headings of each reply

easily visualized. A learner who is returning to a conversation some days later, or catching up on new messages, needs this detail.

The EBBS provides an outline view (Figure 7.1) that contains this information, unlike the earlier version which did not show the message ancestry and only made the first set of replies visible.

Without looking at an outline view, it is easy to get lost in the original early system. It is only possible to see the current message and one step ahead (the links to replies) and there is no view of where the reader has come from. All other structural information is missing. It was at the request of users that the message ancestry was added; a further alteration was to make the message ancestry (Figure 7.2, A) clickable.

The replies beneath the message view have also been enhanced with extra structural information. The numbers after the message heading give an indication of how large the thread is beneath that message. It is possible to tell at a glance then where the active areas are and how much more there is to read.

Navigation

Structural/spatial awareness and navigation are linked. It is important to have a clear picture of how messages interrelate on the system before it is possible to navigate through them. It is desirable to navigate through the dialogues by selecting messages rather than have a set of controls that are apart from the message. Why click a button that says 'next message' when instead you can click directly on the heading for the next message? Navigating via 'remote control' adds an extra layer of complexity to the learner's interactions. In the original EBBS the user had to click on the message number rather than the message heading; it also relied heavily on the next/previous links to move through messages.

The next/previous links are still available in the current version of the EBBS, but evaluation of the system shows they are not used. It is difficult to envisage what next and previous do within a hierarchical tree structure. In the original EBBS these buttons took a user through the messages in the sequence that they were posted (regardless of which thread they were in). This reflected the system's original aim of more casual use where simple comments and questions were more important than ongoing conversations. Now these links step the user backwards and forwards in the tree structure. It is not easy to follow if the 'next' message is a reply to the current message, or is a message that shares the same parent, or the start of a thread much further up the tree. Next and previous may well be removed from later versions of the EBBS.

Again in response to users' requests the system was altered so that replies beneath messages could be unfolded (Figure 7.3). A learner who is making frequent visits to a course may leave the current week's thread unfolded and let it provide a direct root into the active area of a conference.

```
    3 Discussions:

        ▽ #1 Café 10/10/97, Matthew (43/62)
             ▷ #5 logging on and traffic? 14/10/97, Kathryn_t (2/2)
             ▷ #7 System Downtime 15/10/97, Gail_t (3/3)
             ▷ #8 New Cafe 15/10/97, Gail_t (7/7)
          ▽ #25 CD ROM experience 27/10/97, Paolo_p (4/9)
    ▶          ○ #26 shared experience 27/10/97, Kathryn_t
                 ○ #29 yes please 30/10/97, Agnes
                 ○ #31 CD ROM Experience part 1 30/10/97, Paolo_p
                 ▶ #51 CD ROM Experience part 2 17/11/97, Paolo_p (0/1)
                 ▶ #61 CD ROM , CD ROM 2/12/97, Paolo_p (0/2)
                 ○ #70 keeping in touch 3/12/97, Alan_p
             ▷ #28 Books and other readings 28/10/97, Agnes (3/3)
             ▷ #30 Problems with the CD ROM 30/10/97, Huw_r (4/4)
             ▷ #33 Week 2 Summary - good multimedia features 30/10/97, Agnes (0/2)
             ▷ #36 Introducing Palitha 31/10/97, Matthew (2/2)
             ○ #42 Bug report, system down 4/11/97, Arturo_e
             ▷ #43 looking for inspiration! 5/11/97, Kathryn_t (4/6)
             ▷ #54 Multimedia Links 21/11/97, Matthew (1/1)
             ▷ #57 keeping all this for later ? 28/11/97, Kathryn_t (1/1)
             ▶ #58 Corse survivors 1/12/97, Denisew (0/9)
        ○ #2 Late arrivals 10/10/97, Matthew
        ▷ #3 Student Area 16/10/97, Matthew (0/6)
```

Figure 7.3. Unfolding the message outline

Session management

A system which is to be used in a course is one that the learners will need to use repeatedly. They will be interested in following exchanges that will happen over the period of the course as well as finding people's reactions to their own messages. Most Web conferencing systems cater for standard surfers who may visit the site rarely or perhaps just once. A learner requires more from the system. The system needs to recognise them when they return. It should be able to show them where the activity has been since the last visit, what new unread messages there are and remember the learner's preferences.

The EBBS keeps a record of what messages a learner has seen. It is able to highlight new messages. Messages with a solid symbol next to them are messages that have not been seen yet. These symbols are available anytime the message heading is displayed, whether in an outline, message or search window. The replies listed in the message view window (Figure 7.2, D) are followed by a value that shows the number of unread messages in a thread and so then points to the place where the latest activity is taking place.

When learners return to the system, they can choose to see a list of new messages in the conference or a particular thread. This list does not show the context of each message in the hierarchy and some learners find its use problematic and prefer to pick highlighted messages from the message outline.

A satisfactory way of displaying the message context within the list of new messages remains to be found.

Supporting ways of working

Methods of work will be different from learner to learner, and will alter in the same learner depending on the activity underway. A system that can support different learning styles without becoming overly complex to use will be more easily accessible to a greater number of learners. The hope is that if the system is easier to use, then it will be used often. Certainly something that is frustrating to use will have a negative impact on the dialogues that take place.

The EBBS supports different approaches to finding messages. A learner may pick them from the outline, browse through the message navigator, unfold the structure, get a list of new messages, or search on text, heading, or author.

Learners can also collect multiple messages into a single page so that they can print them out or work offline. Learners choose which way to approach the system based either on the activity they want to perform, or through a routine they have developed.

Supporting learners used to other systems

Perhaps surprisingly, evaluation of some of the courses shows that learners who are already familiar with the FirstClass conferencing system (see Chapters 5 and 16) find using the EBBS difficult. These users suffer more difficulties than learners who are new to computer conferencing. FirstClass, while similar in many respects, has some fundamental differences. For a start the messages are stored in a star structure (folders containing many messages all at the same level), rather than a tree structure as the EBBS does. Users of FirstClass may order a long list of messages via date posted, author name, or alphabetically by subject, but are given no support in visualizing the conversation threads. Someone who learns to interact online using FirstClass develops a way of working that the system affords. Users moving between systems take time to adapt to the new structure. However, experience show us that this transition can happen satisfactorily in time.

As part of the continued development of the EBBS we intend to add an interface that mimics the structure of FirstClass. In this way we can provide a more comfortable environment for people who have used star structured systems.

Social dimensions to the history function

Part of the trial of working online at a distance is the feeling of being out of touch. Web conferencing for many distance learners provides an avenue for interacting with fellow students that they would otherwise not have. To get to know others through such an interface can be tricky (though some find it liberating since it is a safe environment where you can be whomever you want).

Any way in which the conference can add to a feeling of community, activity and character should be welcomed. The system as it stands could do more in this respect, but does provide two functions that go some way towards this.

The history function not only shows when a message was added, but also who read it and when. Students use the history to see how busy the conference is, to see how many people have read their message (and not replied) and to see which people have seen their message.

Learners have used the history function to follow their tutors. They can see if the tutor has read the message and chosen not to respond, or has simply not read it yet. In one case, students used this function to follow their tutor and then criticize an apparent lack of activity!

The message icons (Figure 7.2, D) are another way in which a learner can add a sense of identity and community to a message. Currently icons are selected from a list and can be used to provide an interpretation of the message (eg, a clown icon for joking around and a cactus when dealing with a difficult subject). Users tend to select a particular icon and stick with it for neutral messages as a way of providing identity. One learner went further and used HTML to add a picture of himself to his messages. Note how this usage contrasts with the use of icons in Chapter 8, where only a limited set was chosen in order to keep the focus more tightly on the peer review dialogue under way.

Course integration

There are many ways to use a conferencing system as part of an educational course. There are no correct solutions since each course has different objectives. The EBBS has been used for two quite different course styles, described next.

Discussion forum

The Professional Development in Educational Technology (PDET) courses depend heavily on participants sharing their own views and experiences. For example, a week in the multimedia course starts with an activity where different sorts of interactions are compared and an EBBS discussion about the merits of each is started. Tutors in the course try to direct the discussion with an occasional question or remark. These courses are not examined.

Electronic workbook

IET also teaches an MA in Open and Distance Education. The first year of the course uses the EBBS as an 'electronic workbook'. This course does not rely on online discussion for teaching nearly as much as the PDET courses, as the students make much greater use of printed course materials. Students are able to post written answers to the print activities onto the EBBS and therefore get extra feedback from tutors and students. The electronic workbook is also used to ask specific questions about course materials, share resources and chat with other students.

Student activity levels

It appears to be a general rule in computer conferencing (certainly it is our experience) that of the students on a course one third almost never use the conferencing system (for the MA it is possible to complete the first year without using the system). One third read messages but do not add much, and one third are active in reading and posting. The reason for the differences are many. For instance, some students choose distance education since this mode of learning suites their lifestyle. One student observes in a message:

> After a long absence from BBS, I return determined to explore some of its potential. The truth is that I like studying at a distance, even though it's well known that distance students dislike isolation.

For others the conference system is an important part of their learning. One learner has made 390 visits to the system in ten months, nearly ten times more visits than one of the tutors. This student must check the system for new messages more than once a day whereas the tutor is just accessing a couple of times a month at the most. It is important, though, not to jump to conclusions about the level of work put in by these people. The tutor posts many more messages per visit than the student, the tutor preferring to prepare messages offline.

For some students on the MA it is a matter of discipline to post their answers to many of the activities in the work book. Working this way ensures that they follow the course properly (Figure 7.4). Other learners may use other techniques to ensure they spend enough effort in studying.

The PDET courses have a higher student activity level than the MA. These courses rely on the Web conference for the delivery of course content. They are also shorter courses so there is also less time to fall behind (though this is still a problem for some).

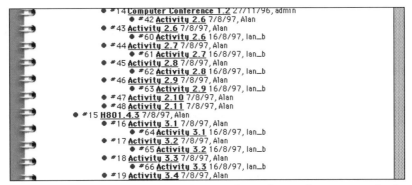

Figure 7.4. Here you can see Ian is the only student to regularly answer all the activities, each time getting a follow-up message from the tutor 'Alan'

The use of the conference is also different. Students are expected to discuss and share as part of their learning.

Encouraging student discussion

It was one of the teaching aims to promote discussion and to this end a tutor response would not only deal with a point raised by someone else but would normally pose a new question as well. A few students found this irritating. A course evaluation showed that for one course many of the students felt that there was not enough tutor input. Tutors add more messages than students on these courses, but not all student points were followed up with a tutor response. The value of the PDET course is the discussion and not a tutor led lesson on a topic. The courses no longer refer to tutors as 'tutors'. The word suggests that some specific teaching will take place. New terms include 'Moderator', 'Discussion Leader' or 'Group Leader'. These titles much better reflect the roles of the 'tutors' on the PDET courses.

Maintaining online discussion

Experience on these courses tells us that for effective discussion the students have to be working on the same topics at the same time. Students who lag behind adding messages to conferences that are a couple of weeks out of date do not get feedback from other students. What is more, they have a stack of messages from other people to read.

Conferences are now managed so that soon after a week of study is finished, the conference area for that week becomes read only. Students who still have something to add can leave messages in a continually open general discussion area. The advice for learners who have dropped behind is to skip work so that they can catch up. Messages in areas they skipped over are still available for review once the course is over.

Improving learning dialogues

We have already seen in Chapter 6 how various personal styles can affect the online experience. We also know that time pressures are felt by most participants who study these courses since they are normally studying part time alongside full time employment. Course design must build time into the schedule for working online as well as set course activities and reading.

Tutors also have time pressures. The course is only part of the work that these full time academics have to do. Not all learners' messages get a tutor reply. Students need to feel a better sense of community; a feeling of being listened to is an important factor in saying anything, so responses from tutors and fellow learners are important. Both tutors and students could be better supported by the system in order to promote better dialogues. This chapter ends by suggesting a few ideas about how this could be done.

Automatic nodding

Tutors observed that they wanted to encourage participants by replying to more messages. But it is not always easy to compose a detailed response to a message. After responding to several learners who have completed the same task it is not always easy to think of something original to say each time. In a face-to-face situation a short reply saying 'that's right' or 'those are good ideas', or even just nodding as a learner talks is all that is necessary to encourage the student. In an asynchronous medium these kinds of messages appear awkward – these moments of encouragement are frozen in time in such a medium just as an odd facial expression can be when we are photographed unexpectedly. Leaving several such messages in a thread to save time is worse, though probably not as bad as giving no feedback. One student on a recent PDET course was so discouraged by only having comments from tutors rather than peers that they would only correspond with the tutor via e-mail.

One possible solution to this might be to have some kind of quick feedback system for both students and tutor once they have read a message, for example a nod, smile or frown button to press at the bottom of the message. Learners when they return to their message can see that it has been read, and what people thought. Other people could also benefit from a better feeling of consensus and community. A potential drawback is that such a feature would be used at the expense of more detailed written replies.

Voting

'Automatic nodding' could be extended into a voting system that allows a tutor or student to propose an issue and have others post a vote on the matter. A voting system may encourage more people to enter into a debate than would normally if more complex or time consuming responses are required. It might also work to spark off new discussions based on the outcomes.

Interactive activities

Voting is just one kind of collaborative interactive activity. It is possible to imagine other activities that could be integrated into a Web conference that provide starting points for discussion. For instance participants could try an online simulation – the results of which feed into a discussion about individual differences or trends across the group. These activities again might help stimulate discussion, enable more people to join in, and take away some of the pressure from tutors to lead and drive discussions. The PubQuiz in Chapter 9 and the problem solving tutorials of Chapter 6 are good examples of this.

FAQs

A well tried system for alleviating the load from conference tutors or moderators are Frequently Asked Questions lists (FAQs). These are a list of questions (and their answers) that are often asked either in the current course or in earlier presentations of the course. A tutor can direct someone to the FAQ list if they ask a question that is already answered there. Building and maintaining such lists is time consuming. An 'answer garden' is one way to approach the building and maintenance of such knowledge (Ackerman and Malone, 1990) and the intelligent agent approach described in Chapter 16 shows how automated assistance can help alleviate some of the pressures.

New roles for students

A further method of eliciting student dialogue is signing students up for particular roles as discussants, summarizers or devil's advocates who are asked to present a contentious view of their own, or cite one from the literature.

Tutor tools

The system should be able to provide tutors with better support and overview tools. Such tools could include things such as:

- *'who's left out'*. Is there a student that has not had feedback from fellow students?

- *'who has not heard from a tutor'*. For a particular thread this tool could highlight who has not had tutor feedback;

- *attendance*. A tool should show an attendance profile: who are regular contributors, who has been lurking (reading not commenting), and who has not even been reading. A prototype attendance tool on the EBBS has the ability to send e-mails to learners who have not been seen for sometime, or send an e-mail each time a new message is added.

If some kind of intelligent agent system, of the sort discussed in Chapter 16, were integrated into the EBBS then there arises the possibility for the agent to help the tutor select information from previous presentations of the courses that is pertinent – or even to automatically make the information available.

Conclusions

This chapter has demonstrated ways in which the technology needs to be adapted reflexively to match and encourage student learning. This adaptation needs to be carried out both at software and courseware levels. Our experience tells us that students are keen to use new technology when it has benefits such as more flexible learning patterns, greater contact with tutors and peers, and better integration with the diversity of media and resources on the Web.

The challenge is for educators to support learners in these new environments.

Chapter 8

New scenarios in scholarly publishing and debate

Simon Buckingham Shum and Tamara Sumner

Mouse clicks and hypertext alone do not take Web-oriented publishing very far beyond the paper-based academic model in which it is rooted. The Digital Document Discourse Environment (D3E) not only fosters a new style of scholarly publishing and debate, but also automates many of the relevant editorial tasks.

Introduction: two scenarios from academic life

A student assignment

An assignment on a distance learning course requires students to critique a conference paper which their tutor has placed on the course Web site. Students are required to construct a critique of it from a number of different perspectives. After the submission deadline, the tutor then allows everyone to see each others' critiques. In a follow-up exercise over the following week, the students and tutor discuss their different interpretations. The students then write a summary essay which they publish as a Web document with links back into the group discussions as evidence for their claims.

Journal review and publishing

A submission to a Web-based e-journal claims that interactive animations are a powerful tool for distance teaching. This is supported by demonstrations embedded in the text, which allow readers to assess these pedagogical claims. This has sparked a lively Web-based review debate between authors, reviewers and several researchers who responded to an open invitation to join in at the open peer review phase. Following the review deadline, the editor sends the authors an acceptance letter, plus required changes. This letter is a Web document which summarizes, and links back into, the debate. The editor also edits the review discussion, removing comments that will have been addressed in the corrected version, but leaving the most interesting issues that are likely to fuel future discussion.

In revising their article, the authors decide to embed an audio-visual slideshow which guides the reader through several screenshots of their animation system, highlighting particular features that were found to be problematic in an evaluation. They download the journal's tool for composing such presentations, import the screen images they have prepared, and record commentary for each one. They then upload the final article to the journal's online markup tool, which gives it the journal's look and feel, and integrates it into the edited version of the discussion. They are able to modify any aspects of the article and navigation around the site until satisfied, after which they e-mail the editor, and the article acquires the status of 'published'. Periodic discussions continue as different readers discover the article. Over the next year, the authors submit (unrefereed) update notes to their article's discussion, reporting evaluation studies and software releases. Readers who have subscribed to the article are automatically alerted to these developments by e-mail.

These two scenarios describe Web technologies most of which are now implemented, and which are being used by students, journal editors and researchers. In this chapter, we describe the approach that underpins our work, and a publishing toolkit called D3E that makes possible the rapid generation of Web sites for scholarly, document-centred discussions as described above.

Paper-based print and scholarly work

Since paper-based print became the dominant medium for information dissemination and consumption, the way in which knowledge is published, sanctioned and debated within scholarly communities has been shaped by the affordances of paper to such an extent that we barely think about it. We talk of 'research papers', making the medium synonymous with its message. Paper is expensive to produce and distribute, so journals are expensive and can only publish a fixed number of articles per year, in issues of a certain, mailable size. Paper-based communication is slow, so the number of discursive exchanges between authors and reviewers is minimized, and coupled with cost, articles take months or even years to be published; following publication, there is no simple way to set up a forum for debate about a paper. The legitimate representations for presenting work are those that paper can support – static text and graphics – even when time-based material is being presented (eg, extracts from verbal protocols or video data), or when computer systems are being described (such as hypertext or simulations), where interactivity is the key feature about which the author is making claims.

Currently, we are witnessing the beginnings of a shift from paper to digital media in the submission, review and publication of scholarly work. In many journals, it is now standard procedure for reviews and submissions to be transmitted electronically. Occasionally, automated systems are in place for matching reviewers with submissions based on keyword analysis or semantic indexing. In many electronic journals (e-journals), the articles may be available to subscribers to print (eg, as PostScript or Adobe Acrobat files). The abstracts for articles may be available in HTML on the Web. In a few cases, the final version of the whole article is published on the Web. In even fewer cases, an electronic discussion forum is offered to journal subscribers, usually in the form of an e-mail list.

From surveying the current state of the field, our conclusion is that most e-journals serve only to demonstrate the extent to which thinking is still 'papyrocentric' (a term coined by Stevan Harnad). Traditional documents are simply disseminated digitally, and traditional activities are facilitated by established technologies such as e-mail and document/journal management systems. The central processes and products of scholarly work have gone unquestioned. This can be ascribed on the one hand to inertia amongst publishers who fear the loss of markets and are unsure of their role in digital publishing, and on the other to inertia in the paper-based academic culture, where traditional print literacy and genres dominate (understandably), literacy with new media is rare, and the pressure to publish in established journals is intense.

Papyrocentric deployment of interactive media does not seem to us, therefore, very imaginative. Some readers may see an apparent irony in our use of a book to disseminate these ideas. We should emphasize that we are not trying to build a case against print or paper, which individually and in combination possess unique interactive and socio-cultural properties that will ensure their life for the foreseeable future (see Nunberg, 1996), for further discussion on why elegies for the book are premature). However, for the first time, the dominant influence of print on our conceptions of documents, publishing and associated scholarly processes is being seriously challenged by the emergence of interactive media and the Internet. In such transitional times as these, constraints previously taken for granted are recognized as merely contingent on paper, and established modes of working are no longer as natural and obvious as they seemed. Such times provide the opportunity for radical and creative reflection on why we do what we do, offering the opportunity to keep the best properties of paper, but to explore alternative scenarios that transcend current paper-based practices.

We recognize from the start that change is more than a question of introducing new technologies. With respect to the economics of publishing, publishers' roles will continue to change, just as academics' roles already are. Okerson and O'Donnell (1995) and Peek and Newby (1996) explore in detail new models for scholarly publishing which achieve the maximum dissemination at minimal cost that scholars seek. New media and work practices exist in perpetual tension, each influencing the other. Our approach is to co-evolve the two in the different contexts in which we are working.

Requirements for promoting scholarly discourse

The intellectual 'cut and thrust' of debate between peers as they contest the ideas proposed in a document is a core skill that we seek to foster in students, and which obviously needs to be supported within professional scholarly communities. As members of these communities become increasingly distributed in time and space, how is this to be facilitated? In conventional teaching situations, such debate normally occurs amongst students when they are brought together in a tutorial context, moderated by a tutor; this is difficult in distance educational contexts. When the object of discussion is a document, we need more elegant environments than an e-mail list in order to easily refer to the different features and conduct parallel streams of discussion. In the context of a journal, such debate is also missing between authors, reviewers and peers with the exception of the few journals which publish commentaries and replies (albeit after a long delay, and with poor support for continued discussion following publication).

Based on our experiences in the roles of teacher, researcher, journal reviewer and editor, we propose that good scholarly debate displays the properties listed in Figure 8.1 – whether at student or professional level (and with lifelong learning the distinction blurs). We discuss the properties in relation to peer review in journals, since this is the most established form of academic debate about documents. However, our critique applies equally to student level debates about the merits of an article in a reading assignment (see also the analysis of 'learning dialogues' presented in Chapter 7).

Good scholarly peer review and debate displays the following features:

- *Open* – to multiple perspectives from all relevant parties. In the review stage, these parties are the authors, reviewers, editors, and possibly the journal's subscribers. Following publication, debate is clearly open to include the public. The conventional journal review process is not open to anyone except the editor and anonymous reviewers. We wish to question the value of reviewer anonymity, and encourage more open dialogue. It can help substantially if one is able to interpret someone's comments in the light of their background; reviewers should be prepared to stand by and defend their reviews.

- *Informed* – by relevant evidence/resources. Participants should have the time to seek out relevant evidence to back their case, and point to relevant resources of which the authors should be aware (eg, other researchers or research institutes; publications; tools). Paper journals support this well, given that there is so much time for participants to prepare their contributions.

- *Dynamic* – the debate should also be quick enough to support dialogue, that is, it should not take so long to reply to a point that the dialogue cannot progress, or moves on to other issues. As already noted, this is a serious problem with commentaries in paper journals.

- *Carefully constructed* – contributions to the debate should be made after appropriate reflection, and not elicited under the pressure of the moment (as can happen in face-to-face debates when, for instance, a long silence must be broken, or a quick reply forced by clever rhetoric). Paper journals do not often place such pressure on reviewers that they have an excuse not to provide careful reviews.

- *Cumulative* – the debate should allow participants to single out and reply to multiple threads in an argument in parallel, so that discussion can proceed on many different fronts, without being confusing. Firstly, paper based texts do not support this multi-threading process very well. It is of course possible to conduct a multi-threaded debate in which one topic after another is addressed in the text, but this is a poor structure for supporting collaborative debate in which any point may turn into a major new thread. Non-linear text is required. Secondly, normal journal review is not cumulative in a fundamental way – the author has no right of reply to an anonymous reviewer. Even if an author finds out who the reviewer is, it is not clear whether it is acceptable to initiate a dialogue about the review. Current scholarly culture adopts a bizarre mentality which is best summarized by the competition warning that 'the judges' verdict is final and correspondence cannot be entered into.'

- *Preserved* – we contend that the debate should be preserved, to accompany the publication. It should be publicly inspectable as a valuable trace which shows how the final product came into being. Normally, this trace is left for scientific historians to uncover in order to shed light on the influences which shaped a theory. The scholarly publication is simply a milestone along a continuing journey, never the end. The discursive process by which it has emerged will continue as the ideas crystallized in an article evolve and are reflected on in the light of subsequent work.

Figure 8.1. Characterising scholarly peer review and debate – skills that we seek to foster in students, and which need to be supported in professional research communities

A process with the above characteristics can be well supported by mixed pace, asynchronous, multi-threaded discussions, tightly integrated with the particular document(s) under debate.

The D3E environment for reading and critiquing Web documents

D3E stands for Digital Document Discourse Environment. The D3E Project began as an action research project to create a next generation e-journal on the Web, with explicit support for critical peer review and interactive media embedded in articles. It became clear that the HTML mark-up effort that required had to be partially automated to make the publishing of such complex Web-sites tractable. It also became clear that there were many contexts where documents need to be discussed in different ways, by different populations. This motivated the requirements for a generic publishing toolkit which could be used to generate different kinds of sites. The concept of a tailorable environment was conceived, with the project's research goals being to better understand the factors that make discussion and debate about media-rich Web documents intuitive and effective. We are concerned therefore with the whole spectrum of design issues, from user interface design and hypermedia functionality (Buckingham Shum and McKnight, 1997), to the computational, cognitive and cultural issues that determine uptake of such novel technologies by professional communities.

Design principles underpinning D3E

D3E is based on extensive research into how hypertext systems can support critical reflection and the analysis of arguments in writing and software design. Over a period of about six years, we have surveyed, prototyped and evaluated the usability and effectiveness of systems designed to support the representation and analysis of arguments to justify decisions, and the smooth switching of attention between building an 'artifact' (whether a written document, CAD design, or program), and critically reflecting it (Buckingham Shum, 1996a, 1996b, 1998; Buckingham Shum and Hammond, 1994; Buckingham Shum et al., 1997; Fischer, Lemke, Mastaglio and Morch, 1991; Fischer, Lemke, McCall and Morch, 1991; Sumner etal., 1997).

From this work on pre-Web hypermedia systems, we formulated several design principles to guide the development of D3E.

A: Avoid over-elaborate discussion structuring schemes.

B: Integrate document media with discourse.

C: Redesign work practices to emphasize discourse.

D: Support the new practices with tools.

Principle A: Avoid over-elaborate schemes for structuring comments and discussions. If users classify their document annotations or contributions to an online discussion, greater computer support can be provided. For instance, one can search for all theory comments that have contradictory evidence, if those categories have been defined and used. Numerous schemes have been proposed for structuring discussions (eg Conklin and Begeman, 1988; Turoff *et al.*, 1991). In the systems we have studied, discussion schemes have required users to categorize contributions as issues, positions, comments, pros, and cons. Schemes of this sort, however, run the risk of burdening people with excessive representational overhead by forcing them to categorize their ideas before they are ready to, or the scheme is too restricted to capture the nature of a subtle comment. Studies from a wide range of work contexts show that at least initially, users are often unable or unwilling to structure ideas in new ways, because the effort is too great for the perceived benefit (Shipman and Marshall, 1994; Shipman and McCall, 1994). The answer is to allow a user community to evolve a richer scheme from a simple one as they deem it worthwhile (this may be in ways that cannot be predicted by an outsider).

B: Computational tools must tightly integrate documents with comments and discussions about them. Many systems place documents in a different application to discussion about them (we see this with e-mail discussion lists for Web e-journals). This separation hinders users from quickly accessing relevant comments when they are most needed and makes it hard to add contextualized comments. Likewise, tools should tightly integrate the textual parts of documents with any computational parts. Research in design support tools has shown that users need to easily bridge the separation between different representations of the design, and between representations and design rationale (Fischer *et al.*, 1991; McKerlie and MacLean, 1994).

C: Work practices must be redesigned so that structured annotations and discussions are integral to the task. Studies show that people often do not contribute to discussions because it is perceived as extra work over and above what they are already required to do (Grudin, 1996). Successful approaches have redesigned work practices to make contributing to a discussion integral to the overall task being performed (Terveen *et al.*, 1993). Others also advocate 'seeding' (providing some initial contents), arguing that people find it easier to contribute to a discussion site with content designed to promote debate, rather than starting from scratch (Fischer *et al.*, 1994). In a course setting, this means providing the right kind of motivation to students to participate in group debates, and seeding the discussion area with appropriate structures and questions. In a journal online peer review setting, this means redesigning the review process to require electronic threading of reviews into a shared space, changing the traditional roles of editor and reviewer, and seeding author-reviewer discussions for readers to build on.

Principle D: Tools are needed to support the new work practices. Many people may lack the technical skills, time, or inclination to engage in hand-crafting new digital document forms. Support is needed for automating the tedious and error-prone parts of the document creation process and to make it accessible to non-technical participants. Tools should be designed to make a good first approximation and then allow for humans to refine and correct the tools' output. The challenge is to create tools that are supportive, yet do not hinder the formation of new practices. Our goal is that the D3E Publisher's Toolkit will enable students,

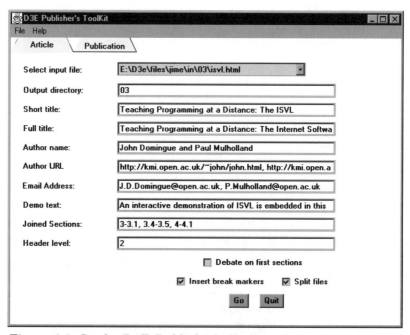

Figure 8.2. In the D3E Publisher's Toolkit, the tutor fills in the details of the conference paper to be published on the Web for discussion

tutors and researchers (as well as professional publishers) to easily 'publish' Web documents in a well-designed discussion environment, without having to worry about the intricacies of HTML.

We now return to the opening two scenarios, and show how they can be implemented using D3E. Unless indicated, everything described is implemented at the time of writing.

Implementing the scenarios

A student assignment with D3E

The tutor in the scenario has downloaded a paper from the Web and obtained clearance to use it for a teaching exercise. She imports the HTML file into the D3E Publisher's Toolkit on her computer, selects the style of publication that she wants to generate (eg, 'Paper for student assignment') which determines the look and feel of the site, and fills in the form with the relevant details (Figure 8.2).

On hitting the 'Go' button, the toolkit creates the environment captured by the screenshot in Figure 8.3.

The toolkit generates the following HTML files to achieve this:

- comment icons (as shown in margin) are embedded in each section of the article which take the reader directly to the relevant area of the discussion space;

- a frameset of the chosen look and feel (defined by HTML templates);

- an active table of contents to navigate around the article;

- two-way links between citations and the corresponding entries in the bibliography, the latter being displayed under the main document frame when a citation link is followed;

- the source HTML file is split up into smaller, faster loading files (corresponding to sections in the conference paper, except where the tutor has specified that they should be joined);

- navigation buttons to the previous and next sections at the foot of each file;

- a 'downloads' page, where for instance, print versions or any required plug-ins can be placed.

Secondly, the toolkit generates a discussion space linked to the document, providing:

eg. Office 2000 discussion functionality within authoring tool

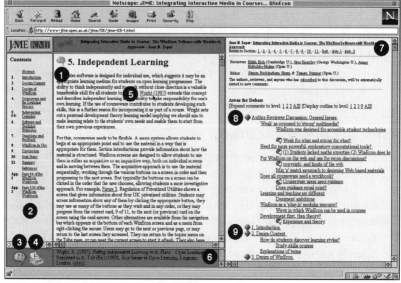

Figure 8.3 (Plate XI). Output of the D3E toolkit from a source HTML article. On the left is the Article Window, on the right the Commentaries Window showing the top level outline view of discussion about the document. (This example is taken from an e-journal peer review debate – see later discussion of scenario 2).

Key: [1] Comment icon embedded in each section heading: displays section-specific comments; [2] active contents list; [3] iconic link to display top level discussion outline, as shown on right; [4] iconic link to download Acrobat version; [5] citation is automatically linked to entry in references, displayed in footnote window; [6] reverse link to citation(s) in the text; [7] links from discussion back into article; [8] general heading (defined in toolkit) for discussion on the whole document; [9] headings for section-specific comments.

- an outline structure of headings matching the paper's section headings;
- areas for general discussion (defined by the tutor in the toolkit) which are inserted at the top for comments not specific to a particular section;
- links back into the different sections of the article, created to facilitate smooth navigation.

When the student logs in to the Website, she is automatically taken to her own private copy of the discussion space; at this stage it is in fact a private, personal annotation space since only she can

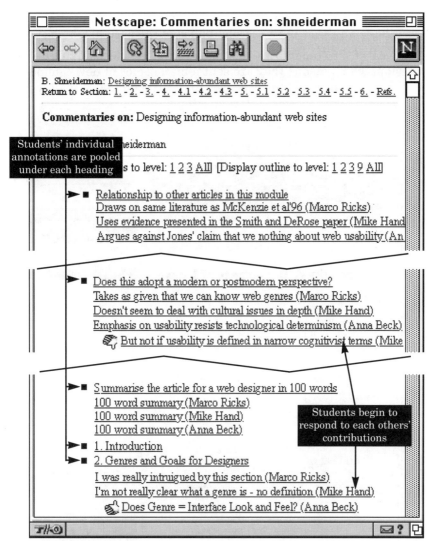

Figure 8.4 The shared discussion space where students can see and debate each other's commentaries on the paper via threaded discussions, with the option of tagging contributions as agreements (👍) or disagreements (👎)

read and write to it. There she develops her own critique of the paper. Each comment she adds is copied to the relevant section of the shared discussion space (yet to be made public). After the submission deadline, all students are sent the address of the shared discussion space which has clustered each student's private annotations under the relevant discussion headings

(Figure 8.4). The students can now view and comment on each other's analyses in the second phase of the assignment.

All of the students are automatically 'subscribed' to this discussion, which means they are sent e-mail copies of new comments. They can also submit responses to the Website via e-mail, which students with slower Web connections find particularly useful.

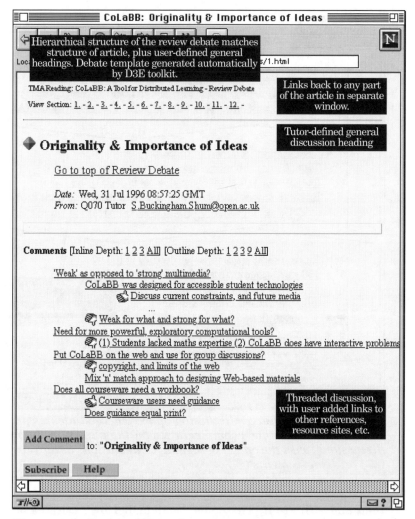

Figure 8.5. Extract from the online review discussion between authors, reviewers, and other researchers in the field who have joined in at the open peer review phase. Five of the contributions shown are from reviewers, five are from the author, one is from the editor, and two are from readers.

In the final stage, the students compose their summary essays. Most of them do this using their favourite wordprocessor, convert it to HTML, and then make the links to the relevant commentaries that they are using as evidence to back up the arguments.

Notice that the threaded discussion environment aims to deliver the power and simplicity of that used in Chapter 7, while maintaining the smooth integration with other course materials as advocated in Chapters 4 and 6. Best of all, the environment itself is generated automatically by D3E.

Journal review and publishing with D3E

The user interface described in the last scenario is also used in D3E-generated e-journals. Examples of these are the *Journal of Interactive Media in Education* (JIME, 1996) and a special issue of the *International Journal of Human-Computer Studies* (Buckingham Shum and McKnight, 1997). The scenario is based on JIME which uses a hybrid peer review system of first assigning a submission to appointed reviewers, and then opening the resulting discussion to the research community. All reviews are entered direct into the threaded Website discussion, as illustrated in Figure 8.5.

The discussion is unmoderated, ie messages are not pre-filtered by the editor, as this would create too much work. To date, professionalism and standard 'netiquette' have proved to be sufficient. However, the editor has a moderator's power to remove inappropriate comments, and to facilitate discussion on themes that he or she judges of particular importance.

Elsewhere, we have discussed in detail the co-evolution of roles with the deployment of D3E in different contexts (Sumner and Buckingham Shum, 1998). Figure 8.6 shows schematically how JIME's review lifecycle differs from the traditional process, and 'who does what when'.

Returning to the scenario, the interactive animation that the authors submit could be a Java applet which loads directly into a Web browser (eg, see the JIME publication by Domingue and Mulholland, 1997b, work also described in Chapter 11). Demonstrations in other JIME publications have used browser plug-ins to provide direct manipulation, video and animations, interactive Websites, and downloadable demonstrations for reviewers and readers to install.

The editorial report that the authors receive following the review process is a Web document with links back into the review

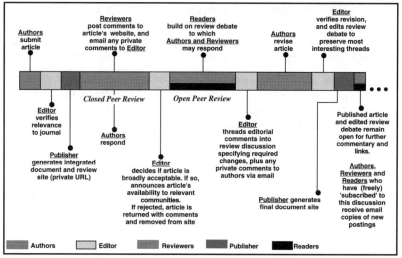

Figure 8.6. Hybrid peer review process in JIME. Firstly, a submission is allocated to appointed reviewers who discuss it between themselves and with the author. Secondly, recognizing that these reviewers cannot make every pertinent point or know of all relevant work, an open peer review phase is announced to the relevant communities, inviting anyone to contribute to the discussion. The results of this are then distilled by the editor into a hypertext accept / reject letter, with links back into the discussion. The final version continues to be open to discussion.

discussion, so the editor does not have to reiterate and recontextualize comments. This is the same genre of document as the student's summary essay in the first scenario, which linked back to student discussions.

In the scenario, to prepare their audio-visual slideshow the authors downloaded the journal's tool. We are planning to implement this as a Java applet; at present, the journal production team uses standard tools to convert authors' images and sound files into presentations. When the authors have recorded their commentary on each slide, the embedded slideshow looks as shown in Figure 8.7 (used by Soper, 1997). This user interface was created from the reusable Web-presentation environment developed in the Stadium project (Chapter 9).

Finally in the scenario, the authors upload their revised article to the journal's Website, submitting it to the markup tool. They then iteratively fine-tune any parts of their article until they are

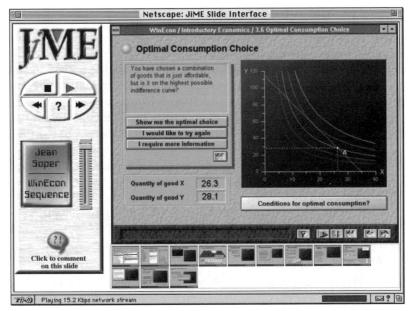

Figure 8.7 (Plate XII). The authors' audio-visual slideshow launched from their article at the journal's Website. Clicking 'Play' takes the reader through the slide sequence with streaming audio. The reader can pause and replay at any point, or jump to another slide via the thumbnail images.

happy with it. A client-server version of the publisher's toolkit is currently in development. The advantage for the journal in keeping the toolkit code on its Website is that it can be modified at any time; the advantage for the authors is that they can immediately see how their articles will appear, including the discussion part of the site (since they will not have this running on their local sites).

Thus, as articles move from being single file, textual documents to complex, interactive Websites, we hypothesize that given appropriate tools and user interfaces, authors will appreciate the hands-on ability to iteratively fine-tune the presentation of their work for publication, thus cutting out endless requests to the publishers to correct and update files. This is of course exactly the pattern we have witnessed over the last 20 years as authors have gradually taken responsibility for producing their own camera-ready figures and tables.

Summary and future directions

This chapter has described how we are seeking to exploit the potential of interactive Web media through user-centred analysis of a mode of working that defines academic life – critical, structured debate about documents. We are as interested in supporting school and university students critiquing course texts and publishing essays, as in supporting professional scholars and researchers engaged in journal peer review and publishing. We have questioned the replication of papyrocentric models which do not address whether the new media make possible new modes of working, and new forms of document. We then described the design principles underpinning the environments for reading and critiquing Web documents that the D3E publishing toolkit generates, and illustrated how things might be different by working through two scenarios of academic document-centred discourse, as supported by D3E.

Given the ubiquity of document-centred work, D3E is also useful in contexts other than academic debate. We see supporting collaborative discussion of documents as important in the broader context of knowledge management in organisations, since documents acquire significance from the debate they provoke (Brown and Duguid, 1996). D3E is being trialled within The Open University as a structured intranet environment for critiquing committee discussion documents. D3E has also been used to publish a national discussion Website to debate the recommendations of a government inquiry into the future of higher education (Dearing Website, 1997). Comments and debate are organized on a recommendation-by-recommendation basis, to facilitate the pooling of related material in constructing responses to the inquiry.

Future plans address our ability to analyse the usage of D3E generated sites in more detail, technical advances in the toolkit, and the exploration of new genres in hypertext scholarly publishing.

We wish to develop better tools for analysing interaction patterns in D3E Websites. We want to be able to define higher level units of analysis than the raw log files generated by standard Web monitoring utilities. This will enable us to quickly ascertain and visualize which of the variety of D3E's navigation methods users prefer, and also to monitor the usage of different annotation and discussion facilities.

The Web is a highly impoverished hypertext system compared to the state of the art in hypermedia technology. Bieber *et al.*

(1997) have analysed in detail how the Web could be usefully extended in many ways. One of these is to store link information separately from the documents, rather than embed them in documents. This makes it possible to view a document through different 'layers' of superimposed links which represent different perspectives. We are currently exploring the potential of one such approach (Carr *et al.*, 1995; Multicosm Ltd) in combination with D3E. We envisage numerous possibilities: students selectively viewing links to commentaries adopting one perspective, and then links adopting a contrasting position; reviewers arbitrarily selecting a particular region of text and making this the anchor for their comment; an editor displaying review comments of different categories (eg, serious objection; supporting evidence; methodological weakness).

Finally, some of the most intriguing new avenues to explore spring from the rich intersection of hypertext with literary and philosophical analyses. It is proposed by some that in contrast to static, predominantly hierarchical documents, interactive hypertext networks make possible important new genres of writing (eg, Kolb, 1997; Landow, 1992). By extension, the Web could form the basis for radically different genres of scholarly writing and argumentation. In our own work, we are moving from analysing support for discourse about a particular document (as D3E does at present), to support for interpretation of a document in relation to other work. We have therefore begun to develop a representational basis for encoding documents in ways that could support the emergence of new genres of publication and discourse over the Web (Buckingham Shum and Sumner, 1997). We are investigating the feasibility of enriching Web documents in ways that support searches for conceptually related documents. Approaches to this problem include HTML metadata (W3C, 1997), and shared, Web-accessible ontologies (see Chapter 13's analysis of knowledge modelling and Web documents, and the technical infrastructure described in Chapter 14). Such a representational scheme could also form the basis for generating graphical views, for instance, of the research literature (eg, Chen, 1997), detailed scientific argumentation, or concept maps (Gaines and Shaw, 1995).

To conclude, in the fast evolving world of interactive media and the Web, it is harder to know how to use the technology than to develop it. This chapter has described how we are interpreting the challenge of designing an appropriate 'Knowledge Web' for the scholarly work of students and researchers as they publish and critique documents.

The Knowledge Media Institute in The Open University's Berrill Building

Plate I

Figure 1.1. Sir John Daniel at IDLCON-97

Plate II

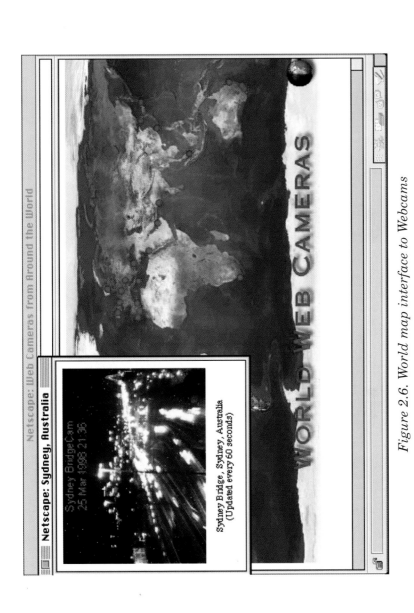

Figure 2.6. World map interface to Webcams

Plate III

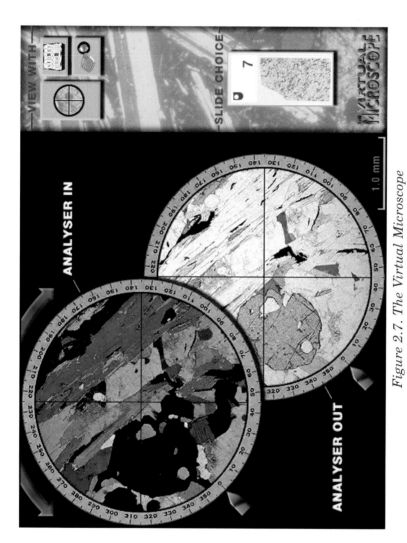

Figure 2.7. The Virtual Microscope

Plate IV

Figure 2.9. First Flight – Wright Brothers plane simulation

Plate V

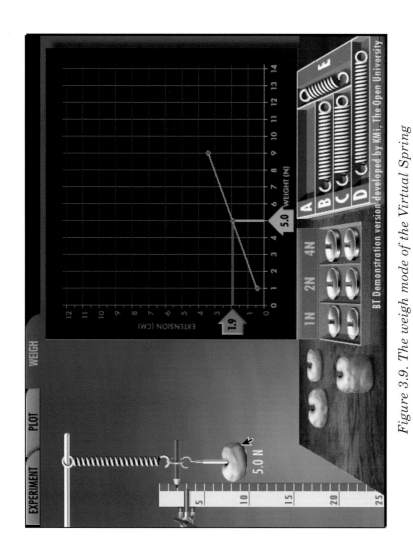

Figure 3.9. The weigh mode of the Virtual Spring

Plate VI

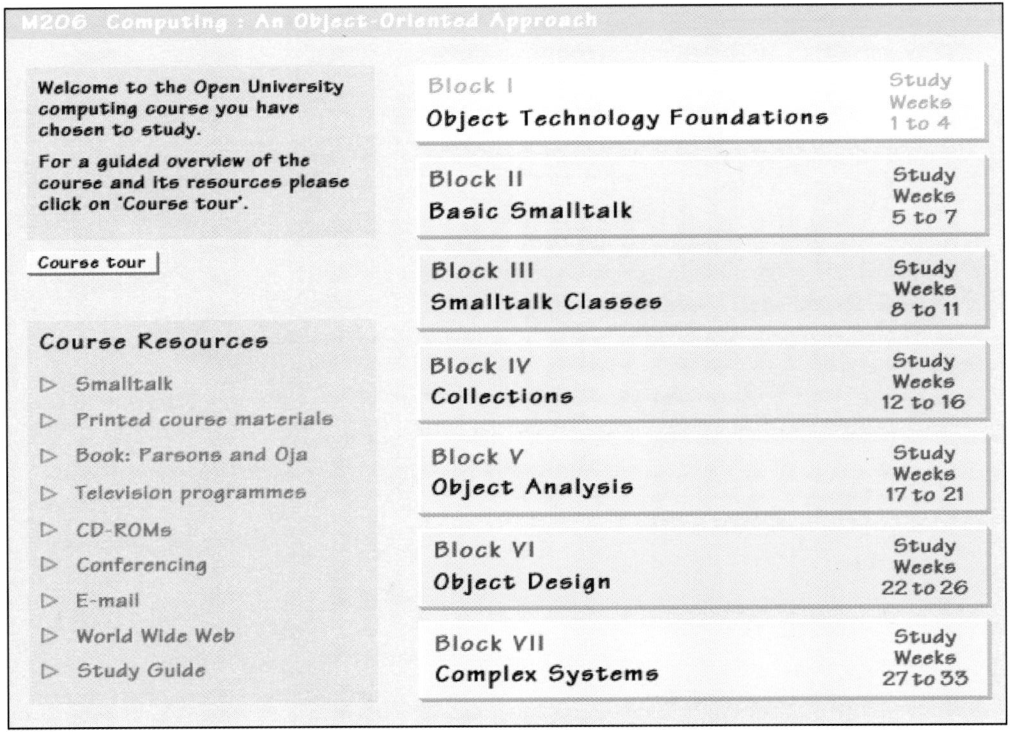

M206 Computing : An Object-Oriented Approach
Welcome to the Open University computing course you have chosen to study.
For a guided overview of the course and its resources please click on 'Course tour'.
Course tour
Course Resources
Smalltalk
Printed course materials
Book: Parsons and Oja
Television programmes
CD-ROMs
Conferencing
E-mail
World Wide Web
Study Guide
Block I
Object Technology Foundations
Study Weeks 1 to 4
Block II
Basic Smalltalk
Study Weeks 5 to 7
Block III
Smalltalk Classes
Study Weeks 8 to 11
Block IV
Collections
Study Weeks 12 to 16
Block V
Object Analysis
Study Weeks 17 to 21
Block VI
Object Design
Study Weeks 22 to 26
Block VII
Complex Systems
Study Weeks 27 to 33

Figure 4.1. The interactive course map

Plate VII

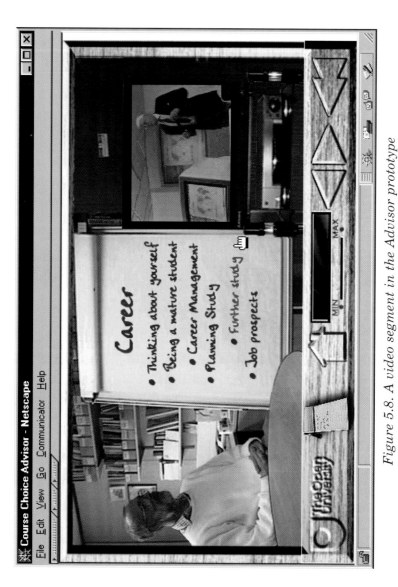

Figure 5.8. A video segment in the Advisor prototype

Plate VIII

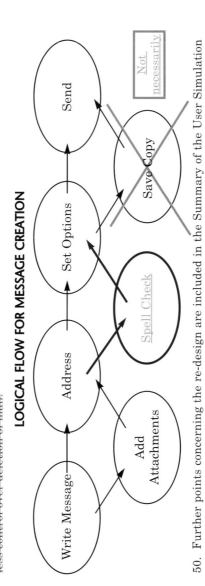

This is not a conceptual issue

Question 3
Did the Re-Design Work

- **Conceptual Issues** – these include -automatic opening of the Address Box when the Create button is pressed, the possible inclusion of a drag and drop ~~method~~ technique for assembling the 'To', and 'Copy To' lists in the Address list, automatic opening of the Priority and Save To dialog boxes when pressing the Send button, automatic query if there is no text in the Subject or Message fields, ~~and less control over deletion of mail.~~

LOGICAL FLOW FOR MESSAGE CREATION

Write Message

Add Attachments

Address

Spell Check

Set Options

Save Copy

Not necessarily

Send

50. Further points concerning the re-design are included in the Summary of the User Simulation at Annex C.
Basically a good answer—see detailed hypertext comment below.

Figure 6.2. Example of a marked assignment

Plate IX

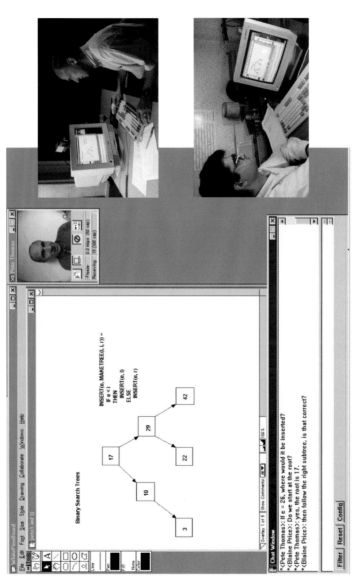

Figure 6.3. Audiographic tutorial student screen dump with inset photos of student and tutor

Plate X

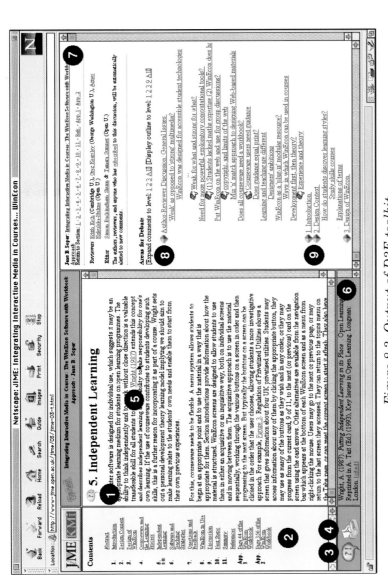

Figure 8.3. Output of D3E toolkit

Plate XI

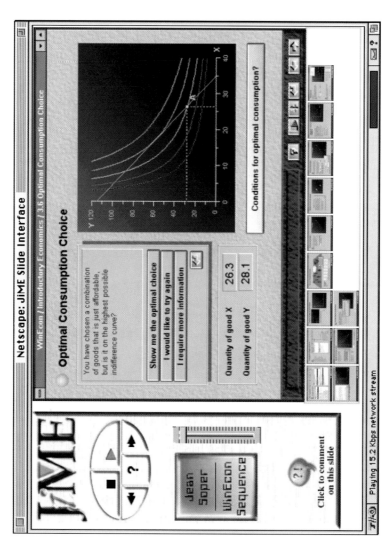

Figure 8.7. JIME slide interface

Plate XII

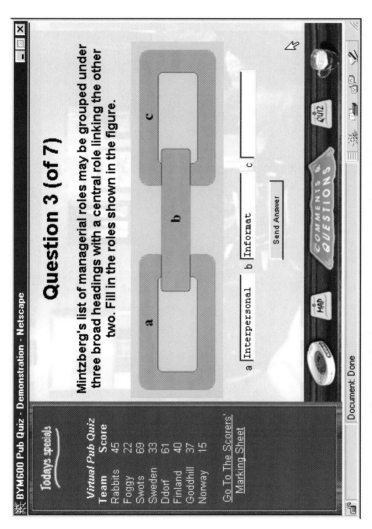

Figure 9.6. A question screen in the Pub Quiz

Plate XIII

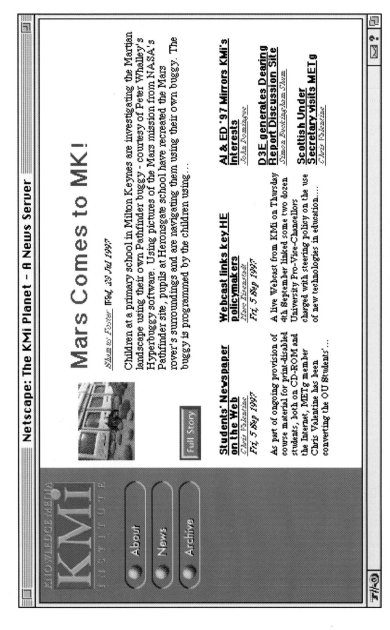

Figure 10.2. A screen snapshot of the KMi Planet frontpage

Plate XIV

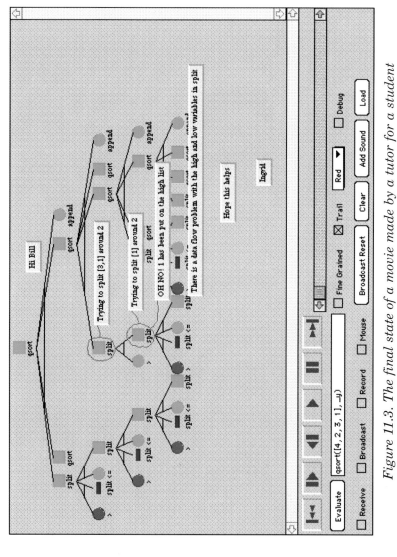

Figure 11.3. The final state of a movie made by a tutor for a student

Plate XV

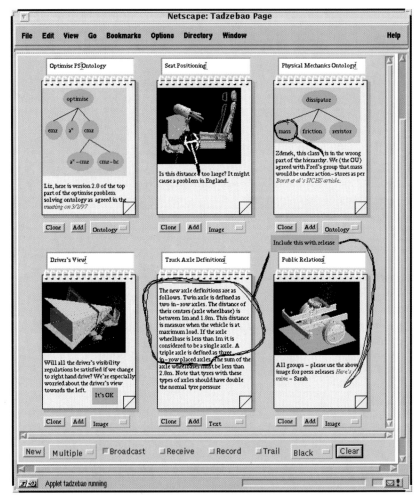

Figure 14.2. Tadzebao from World Wide Design Lab

Plate XVI

Chapter 9

Exploring telepresence on the Internet: the KMi Stadium Webcast experience

Peter Scott and Marc Eisenstadt

There is no substitute for 'being there' to experience the look, feel, excitement and overall sense of presence at an event – be it a tutorial or a concert. When being there is impossible, an alternative is to provide an enhanced experience using the latest Web-oriented media, but only if one understands how best to use these media, particularly audio.

Introduction: real telepresence and the KMi Stadium architecture

The Internet combines many media that can be used in different modes. At the moment, the dominant mode is asynchronous, valuable in many contexts described throughout this book, seeking for information, but more synchronous technologies such as live video and audio are increasing in feasibility. In our telepresence research we explore the power of remote presence that can be created through these live interactions. We argue that the live and synchronous can radically change the nature of the asynchronous in this new medium. Consider the voice – using synchronous audio in Internet media turns out to be much more interesting than simply providing a new telephone technology. On the Internet, the user's live voice must integrate not only with the live audio of others, but with live text and actions of others, and with the full range of non-live media and actions.

Four key themes run through our telepresence research.

- **'Presence'** describes our over-arching aim to create a sense of 'being there' to enhance the nature of the learning experience.

- **'Pedagogically sound'** means that we never work with technology for its own sake, but rather embed appropriate technology as transparently as possible into a carefully thought out learning experience.

- **'Peer group'** emphasizes the really radical ability of the Internet to bring together previously isolated learners into a community. In the long term, meeting and working with peers is one of the best payoffs we can provide for the networked learner.

- **'Pan-synchronous'** is our terminology for the bridge between conventional 'synchronous' activities such as live lectures, and 'asynchronous' activities such as on-demand replays or discussion group e-mails, conferences and newsgroups. To illustrate this point, consider that I could be a facilitator running a live group session on the Internet, where we are discussing the replay of a keynote address recorded yesterday, followed by the offline conference up to now. Is this synchronous, or asynchronous? It's both, and it doesn't even matter.

Much of our telepresence activity can be bundled under the umbrella of 'KMi Stadium'. This is a generic label for a suite of activities and software tools that have been evolving since 1995. The common focus of these activities is large-scale live events and on-demand replays that can give remote participants anywhere on the Internet that sense of 'being there'.

An evolutionary perspective on the progress of KMi Stadium research is illustrated in Table 9.1. There are two key threads to this work: an experimental event thread and a product thread. In the former, we include the range of experiments we have conducted using a mix of technologies to explore very different telepresence event types. The events in this thread have used whatever current technologies were useful to explore the event type at that time – typically with HTTP based client-server platforms and associated plug-ins and helpers. The product based

	Event Thread	Product Thread
1994	Virtual Summer School	
1995	Internet Talk Radio++	Java Inferno Prototype
1996		
	Live Tech – Talks & Tutorials	
1997		
	Big live experiments	
1998		Lyceum

Table 9.1. An evolutionary view of Stadium research

thread has focused instead on the development of our own clean and simple tools for our evolving telepresence model. The tools in this thread have been Java based prototypes.

The first pilot in the event thread, held in 1994, was something we called the Virtual Summer School. In 1995 we graduated to a series of big-name personality interviews to a world-wide audience, in a Net Radio style. This led us, in 1996, into the first of the product based experiments, the Java Inferno prototype. In 1997 we conducted a wide series of innovative interface experiments including a Pub Quiz, a set of lectures and a symposium. Meanwhile, over in the Java product thread, we drew upon our event based experience to abstract from the Inferno prototype a new client, which we call Lyceum. We describe the individual prototypes and experiments in the following sections.

Early experiments and prototypes

In the descriptions which follow, please bear in mind that our 1994 activities took place pre-Netscape, pre-Java, and even pre-28.8Kbps modems.

The Virtual Summer School, 1994

Open University students on many courses must attend residential schools (eg, a one-week summer school to gain experience conducting experiments), providing an additional layer of support. About 10 per cent of students have genuine difficulty attending such residential schools, so we investigated ways of bringing this experience directly into their homes. In August and September 1994, a Virtual Summer School (VSS) for Open University undergraduate course D309 Cognitive Psychology enabled students to attend an experimental version of summer school from their own homes (Eisenstadt *et al.*, 1996).

The VSS was designed to enable students to participate in many of the activities of a physical residential school. Our intention was that they should be able to undertake group discussions, run experiments, obtain one-to-one tuition, listen to lectures, ask questions, participate as subjects in experiments, conduct literature searches, browse original journal publications, work in project teams, undertake statistical analyses, prepare and submit nicely formatted individual or joint written work, prepare plenary session presentations, and socialize.

The technology involved, considered radical at the time, is now of interest because it appears rather arcane. Even then, we knew full well that it was something of a 'lash-up', but this was

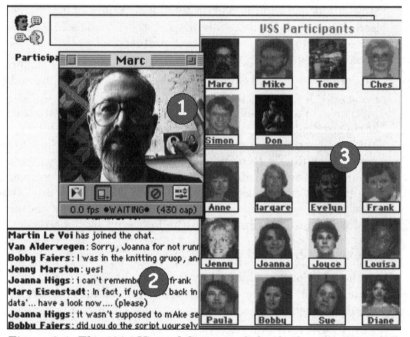

Figure 9.1. The 1994 Virtual Summer School, showing (1) a CU-SeeMe window (upper left), (2) a FirstClass chat window (lower left), and (3) thumbnail photos of participants used to moderate turn-taking (right). In the early days of voice-on-the-net, our 14.4Kbps modem users had to resort to a 17-way telephone conference call, using mobile phones supplied by us!

necessary precisely because no single technology provided an approach for us, and we really wanted to know what could be achieved in this arena. We provided students with e-mail, Usenet newsgroups, live chat lines and low-bandwidth (keyboard) using FirstClass v. 2.5 from SoftArc, and Web browsing via NCSA Mosaic version 1.0.3 (!) Using Cornell's freshly-released Beta of CU-SeeMe, students were able to attend a Virtual Guest Lecture by Apple Fellow Donald A Norman. We even supplied mobile phones for helpdesk and backup audio support, which proved crucial during some of the live events. We also used a product called The Virtual Meeting (from RTZ in Cupertino), which displayed images of all remote participants, and facilitated moderated turn-taking, hand-raising, interactive whiteboard drawing and question/answer sessions (Figure 9.1).

The students clearly loved the peer group interactions and the audio discussions with the guest lecturer. They found the whole experience enthralling and motivating, and did as well academically as face-to-face residential summer school students on their later assignments and exams. However, they were not only overwhelmed by the fragments of technology they needed to wrestle with, but also stunned by the sheer amount of time they ended up investing over a two-week period (a few hours per night, as opposed to the 30–60 minutes per night they were expecting). Poor connectivity due to net traffic and lost packets dogged many of the experiences. Yet the whole activity whetted our appetites and showed the students and us that bigger, better and more effective approaches were possible. Aside from the obvious issues about ease-of-use and minimizing time spent, two key lessons emerged: (i) audio was so important as a vehicle for conveying content, tone and general sense of presence, that we felt we could sacrifice video entirely if necessary, until the technology allowed us to include it for our students; (ii) we needed to think very hard about how to do this on very large scale. We adopted the name 'KMi Stadium' to capture our emphasis on scalability, and undertook a variety of related experiments and prototypes, described in the next section.

NetRadio++

Beginning in 1995 we used a combination of RealAudio, telephone patch panels, and CU-SeeMe to run a virtual seminar series we called 'KMi Maven of the Month'. The format was a 30-minute interview with a leading knowledge media researcher or personality ('maven' = expert or connoisseur), conducted live in the first instance and then available as an on-demand replay, with opportunities for group discussion both during and after the event. Typical personalities included Peter Cochrane from British Telecom and Apple's Alan Kay. These interviews extended the 'talk radio' format by adding static and updateable images, slow-frame video, QuickTime movies, audience questions and sound effects to enhance the presentations. Unlike Internet Relay Chat or conference/auditorium events held at the time by the big on-line service providers, we placed more emphasis on auditory and visual communication to encourage visual and verbal interactions to take place anywhere in the world. Audiences numbered from dozens to low hundreds, with listeners located everywhere on the Internet from Tokyo to Brazil.

First Java prototype

By 1996 we were constructing our first all-Java implementation to address cross-platform and scaleability issues. We also began to experiment with adding some more 'atmosphere' to enhance the user experience. A key theme of this approach was that significant special-effects graphics and sounds would be downloaded and cached in advance on each client machine (either over the net for high-bandwidth attendees or by CD-ROM distribution for low-bandwidth attendees). Then, live events and 'tutor-facilitated on-demand replays' could be run under 'remote control', with low-

Figure 9.2. Adam Freeman's first Java prototype of KMi Stadium, code-named 'Inferno'. Mood buttons at the bottom were polled by the server, and appropriate atmosphere noises were either played locally or injected into the live audio stream, as appropriate.

---

bandwidth audio and mouse events driving synchronous presentations among all clients (clients could of course run their own private on-demand viewings if they didn't want the live group atmosphere).

Our Java-implemented clients handled all of the 'atmosphere' locally (Figure 9.2). This included the look and feel of the Stadium (or auditorium, or classroom, as appropriate), including locally-run animations which depicted heads bobbing in the crowd, doors opening, flags waving, and even moving image sequences of the presenter(s). In anticipation of the worst case (28.8Kbps dial-up modems) the Java client supplied the animated special effects locally, thereby preserving the valuable bandwidth for the main audio stream.

The Stadium servers were themselves implemented entirely in Java, and dealt with the client polling, secure, dishing out the audio streams, and synchronizing the presenter mouse clicks with the behaviour of each client. The resulting architecture was designed to be inherently scaleable, platform-neutral, responsive in nearly real time (up to 20-second delay in the worst case), and deliverable anywhere on the Internet which could guarantee 28.8Kbps dial-up access. Each audio stream typically required 10Kbps of bandwidth, so serving 1000 streams required 10Mbps in the worst case, and was the limiting factor. We relied on 'like minded' linked sites to deliver this capability, arranged on an ad hoc basis, because IP multicasting was still not a reality.

This implementation was mainly useful for 'cutting our teeth' on a heavy duty Java implementation, testing out user interface concepts with a local (intranet) audience, and thinking about ways in principle to scale up to the delivery of events to an audience of 100,000 people, even within the constraints of the limited Internet infrastructure of the day.

Exploring the Webcast context

As word about KMi Stadium development spread throughout The Open University, we received many enquiries and visitors. Open University Associate Lecturers ('tutors') who handle the 'front line' of interacting with OU students said things like the following: 'Webcasting to 100,000 is a wonderful idea for a research prototype, but what I really need is something I can use immediately with my 20 students scattered across Europe, South America, and Africa'. This motivated us to find a route to build rapid prototypes of innovative Webcasting environments, and test

Figure 9.3. Three different Webcast contexts

them on mission-critical events such as Open University course tutorials and in-house seminars and workshops.

In this section we discuss three live Webcasts undertaken within the stadium architecture: a keynote address, a virtual Pub Quiz, and a multi-talk conference symposium session. As we can see in Figure 9.3 the three events all have a very different look and feel, being designed to support very different types of event. The first is the keynote address we encountered in Chapter 1 with one speaker – pictured at a podium on a stage – speaking to slides. The second is an interactive quiz with the remote clients seeing a British pub environment and responding to the audio questions by posting answers. The last is a multi-speaker symposium designed as a roundtable presentation of short slideshow talks interspersed with speaker-led debate around remote participant comments. In all of these environments, the remote speaker can control what slides (or pages, etc) the remote audience sees in synchrony with their audio. The audio is a one-way broadcast with the remote audience typically interacting via a text-chat environment.

Figure 9.4. The IDLCON-97 Keynote Interface, showing the zoomed-in view. The zoomed-out view was presented in Chapter 1, Figure 1.1.

The Keynote Webcast

The IDLCON-97 presentation, included verbatim in Chapter 1, was aimed at a physical meeting taking place in a large auditorium in Washington DC. Open University Vice-Chancellor Sir John Daniel was 'beamed in' via satellite – appearing as TV on huge screens in the auditorium. A Stadium Webcast shadowed the satellite broadcast, using the same audio feed, presented through our Netscape Navigator environment and broadcast free onto the Internet. A short way into the presentation, the satellite video signal was switched in favour of the Internet presentation picked up via a 28.8Kbps modem connected to a local Washington DC Internet service provider.

The keynote interface contained a number of views of the presentation, including a 'zoomed in' view of the slides (Figure 9.4) and a 'zoomed out' view of the speaker and slides. In Chapter 1, we saw the 'zoomed out' view (Figure 1.1) with its depiction of a stage, speaker and audience. This interface is animated so that viewers can see the figure of the speaker move to different positions, along with lighting effects which add to the overall experience and sense of presence. This view is strongly graphic and animated to make an impact upon a large auditorium audience in a relatively short period of time.

The Pub Quiz Webcast

The Pub Quiz was designed to serve the needs of OU MBA students who were preparing for an examination on the Finance course they were taking. The session was webcast on 11 April 1997. Instead of flying to a central site in the UK or continental Europe to attend a large-group revision seminar, this particular cohort of IBM-sponsored students were able to go to a local Technology Learning Centre and partake in a world-wide session run by three course team faculty members at The Open University headquarters in Milton Keynes, UK. Students registered as teams (a typical grouping comprised six or seven sharing a single PC with a projection screen, and a designated 'team captain' to type in the responses; virtual teams of isolated home-bound individuals could also be created). Live streaming audio from the tutors provided running commentary and feedback, and a sequence of questions appearing in a custom browser frame challenged the students to think about their coursework. A special scoring interface enabled the tutors (sitting in Milton Keynes) to score the exams at the end of each round, and an instantly-updated team scoreboard appearing on the left of the screen inspired some friendly competitiveness. A world map indicated the location of

Figure 9.5. The basic Pub Quiz interface

all the participants, and a chat room enabled tutors to field questions and the 'control booth' to deal with any technical glitches.

The Pub Quiz interface uses a simple model based around a British Pub (Figure 9.5). The main controls are present on the 'bar' at the bottom: the ashtray resets the user to the current state of the quiz; the map 'beer mat' shows the live location of other players; the comments and questions 'bar towel' provides an interface for the user to participate in the live text chat; the quiz 'beer mat' is used in the replay to start the quiz; and the 'pint of beer' shows where you are in the quiz – when you are out of beer the quiz is over! The blackboard to the left reflects the current scores of all registered players. NB the link at the bottom is not available in the live version – it is for replay users to see how the marking happened (Figure 9.8).

When the player registers and enters the pub, he or she is connected to the live audio stream which carries the discussion and questions. The area above the bar is the activity area – showing the current state of the session. As the quiz game progressed the teams were led through a series of questions (presented in free text entry forms as in Figure 9.6) and were given a specific time to return an answer. The answers were logged in the Pub Quiz database, which was then accessed by the

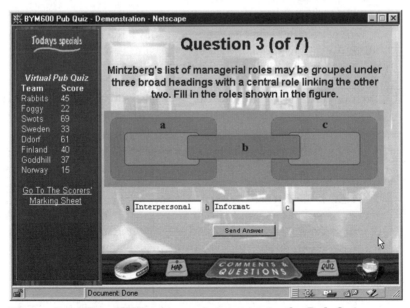

Figure 9.6 (Plate XIII). A question screen in the Pub Quiz

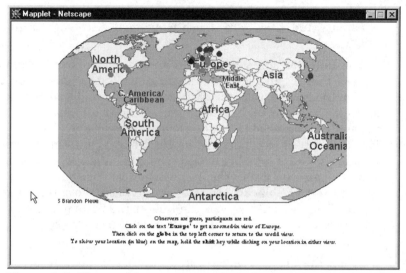

Figure 9.7. The world map view of Pub Quiz participants

markers. Although we could have automated this process by forcing a multiple choice format, we opted to use arbitrary free text answers and real human markers in order to encourage more interesting free form answers. Between each of the three rounds of the quiz, we ran slide-based revision sessions and question and answer sessions based on the activity in the text chat interface.

When one clicks on the map 'beer mat', a window reflecting the current state of participation in the quiz is displayed. In Figure 9.7 we can see that for the 11 April 1997 quiz, the audience was mostly located in the Western Europe time zones. Registered players are shown in red, and observers (barred from participating in the game sections) are shown in green, while this client is shown in blue.

In Figure 9.8 we see the marker view of the Pub Quiz database. The marker here is currently reviewing the team that has called itself 'rabbits' and their responses to some questions in round one. The call to the database server to view a team's entries generates a Web page form around the answers submitted so far (with any marks already given). When the marker has finished marking what has been submitted so far, he or she can submit the marks back to the database – which will then be reflected live on the scoring blackboard in the students' interface.

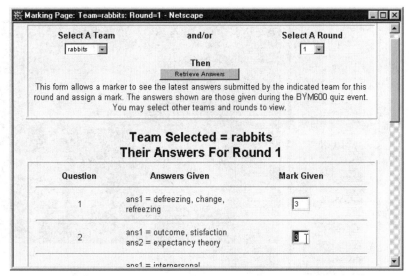

Figure 9.8. The marker interface to the Pub Quiz

The Learning.Org Webcast

Late in 1997, the Stadium architecture was used in a Webcast site in support of a meeting convened by Open University Pro-ViceChancellor for Technology Development Professor Diana Laurillard, under the heading Learning.Org (it should be noted that this name is not an Internet domain name related to this organization). The meeting was designed as a forum for senior university management staff (at Pro-Vice Chancellor level in the UK) with particular responsibility for the overall strategic direction of the use of information technology within their universities. Its aim was to invite these managers to meet and share best practice and experience on the introduction of new technologies into teaching and learning in the UK. The physical meeting was scheduled for 26 September 1997.

In order to make the physical meeting more productive, a number of networked resources were established on a Web site in KMi (http://kmi.open.ac.uk/learning.org). The site included a registration interface, an area for participant self-statements, pointers to other useful sites, and a Web forum implemented using the D3E tools (see Chapter 8). At the centre of these resources was a live Webcast scheduled for 4 September 1997.

The live Webcast event consisted of three 15 minute talks interspersed with roundtable question and answer sessions broadcast onto the Internet from The Open University in Milton Keynes.

Figure 9.9. Contextual stills in the Learning.Org interface

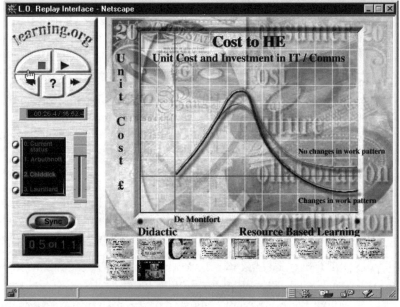

Figure 9.10. A slide from a main presentation in the Learning.Org interface

Participants on the day included Pro-Vice Chancellors from 20 other universities around the UK, all sitting in or near their own offices.

Figure 9.9 shows the Webcast interface, with the main controls over to the left, the main slide panel on the right with a slide tray beneath it. The main panel shows a small collection of stills broadcast to give participants an idea of what was happening remotely, without resorting to the use of video. The main control panel contains a number of obvious buttons – to play and stop the streaming audio, to enter the question and answer interface, to move ahead or back in the presentation. In this Webcast there were four main 'channels' that the user could select: three presentations and one organizing session. To the right of the channel buttons is the volume slider, with the current slide number at the bottom. Figure 9.10 shows a slide from the middle of a main presentation, with thumbnail snapshots in the slide tray at the bottom all selectable by the user.

Running this range of events has led us to a series of important observations, summarized in the next section.

What we have learned

There are six key themes that emerge from the range of stadium developments we have discussed so far:

- **Content creation tools are inadequate:** Presenters' original slides needed significant tweaking (a) to look reasonable within a web browser; (b) to fit within our custom frames; (c) to make clear teaching points to the audience. Slides are nevertheless a familiar medium, and in many cases can be more effective than small slow-frame-rate video images.

- **Front door signposting:** The accompanying Web site needs a clear entrance that distinguishes among (a) the announcement of the event; (b) technical requirements such as plug-ins; (c) a site for participants to test their technical setup; (d) a quick-start 'enter here' sign including automatic testing of browser/plug-in functionality; and (e) a lower-tech alternative in case of problems.

- **Changing state of Webcast site:** To cater for diverse users at different times, the site can benefit by clearly discriminating among (a) pre-event promotion, (b) 'stay tuned' notification on the day of the event; (c) a live 'station ID' and countdown timer in the final hour before going live; (d) a 'live' indicator for latecomers during the event itself; (e) a 'replay available soon' notification as soon as the live event finishes; and (f) a long-term archive with pointers to the location of the replay.

- **Serious production team pays off:** Although 'desktop presentation' involving a single presenter may seem like the ideal, our experience is that for a quality Webcast it pays to have a full production crew on hand, including an event moderator to handle questions and interact with the presenter, a special effects (eg, avatar) controller, a presenter/quizmaster, and people to look after the mix of HTTP, control scripts, and audio servers. In addition, we placed great emphasis on the role of the graphics designer, the audio mixing engineer, the telephone balance unit engineer (for phone-in Webcasts), and the audio encoding technician.

- **Avoiding the weakest link in the chain:** If a server crashes, you need to be able to 'hot-swap' another one straight into its place, or provide an alternative URL for participants. It is also valuable to work with mirror or reflector sites on other continents to help distribute the load, even if this requires one-off dedicated intercontinental ISDN phone calls or dedicated lines to get the signal from A to B.

- **Changing what you do:** In general, presentations benefit from being quite short (10–15 minutes), with lots of audience interaction, including optional competitive elements. Full dress rehearsals are essential, in order to ensure correct timings and synchronization. Audience expectation can be high, so if the event is compared to television, then the low production qualities will be very damaging. One key to overcoming this effect is to make sure you don't try to do the same things, and that you take full advantage of the things that TV cannot deal with, such as interactivity and personalization.

With the above lessons under our belt, we are now setting about addressing the major problems we still face: providing high quality audio interaction among diverse participants, and using this to create an overall quality experience. Note that this is precisely where we began! We have made significant headway through the activities described above, and are now looking to integrate our experiences in the form of a new environment that we call Lyceum, described next.

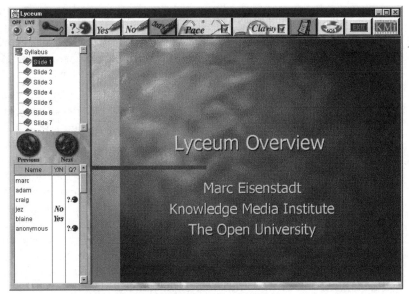

Figure 9.11. Screenshots of the KMi Lyceum

Current work: KMi Lyceum

Design goals of Lyceum

In building Lyceum (Figure 9.11), we were sensitive to several goals: our students, sponsors, and OU course developers use a rich mixture of PCs, Macs and Unix workstations, so we developed in Java to support them all. We needed to deliver to many thousands of students simultaneously, hence our emphasis on scalability. We needed a way to merge audio content and other media types without requiring students to run multiple applications at once, so we put 'seamless integration' as a high priority. We know that audio carries the bulk of the sense of presence on-line, so good audio (an 'audio-centric' focus) was crucial to the functioning of this environment.

We wanted to embed not only slides, but ultimately media of arbitrary types into the main content window, so 'rich content' was another important design goal. Finally, the environment had to be as easy to run as turning on a light switch, and support users over today's dialup modems.

Lyceum functions and features

Lyceum is novel in several respects. Although one hears a lot about streaming audio on today's Internet, it is not widely known that it has been technically impossible, until now, to synchronize a **live** audio presentation precisely with graphical changes on a multitude of different clients. But with Lyceum, the presenter can synchronize changes precisely, taking an audience or tutorial group along on a kind of 'synchronous Web safari' with precision timing to coincide with what is being said in real time.

Anyone with a microphone-equipped multimedia PC can 'have the floor' if the speaker grants them speaking privileges. A participant simply clicks on the question mark 'talking head' icon at the top if he or she wants to ask a question, and then the moderator can grant speaking privileges. At that point, the participant's name will become highlighted, and he or she just needs to click and hold on the microphone icon at the top in order to speak, and be heard by everyone. It is possible to have a free-for-all discussion or just function with one speaker at a time under moderator control. A whiteboard tool can be used to highlight specific slide elements, and slides or other media elements can be selected by the presenter from a storyboard media tray along the left hand side, with the entire audience experiencing the updated images simultaneously.

Why are we doing this ourselves?

Given the plethora of tools and environments on the Internet (and it's an easy prediction that more will be available by the time you read this), why should we be doing basic research and development in this area? A partial answer is that The Open University often has found that an off-the-shelf solution is simply not customisable to the extent we require for our own teaching purposes. Moreover, our approach to dealing with teaching at a distance is somewhat different from others, due to our long-standing emphasis on supported open resource-based learning, as we've seen in Chapters 2, 3, 5, 6, and elsewhere throughout this book. Another partial answer stems from KMi's research role.

Although we are not the inventors of technologies such as streaming audio or Web browsers, we consider ourselves to be 'power users' of those technologies, and feel we can cast them in an innovative light by constructing our own environments with a mixture of existing and custom-built tools. At the same time, we have no intention of re-inventing the wheel, and thus are closely tracking the emerging technologies. Table 9.2 lists related products, and the relevant URL where they can be located and tested. Centra's Symposium, in particular, stands out as a landmark product in this space, because it shares our philosophy of platform independence, ease of use, scalability, and using the interface to create a simple yet compelling sense of presence.

Product [company]	URL
Atrium [VocalTec]	www.vocaltec.com
Auditorium [PlaceWare]	www.placeware.com
CU-SeeMe [White Pine]	www.wpine.com
EventWare Classroom[Collaborataive Systems Research]	www.eventware.com
NetMeeting [Microsoft]	www.microsoft.com/netmeeting
PowWow [Tribal Voice]	www.tribal.com/powwow
Rendezvous [Visualtek]	rendezvous.visualtek.com
Symposium [Centra]	www.centra.com
Voxchat [Voxware]	www.voxware.com

Table 9.2. URL's for Web-based group meeting / virtual classroom products or tools

By building Lyceum ourselves, we aim to maintain several distinct advantages. As stated earlier, true audio/graphic synchronization is extremely difficult to achieve for live events, and doing it ourselves lets us address the synchronization issues directly. Among the many benefits afforded by our own approach is that it is truly cross-platform, and builds on a simple production philosophy based on a slide-show metaphor. While we never advocate slide shows as the best method of teaching, they do have the advantage of being familiar! We have also built it so that different audio compression tools can be plugged in as and when they become available and Lyceum is designed by us to work seamlessly across corporate firewalls.

A final benefit of our own work is that the interface itself is built from modular components whose look and feel can be modified according our own needs.

What is next for Lyceum?

The next phase will provide simplified content production tools, so that PowerPoint slides can just be dropped into a Lyceum presentation a short while before 'going live'. The whiteboard will be enhanced with industrial strength drawing tools, in line with user expectations. The underlying server architecture that we deploy is built from the ground up to handle a very large number of users, and we will also move beyond slide shows to handle modern multimedia presentations.

We plan to experiment with 'minimalist' production modes, as described earlier, so that the presenter can 'fly solo' rather than require the full audio, graphics, and server monitoring production team. The Lyceum architecture is secure and extendible so that examination and advanced administration functions, such as user logging and box-office payments for events, can be added.

Concluding remarks

We began by looking at ways to provide a compelling user experience for students at a distance: what we like to call 'real telepresence'. This approach emphasized ways to augment the real experience, in the spirit of Buxton's (1997) 'augmented reality', rather than embed the user in a potentially daunting virtual reality environment. We want our students to be able to share (with one another and with their mentors) the best of the learning experiences that we can provide, even in relatively isolated circumstances.

The harsh reality is that the 'virtual classroom' can be a very unrewarding experience for two reasons: (a) the technology can easily get in the way; (b) even if the technology works brilliantly, the real classroom experience itself is usually pretty depressing – what an awful thing to look forward to! Therefore, we have tried to address both the technology and the way it is used. Our experiments and prototypes have suggested ways forward: we now know a great deal about the ingredients of a successful synchronous event on the Internet, and can use the emerging technology to convey innovative experiences such as the Pub Quiz which go beyond the rather tedious classroom metaphor.

Chapter 10

KMi Planet: putting the knowledge back into media

John Domingue and Peter Scott

The Web is a great medium for disseminating news externally and internally. Many of the mundane tasks of alerting readers, soliciting, gathering, and formatting stories can be handled by intelligent agents. The challenge, taken up by KMi Planet, is to integrate these tasks in a compelling fashion with minimal overheads for the in-house reporters and maximal benefit for readers.

Introduction

In this chapter we describe KMi Planet, a Web based news server which facilitates communication and allows the wider community to access KMi-related items of interest.

Most news-of-the-future projects, particularly those based upon the concept of intelligent agency, focus on the idea of personalized news feeds (eg, Chesnais *et al.*, 1995; Kamba *et al.*, 1997). In these systems the reader delegates the activity of finding interesting stories, possibly from a wide variety of sources such as the Web and usenet newsgroups, to an agent which 'knows' the reader's interests. Within the KMi Planet project we have investigated how a newsroom-agent could aid in the task of creating a high quality Web based news page from widely accessible input. Our aim was to enable 'journalists' to send in stories from the 'front line' with minimal hardware constraints.

The Planet architecture is based upon the LispWeb server (described in Chapter 12). Within LispWeb, HTTP requests are handled by arbitrary Lisp function calls. As Lisp is the *de facto* standard in AI research the server architecture greatly facilitates the construction of Web agents. The Planet is implemented as a set of Lisp modules replicating some of the activities found within news agencies.

Communication within an organization

Organisations need to keep members informed. Most organisations of a significant size do this via an internal publication. The major problems with internal publications is the effort involved in getting a story from a member of the organisation into the publication, and the delay in getting the publication to all the members. The hurdles include:

- *transcription* – transcription software is not readily available when the story is 'hot'. There follows a time delay after which members may suffer from motivation and recollection problems,
- *distribution* – paper based techniques necessarily have a time delay,
- *archiving*, and
- *searching*.

Within some organisations internal mail lists are used to keep members informed. While alleviating the problems of distribution and archiving, messages within a mail list constitute a low quality medium (single font and style used, graphics can be attached but are not in place or laid out).

Many organisations are now deploying electronic and networked news delivery to facilitate organisational communication. Distribution techniques vary from e-mail lists and sites in HTML, to the use of commercial news feed systems like PointCast (1998), Headliner (1998), and WebCast (1998). A number of organisations (eg Apple and EuroParc) use large screen displays in social areas to increase employee awareness. Even with commercial news feed systems, which can provide the news very effectively to the news-user, the construction of high quality news articles still represents a substantial editorial and journalistic effort that can take up a great deal of time.

Our approach – a news room agent on the Web

Our approach to alleviating the above problem is to provide a news server which accepts stories submitted in the lowest common denominator medium – an e-mail message – yet is able to create a high quality Web page. The key to our rationale is that the submission must be as simple and easy as possible so that it will be genuinely used. The system should take the pressure off the journalist and editors by making their contributions entirely lightweight – by having a software agent taking on much of the work.

One key aspect of agent systems (as discussed in Chapter 15, and also by Maes, 1994; Milewski and Lewis, 1997) is that their

Figure 10.1. A screen snapshot of a full story displayed in KMi Planet

users delegate responsibility to them for some task on which they work autonomously. As Chapter 15 shows, this very notion of autonomy raises some very interesting challenges. In our model the Planet is given stories directly by researchers, who in this context play the role of journalists, and takes on the responsibility of editing these and presenting them to the research community as news. In this simplest communication model a journalist sends an e-mail message to the KMi Planet story account. The subject line of the mail message becomes the headline of the story. The body of the message becomes the text of the story. If the journalist attaches an image to the mail message, it is added into the story in an appropriate place. In Figure 10.1 we see a single story Web page rendered from an e-mail message. The story headline is displayed at the top, the attached image follows beneath and then the name of the 'journalist' who sent the message (linked to his or her home page) and the date of the submission. The message body is shown below, with Web links appropriately anchored to their destinations. In the current Planet view this is what single stories look like. Although the human journalist is responsible for sending in a good story, all the rest of the process is handled by the software.

Figure 10.2. (Plate XIV). A screen snapshot of the KMi Planet frontpage

Given that we have a database of such stories then we could present them in a number of different ways. The most obvious is the newspaper-like multiple story page where the submitted story is presented in the context of other stories. A snapshot of a KMi Planet multi-story news page is shown in Figure 10.2. Here we see the story from Figure 10.1 occupying the top half of the page with three story columns beneath it. The top story image has been scaled to fit into this page design as an illustrative graphic and the body text has been truncated to fit into the cell. Finally, a button has been added to lead one back to the full story (of Figure 10.1). In the columns beneath we see two further truncated story views – in the left two columns we see less of the body of each story, with no illustration, while in the rightmost column are only some headlines and authors' names. In the current Planet view, this is what the Planet front page looks like.

Finally, in the screen snapshot of Figure 10.3 we see a very simple headline listing of a large set of stories – listed in this case by date. In the current Planet view, this is what the story archive looks like.

As can be seen from Figure 10.4 the KMi Planet architecture, built on top of the LispWeb server (see Chapter 12), has four main components:

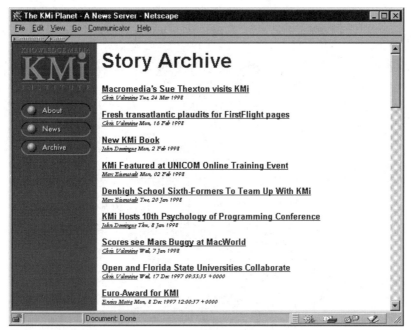

Figure 10.3. The KMi Planet archive of stories

- *an executive editor* – which has overall control, and can respond to commands from the human editors and generate requests for the other modules or human agents;

- *a story processor* – which can take story submissions and maintain the database entries for them;

- *a story presenter* – which presents the Planet stories to the client;

- *a set of databases* – which include the stories that make up the Planet's news; the journalists who may contribute the stories; the images that the story presenter may use to illustrate the stories; and a small database of presentation formats.

The Planet databases

The stories database contains the text of the stories that have been provided to Planet by the journalists. The stories are stored in a simple text form, and have been processed by the story processor to identify unusual text characters.

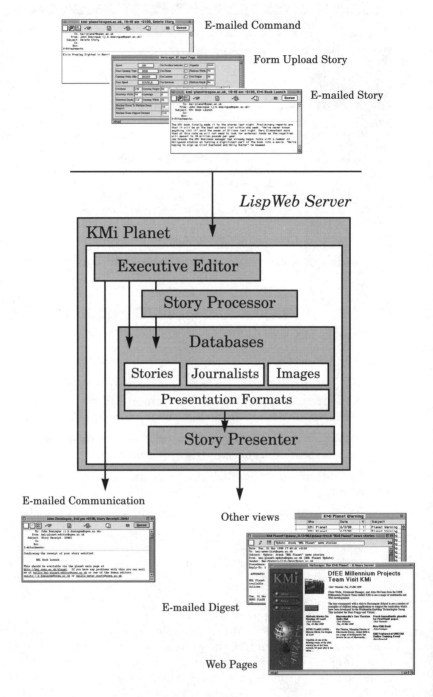

Figure 10.4. The KMi Planet architecture

The journalists database is maintained by the executive editor and is a record of all the people who are registered to contribute to the publication. In the case of the KMi Planet, all researchers in the Knowledge Media Institute are registered as 'journalists' with this system. The database holds each journalist's e-mail address and the address of his or her home Web page and a picture of the journalist. The picture is used in some presentation formats, particularly for a detailed Web page in which no other suitable image can be found.

The images database is a collection of the images that can be used to illustrate stories. The main source of these images is from journalists who add GIF attachments to their e-mailed stories.

The presentation formats database is a set of templates and instructions that can be used by the story presenter to format stories for output. So, for example, the Web front page format is an HTML framework into which stories may be added when the story presenter receives a request for the Planet front page. Other formats include the Web page archive view, the Web single story view, the Apple PlainTalk (1998) speech output interface (described below) and even the plain text view. The templates are easy to change and therefore afford different styles of presentation in each of these views.

The executive editor

As its name implies, this component is in overall charge of the system. As can be seen from Figure 10.4 it takes input from various sources (usually e-mail) and can respond using e-mail. It can write directly to any of the Planet databases or through the story processor.

At the core of the executive editor is an e-mail processor – this module is responsible for maintaining a number of e-mail accounts that relate to the work of the Planet. The executive editor reads mail in these accounts and acts appropriately. The message could cause the module to change a database entry directly, to generate an e-mail reply or even be passed on to another module. At the moment there are three main e-mail accounts: a demo account, a story account and a command account.

The first is the easiest to deal with as messages to the demo account are deemed insecure and for demonstration purposes only and so are passed on directly to the story processor with the injunction that they not be added permanently to any database. These entries are ephemeral and only used to test out the

Planet – to see for example, how a story might look if it were to be submitted to the Planet properly – or to show a visitor a temporary example of the use of the system. For both the other accounts the module first checks with the journalists database that the mail is verified as coming from a registered source. If this is not the case then the executive editor generates a polite refusal reply message inviting the contributor to contact the human editorial team. Only registered journalists can contribute to the second account and entries from these are assumed to be story contributions which are passed on to the story processing agent. Some journalists are members of the human editorial team and allowed to contribute to the command account.

Through this channel they are allowed to mail editorial commands. The human editors can instruct the executive editor to perform simple actions. For example, simple commands at present include:

- add, delete or edit stories in the story database,

- add or delete registered journalists, and

- change the layout of the Web news page, for example change the top story or change the number of stories displayed.

The executive agent can use e-mail to respond to submissions. For example, it acknowledges the receipt of all stories. However, it can also use e-mail proactively. For instance it can use simple heuristic measures to chase up stories from journalists. At the moment, the Planet notices when the top stories fall below simple thresholds – set on command, by the human editors. When these thresholds are exceeded (eg the latest story is deemed to be too old) the executive mails a message to this effect to the editorial team. It can then be instructed to chase up journalists for fresh copy.

The story processor

The executive editor feeds stories from registered journalists to a story processor which is primarily responsible for maintaining the image and story databases.

On receipt of an e-mailed story an entry in the story database containing the e-mail message's author, date and subject line, as well as the body of the message and a pointer to any attached elements is created. If the attachment is a GIF image then it is decoded before adding it into the picture database. If any problem is detected in processing the story, the journalist is e-mailed about the problem. Typically, this will involve a problem processing the image. The journalist can then send the image again. If the story is sent as an upload from an HTML page the procedure is much the same.

The story presenter

Whenever an HTTP request comes from a Web browser client the LispWeb server passes the request on to the story presenter. This module uses the formats database (described above) to generate an appropriate response. So, for example, if requested to deliver the front-page (using a front page multi-story format) the story presenter will create a page of stories where each displayed story is composed of the following:

- *a headline* – taken from the subject line of the mail message,

- *an author* – taken from the author of the mail message,

- *a date* – taken from the date of the mail message,

- *a story* – taken from the body of the mail message, and

- *an associated image* – a GIF image either sent as an attachment with the story or an image of the author taken from the journalists database.

Note that in the front page format shown in Figure 10.2 the image is only used for the story that is presented as the top story of the page.

In addition to providing Web based news pages the KMi Planet can also serve its news via multiple other routes since generating most text based formats is no trickier than generating HTML.

One of the more proactive formats is the mailing list. The executive editor sets the parameters for the mailing list format via simple flags in the relevant format database entry. So for example, in the current mailing list format, a mail-out threshold is set to six submissions. When six new submissions have been received the story presenter will construct a condensed text digest of these stories and e-mail them to a subscription based mailing list. A screen snapshot of part of a mailed digest is shown in Figure 10.5.

Another format which we currently employ is text to be read by a text-to-speech processor. So, for instance, one of the formats in the database used by the story presenter allows it to perform some simple formatting to assist the Apple PlainTalk software that benefits from some elementary phonetic pre-processing help. For example, at the moment, PlainTalk reads our unprocessed logo (KMi) as 'ke-mee' rather than the 'kay-em-eye' which we would prefer. Similarly, the version we are using has problems

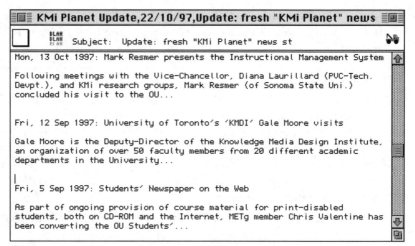

Figure 10.5. A screen snapshot of the news digest sent out by Planet

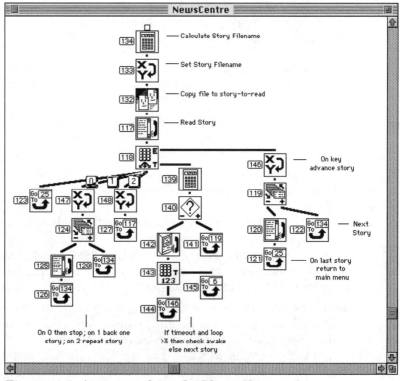

Figure 10.6. A segment from the Planet Voicemail system

reading HTML text anchors and e-mail addresses correctly. We have defined a set of formats and filters to avoid some of these problems. One use of text-to-speech systems like PlainTalk is to 'can' arbitrary text as speech for presentation in a number of interesting ways. In the Planet experiment we have shown how this may be applied to a Voice-mail interface to the system.

In Figure 10.6 we present a small segment from the KMi Planet Voice-mail interface. This program is written using the Bing Software PhonePro software (1998) for Macintosh. The software uses touch-tone phone controls to allow audio access to the KMi Planet stories. In this manner, the phone system leads users quickly and effectively to any story that they want to hear, reading it over the phone using Apple PlainTalk. The usefulness of the Planet Voice-mail system is derived from its simplicity and the use of the story presenter to give the phone interface the appropriate files from the Planet story database in the best form to read. The potential of this capability for visually impaired users meshes strongly with the ethos described in Chapter 2.

Ongoing work

We are currently working on a number of different developments of the KMi Planet project. At the simplest level we are extending the system to handle different image encodings, we are adding in new formats for presentation and also looking at increasing the support Planet can give to the communication between human journalists and editors. Let us consider ongoing innovations in each part of the system in turn.

Innovation for the executive editor: most of the commands that the executive editor responds to are simple flag settings and database manipulations. Our goal is for the executive editor to be able to manage the team of journalists, setters and printers. One obvious development is in the proactive e-mail correspondence with the editors and journalists. Current use of e-mail is crudely based around very simple settings and heuristics which should be much more flexible and sensitive. For example it might notice a story (perhaps through the tagging below) that would naturally benefit from a follow up and invite the journalist to do so, if the submission rate falls.

Innovation for the story processor: there are a number of mundane developments that we are undertaking in processing incoming stories, for example at the moment any attached graphics must be GIF format and either base64 or uuencoded – so it would be very useful for the processor to be able to deal with a number of different formats, eg JPEG. More interesting innovations include the tagging of stories so that they can be more effectively presented in different ways.

We plan to hook the story processor to a KMi story ontology which we are currently developing in our Web accessible knowledge modelling language (Domingue, 1998; Motta, 1998), described in Chapters 13 and 14. We envisage that editors would tag incoming stories using the ontology. This enriched story repository could then be used to facilitate semantic searches and individualized presentations. We will also investigate the extent to which ontologically enriched stories could provide an organizational memory for KMi and promote organizational learning. Thus far we have created the first three levels of the ontology from an analysis of the first 50 stories. The top level classes in the current ontology are: trip report, use of KMi technology, KMi visitor, and donation to KMi.

We are also extending the Voice-mail interface – to add voice notes to the stories. We have already prototyped a simple interface for journalists to dial in to a Voice-mail server and leave voice messages that can be linked to individual news items. The voice note is converted to RealAudio format, copied to the server and a suitable link is added.

Innovation for the story presenter: we have already indicated that it is possible for the story presenter to write out stories from the database in any format. We are currently adding to the number of presentation formats that it can write to: eg push technology and other delivery mechanisms such as HeadLiner, PointCast and WebCast. Each of these supports a database format that, in principle, the story presenter could write to.

We also aim to increase the system's adaptability in recognizing the differing capabilities of different browsers and even the differing needs of different end-users through the use of ontologies. We intend to investigate how the use of ontologies can support the automatic selection of pictures to illustrate stories and aid in page layout.

Innovation in services: as well as serving the KMi research lab and its community, a version of the Planet is currently also being developed for The Open University Business School. We need to consider how we may use this architecture to serve other news and publishing services that share these problems such as the publishing challenges described in Chapter 8. Our ideal would be to provide a simple direct manipulation authoring environment for creating your own Planet so that the system can work for you with the minimum of coding on your part.

teaching + learning?

Chapter 11

Sharing programming knowledge over the Web: the Internet Software Visualization Laboratory

John Domingue and Paul Mulholland

Seeing what a program is doing can be the key to understanding how it works or how to fix it. The Internet Software Visualization Lab extends earlier efforts by making it possible for student / tutor groups to share and clarify hitherto opaque programming scenarios, even over low bandwidth connections.

Introduction

Software Visualization (SV) systems have been used to aid computer science teaching and to locate program bugs with varying degrees of success over a number of years (Mulholland and Eisenstadt, 1998). Their primary use, however, has been within a one-to-one setting. A student or professional programmer views a visualization on his or her own, on a single user workstation. To share an SV one has to bring the participants around the same machine. Unfortunately, there are many instances when this is not feasible.

At The Open University our undergraduate and Master's courses are taught at a distance. On our larger courses students benefit from face-to-face tuition from a local tutor or 'Associate Lecturer'. We have a number of programming courses however, where because of relatively small student numbers we cannot provide a local tutor. On these courses communication between the tutors and students is restricted to telephone and e-mail contact. The tutors often comment on how difficult it is to conduct technical discussions using these impoverished media. For example, tutors will often have to deal with a student's programming problem over the telephone. This makes it difficult for the tutor to establish what the student needs, meaning either the tutor has to guess and plough through areas of the course (which could confuse the student further) or require the student to undertake the difficult task of explaining what it is that they do not know. Also, Open University students study part-time and have to fit their course work around other work and personal commitments. This means asynchronous communication is at least as important as synchronous communication.

Our Masters-level Prolog course uses a graphical SV called the Transparent Prolog Machine (TPM) (Eisenstadt and Brayshaw, 1988; Brayshaw and Eisenstadt, 1991) throughout the course materials, though the visualizations cannot be used when communicating with a tutor or fellow student. Our approach to solving this problem is to allow SVs to be staged on the Web. Using our software tool, the Internet Software Visualization Lab (ISVL), novice and expert programmers can create live broadcasts or recorded movies incorporating visualizations of their own programs. These can be viewed using any Java aware Web browser.

The rest of this chapter is structured as follows. In the next section we outline the design considerations that motivated ISVL. We then describe a system constructed in ISVL and ISVL's architecture. This is followed by a description of related work, and a discussion of the general issues involved in communicating programming knowledge over the Web.

Design considerations

Four main considerations motivated the design decisions underpinning ISVL. These were: integrating new technology into an existing course; a study of novice programmers using TPM; general findings from empirical studies of SV; and our experience of teaching programming at a distance. The design considerations are summarized in Table 11.1.

First, distance education courses, even when taught to some extent over the Internet have a definite life cycle and cannot be transformed overnight. This is not only true when the course as a whole is changed. It also applies even when one component is altered. As one can appreciate from the descriptions of rich media integration in Chapters 4 and 6, alterations to one component of the educational materials can have serious knock-on effects. As was mentioned earlier, the Prolog course uses the TPM notation throughout. Although problems have been noted with TPM (see below), providing extra materials using a completely different notation could do more harm than good. Even if the new notation has been found to be a very effective educational tool, imposing more notations on the students could just cause confusion and detract from the aim, which is simply to teach Prolog. For this reason, ISVL is integrated with the existing materials, providing

Motivation	Design decision
Integrating new technology into an existing course	Consistency with existing materials
A study of novice programmers using TPM	Help students – map between TPM and the code – see temporal development of the SV – deal with multiple views
General findings from empirical studies of SV	Active and collaborative use
Experience of teaching programming at a distance	A/synchronous communication Platform independence Efficient use of bandwidth resources

Table 11.1. Design decisions underpinning ISVL and their motivation

a laboratory for course development, allowing evaluation studies to be conducted more easily.

Second, our recent empirical work has looked at how students are able to use TPM in the early stages of learning Prolog (Mulholland, 1997, 1998). The students were studying undergraduate Cognitive Psychology which involved some simple Artificial Intelligence programming in Prolog. Their expertise can be paralleled to that of students in their first few weeks of the Masters course. The study compared TPM to three other SVs. The study identified three areas where students need further help in using TPM: (i) they need to be better supported in working out how to map effectively between the tree representation and their textual code; (ii) they need help in understanding the temporal position within the execution and its historical context; (iii) previous implementations have required students to navigate multiple views within the SV effectively, creating extra learning demands not directly related to their studies.

Third, other studies have illustrated that the educational benefits of SV are not as clear cut, nor as easy to establish as many thought. Stasko *et al.* (1993) considered the educational benefits of SV in their study of a visualization of a priority queue algorithm. Half of the students were provided with the visualization and the program, while the other half were just given the program. The SV was found to only slightly assist student compre-hension. They suggested one of the reasons the SV may have been of little help was that students were not aware of how their knowl-edge was to be tested prior to viewing the visualization. The students therefore had no clear goal to pursue during the compre-hension phase of the experiment. They suggest a clear task motivation may have helped the students to gain far more from the representation than they actually did. This interpretation was borne out by a further study by Lawrence *et al.* (1994). They found that students who were able to act interactively with the algorithm as well as view it in a classroom setting had a deeper understanding. Similarly, Byrne *et al.* (1996) found that students who were encouraged to predict how the algorithm would develop rather than just passively viewing it developed a greater under-standing. Overall, these findings suggest that the extent to which the student is actively involved when using the SV affects their learning outcomes, though even when students are actively involved, they can interpret the SV incorrectly, rather than learning from it. Students therefore should be encouraged to use the SV interactively to meet some set objective, though they should be monitored or scaffolded when learning by exploration to keep them on track. ISVL should therefore both allow students to interact with the SV and also be usable in collaborative ways with the tutor to counter circumstances when personal explo-ration can run into difficulties.

Fourth, teaching any course at a distance involves two kinds of staff: the course team and the tutors. The course team are responsible for developing the course. The tutors work on the 'front line', teaching the course developed by the course team to the students. The tutors are the ones who communicate directly with the students, as well as marking and providing feedback on assignments. Larger courses may provide opportunities for face-to-face contact between tutors and students at tutorials and residential schools. This is not feasible on more specialized courses, having a small number of students spread over a large area. This is the case for our Masters-level course in Prolog programming, where communication between tutor and students is restricted to telephone and e-mail contact. Tutors have often commented how difficult it is to conduct technical discussions using these impoverished media. Providing a rich synchronous communication medium will not however solve all of the problems inherent in teaching at a distance. Students study part-time and have to fit their course work around other work and personal commitments. In these cases, e-mail is currently relied upon as the sole form of communication. Unfortunately though, like the telephone, e-mail is an impoverished medium in which to communicate programming concepts. This is particularly the case when the student conceptualizes the problem in terms of the graphical TPM notation which is used throughout the course, and is not particularly amenable to the ASCII character set. It is therefore important that ISVL allows students and tutors to work asynchronously, enabling students easily to leave meaningful queries or thoughts for the tutor or other students to view at later times. Additionally, in order to keep costs down we can only assume that students have a run-of-the-mill computer and standard modem which can not transmit high bandwidth data such as video. Also students will be connecting via a modem from home, meaning bandwidth must be efficiently used. ISVL must therefore use the Internet in way which is both platform independent and makes efficient use of the bandwidth resources.

These issues motivated the design of ISVL, which is described in the next section.

An example system: Web-TPM

We are currently testing a visualization constructed in ISVL within a teaching context: we are running an Internet version of our Masters level Intensive Prolog course (Eisenstadt *et al.*, 1988) using a visualization based on the Transparent Prolog Machine (TPM) (Eisenstadt and Brayshaw, 1988; Brayshaw and Eisenstadt, 1991). TPM uses an AND/OR Tree model of Prolog, where execution is shown as a depth first search.

Figure 11.2 shows the ISVL Prolog client running on a Netscape Web browser. The client contains a visualization of the grandparent rule shown in Figure 11.1 obtained in the following way.

```
parent(pam, angela).
parent(angela, ann).

grandparent(X, Y) :-
    parent(X, Z),
    parent(Z, Y).
```

Figure 11.1. The Prolog code for the grandparent program. The program asserts that Pam is a parent of Angela, and Angela is a parent of Ann. It also asserts that for all X, Y and Z, X is the grandparent of Y if X is a parent of Z and Z is a parent of Y.

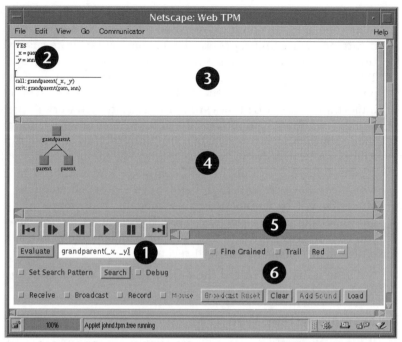

Figure 11.2. The ISVL Prolog client showing the visualization of the grandparent program in table 1. Key: [1] Prolog query; [2] result of query; [3] fine-grained view of execution; [4] coarse-grained view window; [5] speed of replay control; [6] control panel.

First the code in Figure 11.1 was pasted into the fine-grained view window. Then the query 'grandparent(_x, _y)' (find an X and a Y such that X is a grandparent of Y) was typed into the Prolog Query window (1). Then the 'Evaluate' button pressed. The result of the query, 'YES' (indicating that the query has succeeded), the values of the variable _x and _y, and a TPM coarse grained view were then returned (2 & 4). A fine-grained view of the top (root) node was obtained by clicking on it (3). The user can step through the execution using the video recorder style buttons in the control panel. A visualization is played using the 'play' button. The speed of the animation is controlled by the scroll bar (5) in the control panel.

ISVL allows synchronous communication via the 'Broadcast' and 'Receive' buttons. When the broadcast button is selected all the interface actions are copied onto the screen of all receiving clients. Asynchronous communication is facilitated by a record mode. In record mode all the interface actions are stored in a movie which can be retrieved and replayed later. ISVL provides

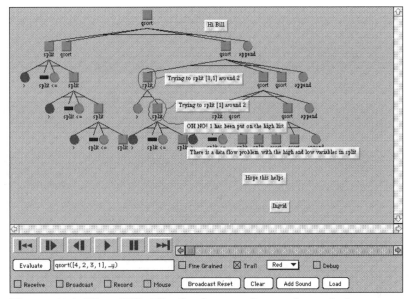

Figure 11.3 (Plate XV). The final state of a movie made by a tutor for a student

drawing and labelling tools allowing visualizations to be annotated. Figure 11.3 shows the final state of a movie made by a tutor for a student.

In this example, the tutor (Ingrid) has annotated the program that the student had been working on before reaching an impasse and asking for help. Using ISVL the tutor can access the student's program, see how it works and view the student's annotations, indicating their current understanding.

Once we've deployed ISVL we expect the number of movies to grow rapidly. From our previous experience of teaching programming and from our studies we know that in each presentation of the course, students will have problems similar to students from previous presentations. We thought it would be useful if students and tutors could search for relevant movies within the movie database, in effect asking 'has any other student had this problem before?'

ISVL provides a search facility based on the search agents found in the Multiple Representation Environment (MRE) (Brayshaw, 1993). MRE allowed users to create different types of search agents which would then search the execution space of PARLOG programs.

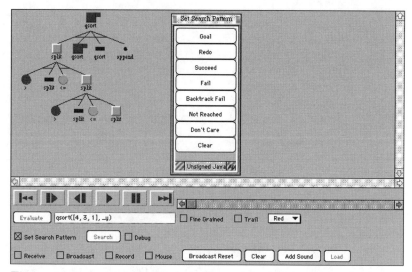

Figure 11.4. A screen snapshot of a user creating a search pattern within ISVL

Figure 11.4 shows a screen snapshot of ISVL whilst a student is creating a search pattern. The student is developing a program and has hit a bug that she cannot solve. She decides to select a pattern occurring in the visualization of the program and search for movies containing that pattern. She does this by:

i) selecting the 'Set Search Pattern' button,

ii) clicking on the desired nodes and then selecting one of the event types ('Goal', 'Redo', 'Succeed', etc) from the pop-up menu (shown in Figure 11.4), and

iii) deselecting the 'Set Search Pattern' button.

ISVL displays the pattern by placing a small square next to each of the selected nodes. Clicking on the 'Search' button causes ISVL to search through all the movies within the movie database for the pattern. A Web page is created containing a list of all the movies which contain at least one match. Figure 11.5 shows a matching movie with the pattern highlighted.

The matching movie is a tutor's explanation of a common bug. It is the same bug as the one the student was unable to solve. After viewing this movie the student is able to fix her own program. This illustrates how ISVL allows knowledge to be reused as well as shared, themes which permeate other chapters throughout this book.

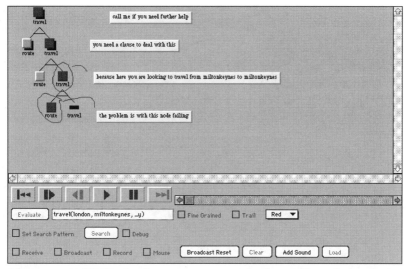

Figure 11.5. ISVL displaying a movie which matches the pattern selected in Figure 11.4

It should be noted that for explanation purposes the example programs presented above are small. Like the original TPM, Web-TPM contains features (for example the ability to compress the subtrees of certain predicates) which enable it to scale up to arbitrary sized programs.

Architecture

ISVL uses an architecture based on a client written in Java and a customized Web server. Using a Java aware Web browser users can connect to the ISVL server and download an ISVL client. Using the client, users can upload and run their programs on the server and receive back visualizations. Users can also use the client to view visualizations collaboratively.

As shown in Figure 11.6, the ISVL server is composed of a customized Web server, a generic software visualizer and a specific programming language. The customized Web server is based on LispWeb which is described in Chapter 12. In addition to implementing the standard HTTP protocol, LispWeb offers a library of high-level Lisp functions to dynamically generate HTML pages, a facility for dynamically creating image maps, and a server-to-server communication method.

The generic visualizer is an extension of our framework for creating software visualizations called Viz (Domingue *et al.*, 1992). Within the Viz framework, we consider program execution

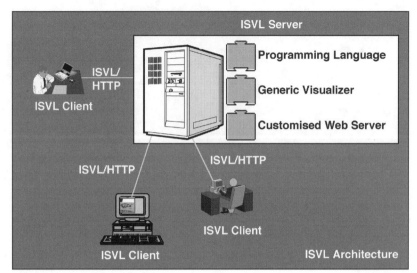

Figure 11.6. The general architecture of the Internet Software Visualization Laboratory

to be a series of history events happening to (or perpetrated by) players. To allow SV system builders considerable freedom, a player can be any part of a program, such as a function, a data structure, or a line of code. Each player has a name and is in some state, which may change when a history event occurs for that player. A player may also contain other players, enabling groups of players to be formed. History events are like Brown's (1988) 'interesting events' in BALSA – each event corresponds to some code being executed in the program or some data changing its value. These events are recorded in the history module, which allows them to be accessed by the user and 'replayed'. Events and states are mapped into a visual representation which is accessible to the end-user (the users of the SV system, not the SV system builder). The mapping is not just a question of storing pixel patterns to correspond to different events and states – we also need to specify different views, and ways of navigating around them. The main ingredients of Viz are:

- *histories:* a record of key events that occur over time as the program runs, with each event belonging to a player; each event is linked to some part of the code and may cause a player to change its state (there is also some pre-history information available before the program begins running, such as the static program source code hierarchy and initial player states)

- *views:* the style in which a particular set of players, states or events is presented, such as using text, a tree, or a plotted graph; each view uses its own style and emphasizes a particular dimension of the data that it is displaying

- *mappings:* the encodings used by a player to show its state changes in diagrammatic or textual form on a view using some kind of graphical language, typography, or sound; some of a player's mappings may be for the exclusive use of its navigators

- *navigators:* the tools or techniques making up the interface that allows the user to traverse a view, move between multiple views, change scale, compress or expand objects, and move forward or backward in time through the histories.

The Viz framework is equally at home dealing with either program code or algorithms, since a player and its history events may represent anything from a low-level (program code) abstraction such as 'invoke a function call' to a high level (algorithm) abstraction such as 'move this item to the head of the queue'.

A programming language is interfaced to Viz by inserting 'create player' and 'note interesting event' hooks into the interpreter or compiler. To date we have created over a dozen visualizations using Viz (see Domingue 1994 for a sample).

Related work

Recent work within the Algorithm Animation community has led to the creation of a number of systems which allow pre-written animations to be viewed remotely. These systems primarily concentrate on delivering animations synchronously as part of a classroom style tutorial.

The Collaborative Active Textbooks (CAT) of Brown and Najork (1996) is a Web-based environment, which allows the same animation to be run simultaneously on a number of machines. Intended for classroom style teaching the view and speed of the animation can be controlled remotely by the tutor. This form of synchronous demonstration of programs is possible within ISVL, though within ISVL the animations are not canned, being created on the fly from the program submitted. A Java version of Collaborative Active Textbooks (JCAT) has been developed (Brown et al., 1997) which can be used with standard Web browsers.

The client-server architecture of ISVL is similar to that of the Mocha system (Baker et al., 1996) whereby the bulk of the work is done on the server and the interface is created by a Java client. Like CAT, Mocha is primarily designed for the synchronous delivery of algorithm animations. The Jeliot system (Haajanen *et al.*, 1997) uses a similar client-server architecture to allow students to visualize algorithms abstracted from Java code to be viewed through a Web browser.

As stated in the previous section, to reduce bandwidth requirements, ISVL pictures are not directly transferred over the Web. They are defined textually and created on the client. This is similar to JSamba, a Java implementation of Stasko's (1996) Samba. JSamba allows animations to be defined textually and displayed in a Java applet.

Discussion

ISVL is a Web based tool which allows tutors and students to have synchronous and asynchronous dialogues on software visualizations. We have briefly described Web-TPM, which was constructed using ISVL, outlining its design requirements and showing a scenario of it in use. Our research group has been developing tools for teaching programming at a distance for a decade and a half. Below are the issues we have identified as being crucial to developing effective support environments for novice programmers.

- *Focus on debugging rather than design.* Contrary to perceived wisdom from the Software Engineering Community, our studies (Eisenstadt and Breuker, 1992; Mulholland and Eisenstadt, 1998) show that the common problems students tend to have are related to programming debugging rather than programming design. Students often spend large amounts of time locating trivial bugs. This task needs to be supported.

- *Clear execution story.* As eloquently argued by Brayshaw and Eisenstadt (1991) and Pain and Bundy (1987) presenting a virtual machine which is easily understandable and learnable is of great importance.

- *Cradle to grave vs. stage appropriate environments.* Eisenstadt and Brayshaw (1988) argued for the necessity of providing a cradle to grave environment. The benefits of this were that novices would not have to abandon one environment and learn another, and that many of the 'power user' features were of potential benefit to novices. We have found in our studies (Mulholland and Eisenstadt, 1998) that novices have problems with notations designed for expert users. There is a trade-off between giving novices representations appropriate for their current stage of learning and requiring them to learn new notations.

- *SV distance to source code vs. scalability.* Again we found in our studies (Mulholland, 1998) that novices have trouble mapping between their source code and abstracted representations of it. Although detailed visualizations close to the source code are helpful for novices, they have scalability problems, and are often unsuitable for visualizing large programs.

- *Integration with framework and tasks vs. maintainability.* As postulated by Stasko *et al.* (1993) and demonstrated by Lawrence *et al.* (1994) novices benefit most from visualizations if they interact with them rather than passively view them. This can only be achieved if the tasks the students are asked to carry out (within the course exercises and assignments) use the visualizations. Unfortunately, courses which have this tight integration suffer from maintainability problems. Any change to the visualization, due to changing circumstances or results of an empirical study, requires changes across multiple media and is therefore very costly.

- *Showing what you don't know.* Most software visualization systems focus on communicating the execution of a standard working program or algorithm. These systems are of less use when the student wishes to understand a program which does not work. For this reason ISVL provides an environment which supports not only the tutors in communicating what they know to students, but also supports the students in communicating what they don't know back to their tutors.

ISVL provides a rich medium within which to communicate programming knowledge. The design appreciates the importance of supporting both synchronous and asynchronous forms of communication. The architecture underpinning ISVL is generic, allowing the domain language or visualization to be changed. The efficient client-server communication protocol allows its application even when bandwidth resources are limited. We hope to extend our work further and eagerly anticipate the extension of its use within educational and industrial communities.

Part III
Knowledge Systems on the Web

Chapter 12

Accessing artificial intelligence applications over the World Wide Web

Alberto Riva and Marco Ramoni

Artificial Intelligence applications can benefit from being acces-sible on the Web. The LispWeb server avoids both the conventional clumsy Web interface to external applications ('CGI') and the aspects of Java which make it inappropriate for AI.

Introduction

It is well known that the success of a computer-based system depends not only on the functionalities it provides, but also largely on how easily such functionalities are available to the largest possible number of users. Failure to meet with accessibility, usability and availability requirements can compromise the usefulness of most applications (Riva and Bellazzi, 1996).

The constantly growing size and pervasiveness of the World Wide Web has opened up new perspectives with regard to the problems just mentioned. The push to add 'intelligence' to the Web has always been very strong, and is motivated by the realization that its open, distributed and powerful infrastructure can be exploited to effectively provide services that go beyond simple document distribution.

Two possible strategies can be followed to pursue this goal. The first one makes it possible for a server to invoke external appli-cations through the CGI interface and to display the results as HTML pages. The second one aims at delivering intelligence to the client, in the form of a program written in a language that the client is able to execute (eg, Java). Both solutions have their limitations: interaction with an external application through CGI is slow and clumsy, and does not overcome the connectionless nature of the HTTP transactions (Cimino *et al.*, 1995). It is there-fore necessary to retrieve and save the state of the system with each connection, something that can become impractical for large, knowledge-intensive applications. On the other hand, languages like Java have inherent limitations due to security concerns, are not supported on every platform, and make it impossible to reuse legacy software written in different languages (Dossick and Kaiser, 1996).

In our view, such tools are not powerful enough to support an effective interaction with complex applications, especially in the field of Artificial Intelligence (AI). AI applications are usually large pieces of software that require powerful computational resources and sophisticated user-interaction facilities. It's no wonder that most of the concepts behind modern graphical user interfaces originated in the AI field, from the necessity to be able to interactively inspect and manipulate complex knowledge representation structures. Moreover, those systems often required specialized hardware, and this had severely limited their dissemination.

In order to overcome the low accessibility problem, one of the major limitations of AI systems in the past, we developed an HTTP server written in Common Lisp, called LispWeb (Riva and Ramoni, 1996). Lisp applications can be made accessible over the World Wide Web by loading them inside the LispWeb server itself and writing a set of functions that call the application and display the results as HTML pages. The main advantages of this approach are the wide availability of powerful client software and the uniformity of the resulting user interface (Rice *et al.*, 1995). The KMi Planet (Chapter 10) and the remaining chapters in this section of the book all rely to some extent on LispWeb. Readers who wish to skip over some of the technical details should jump ahead to the section entitled 'Applications'.

The LispWeb server

LispWeb is a Common Lisp development environment for distributed applications over the World Wide Web. It consists of two main modules: an HTTP 1.0 server, and a library of functions to create HTML pages. The HTTP server handles the GET, POST, HEAD, PUT and DELETE methods, performs IP-based and password-based access control, provides request logging and timing, and serves standard HTML pages, images, Java applets and generic binary files. Thanks to its object-oriented nature, it is fully configurable and extensible: for example, users can easily define new methods, specialize the response function for particular classes of requests, or customize the request logging function. The server can be controlled through an HTML interface or by connecting directly to the Lisp interpreter through a Telnet session. The server is also able to act as a TCP client; it can therefore communicate with other servers in a distributed computing environment (databases, mail servers, etc).

The second component of LispWeb, HALL (HTML Authoring Lisp Library), offers the developer a set of tools to create sets of dynamic HTML pages. Pages are defined using a syntax similar to the one used to define Lisp functions, and are internally represented by the server as Lisp functions; such functions can then be associated with a specific URL, and are run by the server whenever the corresponding URL is requested. The functions, which can take arguments and access global variables defined in the Lisp environment, are responsible for generating the HTML code that will be sent to the client.

HALL also provides the developer with a library of HTML-producing Lisp functions, that range from simple tag insertion to high-level formatters able to produce large blocks of HTML code. For example, the LIST-TO-TABLE function takes a list of lists (lists are a primitive data type in Lisp) and produces an HTML table whose rows are the subsets of the input list. Optional arguments can be used to specify additional features of the table, such as border width, cell alignment, and so on. Such a tool can be extremely powerful, especially in cases where the input list is not known a priori, so that a manual generation of the HTML code would be impossible. Moreover, new functions can be defined to generate frequently-used code fragments (eg, page banners), thus avoiding unnecessary and time-consuming repetitions on the part of the developer. Finally, this approach guarantees that the resulting HTML code will always be syntactically correct and compliant with stylistic recommendations (all pages must have a TITLE, the HTML, HEAD and BODY tags are automatically inserted, etc). Other functions allow the values of the header fields, and of the form fields in the case of a POST request, to be examined and possibly modified. This eliminates the need for external CGI scripts, since the same Lisp function can access the field values and generate the appropriate response page.

The STSP

The Server To Server Protocol (STSP) is an extension of the HTTP protocol designed to enable more complex forms of communication between the LispWeb server and its clients. From the syntactic point of view, an STSP transaction is composed of two distinct parts. During the first stage, the client sends to the server an STSP request composed of a request line (in the form 'STSP request HTTP/1.0') and zero or more header lines (in the form

'Header: Value'). After examining the request and the supplied header lines, the server sends to the client an STSP reply composed of a response line ('HTTP/1.0 code reason-phrase') and zero or more header lines. The STSP reply should communicate whether the client's request is acceptable and, if not, why it was rejected. For example, the header lines in the request could be used to transmit client identification information or accounting data in case a payment is required to access the desired services.

Up to this point, the protocol is identical to the standard HTTP one, except for the use of the STSP method in the request instead of the standard ones (GET, POST, etc). After this initial negotiation phase, on the other hand, the client and the server are free to exchange information in a totally arbitrary way, thereby abandoning the strict request-response scheme typical of a normal HTTP transaction. The name of the STSP emphasizes the fact that in this case the distinction between a client and a server role is no longer applicable. It is of course required that the client and the server agree on the pragmatics of the communication (ie, what information to transmit, when, and under which form), since the protocol itself has no way of performing correctness checks.

STSP requests are formulated in terms of tasks and actions. A task is a collection of actions related to the same application, while an action is an atomic transaction that is carried out with a single connection between the client and the server. Tasks and actions are defined on the server as Lisp functions and become automatically known to the dispatch mechanism. Since actions can take arguments, the general form of an STSP request is the following:

/task-name/action-name/argument/argument/...

There are two main advantages in using STSP. First, since its syntax is almost identical to that of HTTP, very few changes are required to pre-existing HTTP client and server software; in particular, all the code to interpret the request, to parse the header fields and to perform dispatching need not be duplicated. Second, the dynamic nature of the LispWeb server allows task and actions to be easily added, modified and deleted without affecting the other functionalities of the system.

Applications

In order to illustrate the potential and the capabilities of LispWeb, this section describes some exemplar applications developed with it.

The ERA system

ERA (Epistemological Reasoning Architecture) is an automated reasoning system able to represent and handle uncertainty. It provides a good example to illustrate the model of distributed computation suitable for the WWW. The core of ERA is a Belief Maintenance Systems (BMS) based on probabilistic logic, and therefore called Logic-based BMS (LBMS) (Ramoni and Riva, 1993). A BMS is a Truth Maintenance System (TMS) able to use probabilistic rather than Boolean truth-values. A TMS is an independent reasoning module, which incrementally maintains the beliefs for a general problem solving system, and enables it to reason with temporary assumptions on the basis of incomplete information. Its use endows the problem solver with the ability of assuming and retracting beliefs, detecting contradictions, and identifying the assumptions responsible for its conclusions.

Although its computational requirements are relatively small, in order to be effectively used with large knowledge bases the ERA system requires a fair amount of memory and high processing speeds. Moreover, the ability to reason on the basis of incrementally added information fosters an interactive use of the system. The user should therefore be allowed manually to build the network of clauses and propositions, possibly using a graphical user interface, to perform assumptions and immediately to see the results produced by the propagation algorithm. In a previous version of ERA, the user interface was realized using a Lisp-based GUI builder (LispView). This approach posed serious portability and availability problems: although the system itself is written in the ANSI standard Common Lisp, the user interface was tied to a single Lisp implementation on a single platform.

Thanks to LispWeb, it was possible to make the ERA system accessible over the Web, thus overcoming the availability and accessibility problems outlined above. The user interface of the new version of ERA is based on a Java applet that allows the user to create and position the network nodes, to connect them with logical connectives, and to assign the initial probability values to them. Every user action that causes a change in the state of the network is communicated to the server through appropriate STSP actions. In this way, the Java component of the system acts only as the graphical user interface, while the actual computation is performed by the ERA application loaded inside the server. In our opinion, this policy represents one of the most efficient ways to split an application between the client and the server in a distributed environment. The use of Java provides a flexibility and a graphical power that could not be matched by simple HTML. On the other hand, using Java for the whole application would have forced us to rewrite the entire system, without being able to reuse any of the previously developed code, and would have increased the size and complexity of the applet, highly reducing its usability. Figure 12.1 shows a snapshot of the main window of the Java Grapher during an ERA session.

The T-IDDM project

T-IDDM is an EU-funded project whose goal is to develop a distributed telemedicine system to assist in the routine management of insulin-dependent diabetic patients, by offering to patients and physicians a set of services designed to increase the effectiveness of the therapy (Riva *et al.*, 1997). The system is composed of several cooperating modules; one of them is located at the patient's home (the Patient Unit), while all the others compose the Medical Unit, usually located inside a Hospital Information System. The task of the Patient Unit is to collect patient data coming from daily self-monitoring (eg, blood glucose

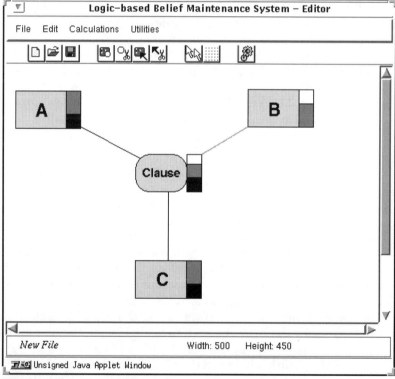

Figure 12.1. Java Grapher

values), to store them in a local database and to upload them to the Medical Unit during periodical connections over a telephone line. The Medical Unit stores the data coming from all the patients being followed, and provides the physicians with tools to retrieve the data, analyse them, and modify the therapy the patients are following according to their clinical situation.

The LispWeb server plays a central role in the architecture of the T-IDDM system. Physicians who wish to use the system may connect to it using a common Web browser, and interact with the system modules through dynamically-generated HTML pages. In order to fulfil the users' requests, the server can communicate with the other software agents present in the distributed system (eg, the database) using the STSP described above. In this way, the complexity of the underlying environment is hidden behind a uniform and intuitive interface. Figure 12.2 shows a schematic view of the T-IDDM architecture.

It may be interesting to look more closely at the conceptual architecture of the T-IDDM system, since it offers a good example

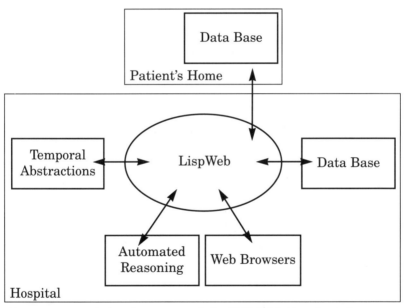

Figure 12.2. The architecture of the T-IDDM distributed system. The LispWeb server communicates with the Patient Unit to receive patient data, with a database to store them, with an automated reasoning system and a temporal abstractions service to analyse them. The users can access all the system functionalities through standard Web browsers.

of the power of a Lisp-based system on the Web. The Medical Unit includes a knowledge base that stores in declarative form all the system's knowledge about the domain of insulin-dependent diabetes. The knowledge base is represented by a collection of frames, hierarchically organized into taxonomies, each of which describes a relevant concept or entity; each frame is characterized by a set of slots that can hold one or more values. In our case, in addition to the information needed to describe the domain from the medical point of view, we have added information that describes how to represent a frame using HTML, both for input (eg, a fill-in form) and for output (eg, a table). In particular, it is possible to associate to each frame functions that describe how to lay it out on an HTML page, how to render the value of each one of its slots, how to acquire each slot from a fill-in form and so on. These functions can be automatically inherited, or specialized in case an object requires a special treatment: for example, when a slot can only receive a value taken from a fixed list of choices, the server will generate a pull-down menu for that slot instead of the default text field. Figure 12.3 shows an example of an automatically generated HTML form to acquire information about the insulin doses that make up a therapeutic protocol.

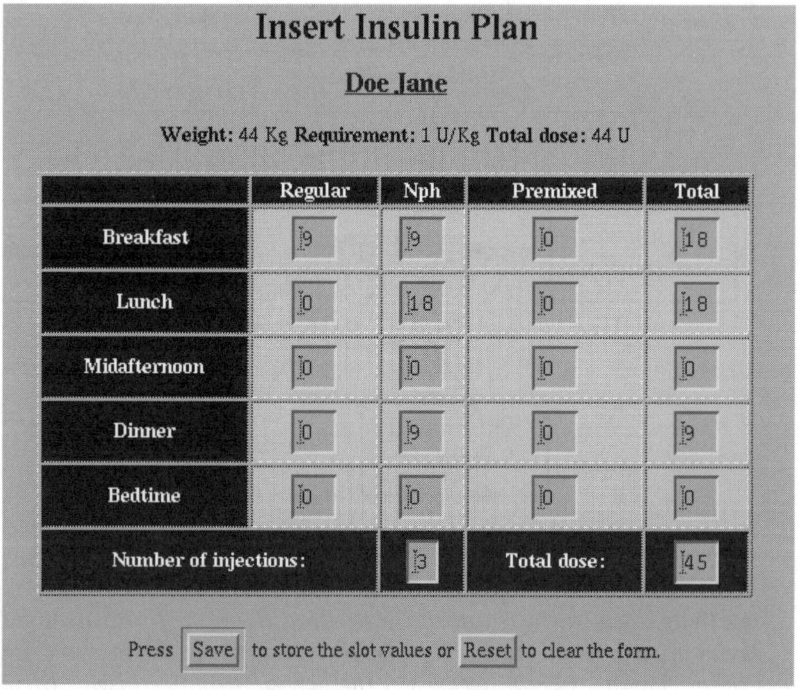

Insert Insulin Plan

Doe Jane

Weight: 44 Kg **Requirement:** 1 U/Kg **Total dose:** 44 U

	Regular	Nph	Premixed	Total
Breakfast	9	9	0	18
Lunch	0	18	0	18
Midafternoon	0	0	0	0
Dinner	0	9	0	9
Bedtime	0	0	0	0
Number of injections:		3	**Total dose:**	45

Press Save to store the slot values or Reset to clear the form.

Figure 12.3. An automatically generated HTML form to acquire the values of an insulin administration protocol

Pointers

Several projects and applications described in this book rely on the use of LispWeb as a dynamic interface to the World Wide Web for intelligent systems. Chapter 11 describes the Internet Software Visualization Laboratory (ISVL), which enables novice and expert programmers to create live broadcasts or recorded movies of their interactions with software visualizations.

As expected, LispWeb is also used in some strongly AI oriented applications and collaborative distributed systems. Tadzebao (Chapter 14) uses LispWeb to support both asynchronous and synchronous discussions on design and the architecture of knowledge bases, know as ontologies. The successor of Tadzebao, WebOnto, was designed to support the collaborative browsing, creation and editing of ontologies and to foster the direct manipulation interface displaying ontological expressions using a rich medium. WebOnto was aimed to be easy-to-use, yet have facilities for scaling up to large ontologies.

Last but not least, we should add that some of the applications of LispWeb are tools, systems and services used in every day life at KMi. KMi Planet (Chapter 10), the intelligent newsletter of KMi, uses LispWeb to dynamically generate and dispatch news pages. Luigi, (Chapter 15) the intelligent agent in charge of arranging meetings in KMi, exploits LispWeb to support its World Wide Web user interface.

Conclusions

Our goal in this chapter was to show how the two apparently remote fields of Artificial Intelligence and World Wide Web technology can receive mutual benefit from their close integration. The Web can be an extremely powerful access medium to deliver the power of AI applications to remote users, independently of their location and of the computational facilities available to them. Thanks to the LispWeb server, applications become accessible over the WWW as a set of dynamically generated HTML pages, can exploit the capabilities of the Java programming language to realize a graphical user interface, and can be used via STSP requests.

We have shown how carefully designed applications can be easily adapted to run in the environment just described, by specializing the relevant input/output methods and by defining the corresponding set of STSP actions. Such a process is, of course, not always straightforward; in the future, we plan to investigate the design requirements that an object-oriented application must satisfy in order to be easily and seamlessly integrated in the WWW environment.

Finally, the ability to run an application using STSP gives a new meaning to the word accessibility: applications become available not just to a wider number of human users, but also to other software agents present in the network. In this perspective, the methodology we have described can become the backbone of a Distributed Artificial Intelligence infrastructure based on widely available and low-cost technology and take advantage of existing knowledge representation languages for distributed environments, such as the Agent Communication Language (Genesereth and Ketchpel, 1994).

Chapter 13

Knowledge modelling: an organic technology for the knowledge age

Arthur Stutt and Enrico Motta

Our culture now accepts the notion of 'knowledge workers' and 'smart buildings'. While these terms suggest a shift towards a knowledge-focused society, our contention is that this trend needs to be anchored in a solid understanding of how to represent and model knowledge.

Introduction: the ubiquity of 'knowledge'

While it is impossible to compare our own age with that, say, of renaissance Italy or fifth century BC India, it is likely that our own time is unique not perhaps in its concentration on knowledge but in its appropriation of the term 'knowledge' and its cognates (intelligence, expertise, smartness). The examples are legion: we talk of knowledge management, knowledge workers, knowledge modelling, knowledge systems, knowledge engineering, knowledge media, knowledge mining, intellectual capital, intelligent machines, expert systems, smart bombs, smart medical alarms, smart buildings. In this chapter we refer to this phenomenon as the *epistemification* of culture with our main focus on one particular aspect – the epistemification of technology – which we see as a crucial aspect of the emerging Knowledge Age.

We will begin our analysis by outlining some of the facets of the Knowledge Age, emphasizing the primary role played by the World Wide Web both as a medium supporting the production and consumption of knowledge and as the locus where a new cyber-society is being constructed. We will then go on to suggest that knowledge modelling (Motta, 1997; Gruber, 1993; Newell, 1982; Schreiber *et al.*, 1994) is (or will become) an organic technology characterizing the unfolding of the Knowledge Age in its natural locus (ie, in the World Wide Web). In a nutshell, our contention is that knowledge modelling technology will play a crucial role in supporting the epistemification of the Web and the creation of virtual communities, sharing, consuming and producing knowledge.

We will substantiate our thesis by means of a scenario which shows how knowledge modelling technology can be harnessed to support knowledge production and consumption on the WWW.

Trends in the Knowledge Age

We have identified three main trends which are representative of the Knowledge Age. These are: the move to a knowledge economy; the epistemification of machines; and the emergence of Cyber-Knowledge. These trends are discussed in the following sub-sections.

The move to a knowledge economy

A number of authors have indicated that recent years have witnessed a change from a manufacturing to a knowledge economy. This transformation involves a shift from tangible to intangible assets and a view of knowledge as both a commodity and a crucial asset in gaining competitive advantage.

Thus, we have seen the rise of the 'knowledge-creating company' (Nonaka and Takeuchi, 1995) with its knowledge workers and knowledge directors. In some ways there's nothing new in this since financial institutions have long been involved in the management and communication of information. What is new is the interest in technology as a means of storing and making available the knowledge resources of a company both to increase profitability and as a possible source of income. As a result, various tools for knowledge management, data mining and knowledge discovery have been proposed.

The epistemification of machines

While knowledge and information are increasingly valued commodities, we still need artefacts such as cars and washing machines. In the Knowledge Age these artefacts have also been transformed: they are now more intelligent, knowledgeable and autonomous. Value has been added to otherwise non-intelligent machines by introducing smartness – for example, washing machines which use fuzzy logic to determine the correct wash-cycle. In terms of software we have seen the growth in intelligent or knowledge systems (Stefik, 1995) and autonomous agents (Bradshaw, 1997) – for example, those used by search engines on the World Wide Web.

Cyber-Knowledge

As we become aware of the variety of competing world views, ideologies and theories of the world (as magnified through the lens of the Web) our view of knowledge changes. We now emphasize knowing rather than knowledge. We see knowledge as constructed by and relative to the world views of knowledge communities (Collins, 1990). We see knowing as implicated in power structures (see, eg, Rabinow, 1986, for Foucault's views on this), multifarious, less well-founded, and not necessarily progressive. In addition, we attribute various epistemic abilities to machines. In this chapter, we use the term Cyber-Knowledge to stand for knowledge which is intelligible to both machines and humans.

The World Wide Web as metonym for the Knowledge Age

The Web can be conceived both as a locus where the boundaries between real and virtual, human and artificial, are dissolved and as a medium for the transmission and collaborative construction of artefacts embodying hybridized knowledge forms. Thus, it can be taken to exemplify (ie, it provides a metonym for) the Knowledge Age. The following are the main ways in which the Web can be viewed as epistemified:

- it acts as a distributed repository of data, opinion and knowledge;

- it serves business, education and the research community as a two-way channel for the flow of information, opinion, argumentation, software and other commodities;

- as a two-way channel it can be used as a communicative tool in the collaborative construction of arguments, research papers, software, buildings;

- it is populated by epistemic agents: spiders, bots, search engines;

- it serves as a forum for the mediation between multiple intelligent agents (whether software or human);

- it is itself an intelligent entity, adaptive, evolving (De Kerckhove, 1997).

Knowledge modelling as epistemic engineering

Having emphasized the crucial role of knowledge (as process and commodity) and the Web (as locus and medium) the obvious next step is to enquire what technology is available to support this process of constructing and sharing knowledge. In this chapter we will concentrate on one particular technology, knowledge modelling, which we regard as an organic technology for the Knowledge Age.

Characterizing knowledge modelling

The term knowledge modelling refers to a particular approach and set of techniques developed in the context of knowledge engineering research (Feigenbaum and McCorduck, 1984; Gonzalez and Dankel, 1993; Stefik, 1995). Knowledge engineering is the discipline which pertains to the construction of knowledge systems (Stefik, 1995). These are decision-making agents which rely on explicit problem solving knowledge (ie, knowledge which is used to make decisions in uncertain conditions) to select the actions required to reach a goal.

Because knowledge systems rely on problem solving knowledge, knowledge acquisition is an important activity in the knowledge engineering life-cycle. In the early days of expert systems (Hayes-Roth *et al.*, 1983) this expert knowledge was acquired and directly encoded into a rule-based formalism (Davis, 1979). This approach is often called 'knowledge acquisition as mining'. The assumption here was that knowledge could be directly transferred from an expert to a computer in a form suitable for problem solving.

This reductive view of expertise was criticized on cognitive (Ford *et al.*, 1990), philosophical (Winograd and Flores, 1986) and engineering (Wielinga and Breuker, 1986) grounds and, as a result, a new paradigm emerged, often called 'knowledge acquisition as modelling'. The main features of the modelling paradigm are the following.

- Knowledge acquisition should not be characterized as a process of mapping expert knowledge to a computational representation, but as a model-building process, in which application-specific knowledge is configured according to the available problem solving technology. In the words of Ford *et al.* (1990, 7.1), 'The mining analogy notwithstanding, expertise is not like a natural resource which can be harvested, transferred, or captured, but rather it is constructed by the expert and reconstructed by the knowledge engineer'.

- It is useful to describe such a model of problem solving behaviour at a level which abstracts from implementation considerations. Newell (1982) calls this the knowledge level. This approach has the advantage of separating problem solving from implementation-related issues.

As a result, knowledge modelling can be characterized as a set of techniques which focus on the specification of static and dynamic knowledge resources. These knowledge models are characterized independently of the nature of the knowledge source. This aspect of knowledge modelling research is especially important since it allows us to discuss the various types of agents as epistemic entities, independently of whether they are software or human agents (this theme is pursued in Chapter 15).

Knowledge modelling techniques

A number of researchers have elaborated on these ideas – in particular situating knowledge modelling technology within a strong constructivist framework (van de Velde, 1994). Here, we wish to highlight two specific knowledge modelling technologies, ontologies (Gruber, 1993) and problem solving methods

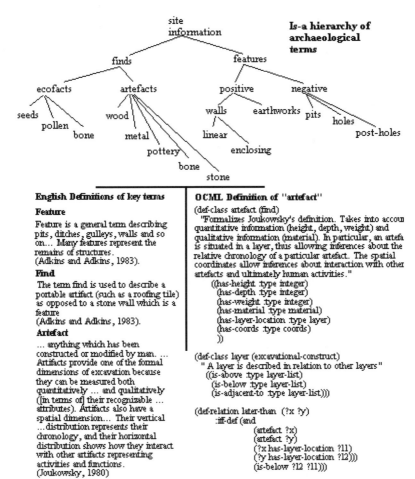

Figure 13.1. Graphical snapshot of part of a generic archaeology ontology. OCML is Motta's 'Operational Conceptual Modelling Language'

(Benjamins, 1993; Marcus, 1988; Motta and Zdrahal, 1997), which we regard as crucial to the creation of the Knowledge Web.

An ontology is a partial specification of a conceptual vocabulary to be used for formulating knowledge-level theories about a domain of discourse; ie, ontologies provide a way to formalize a common vocabulary for describing some area of interest. For instance, Valente and Breuker (1996) suggest an ontology of core legal concepts which can provide the basis for reusing and sharing legal knowledge. The idea is that once a number of agents (human or artificial) agree on such a vocabulary, then they can share and reuse knowledge. Thus, ontologies provide the means to build communities of problem solving agents which subscribe to a common view of some domain. An example of an ontology which supports the specification of knowledge models in archaeology is shown in Figure 13.1.

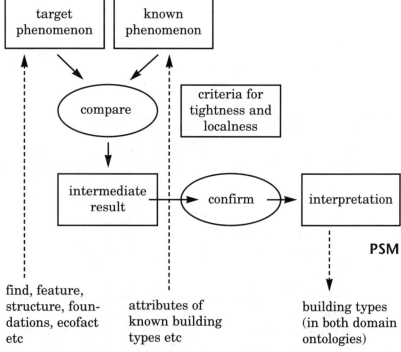

Figure 13.2. Graphical snapshot of interpretation in Romano-British archaeology. TLA compares an unknown (target) phenomenon with a known (base) phenomenon. If the criteria for tightness (many instances of different types of similarities) and localness (spatially and temporally close) are met, the target can be interpreted in terms of the base (see Hill, 1994).

Problem solving methods (PSMs) can be seen as the 'dynamic' counterpart to ontologies. While the latter provide the means for establishing common conceptual schemas, problem solving methods provide the building blocks (control and inference structures) which support the specification of problem solving behaviour. This behaviour is specified at the knowledge-level and in an application-independent style, so that it can be reused in different problem solving contexts.

A partial specification of a PSM is shown in Figure 13.2. The figure shows the inference structure of a PSM for interpretation tasks. This PSM relies on a generic method ontology (target phenomenon, known phenomenon, intermediate result, criteria, interpretation), which describes the terminology required to specify interpretation problem solving at a domain-independent level. The application of this PSM to a particular domain (in this case, archaeology) can be carried out by means of the relevant mappings between PSM and domain ontologies. For instance, in this case, we want the interpretative process to identify building types, hence the mapping from interpretation to building types.

The development of shared ontologies and problem solving methods and the publication of these technologies on the Web are important steps towards its epistemification. By producing ontologies, a community can publish a particular view about some phenomenon. By reusing an ontology, a researcher can then join a community, subscribe to a world view and share knowledge – for instance developing a particular instantiation of an ontology. The development and publication of problem solving methods means that not just 'static' conceptualizations, but also problem solving behaviour can be specified, shared and reused. In a nutshell the emergence of reusable knowledge services on the Web is an important step towards the creation of virtual epistemic communities sharing, consuming and reusing knowledge. In the next section we will substantiate this point by discussing a scenario which shows how knowledge modelling technology can be used to support knowledge sharing and learning on the Web.

A tripartite scenario

The scenario is intended to show how knowledge modelling can be applied to collaborative knowledge work on the Web. In particular we wish to illustrate the resulting benefits in terms of better comprehension (texts partially include their own semantics), more productive search mechanisms, explicit argumentation structures and the simulation of reasoning as well as the more educationally oriented cognitive and meta-cognitive gains. Since many of the archaeological facts and theories are fictional, the scenario is emphatically not intended to teach novice archaeologists.

In the scenarios discussed here we assume that, as in the (KA)2 initiative (Benjamins and Fensel, 1998), a network of enriched Web pages exists which supports knowledge sharing in archaeology. We call this fictional space, ArchWeb. ArchWeb uses dozens of different ontologies, including generic ones for archaeology, specialized ones for Roman archaeology, ontologies for academic publishing and research (discussed in Chapter 8), and for argumentation. ArchWeb goes beyond (KA)2 as it makes use of PSM representations (the second aspect of knowledge models), using ideas from the IBROW3 initiative (see below).

Scenario 1 – Intelligent search and ontology mark-up
A student interested in the archaeology of the Roman Imperial army asks ArchWeb for all the sites where Roman hospitals have been identified. Since the pages in ArchWeb are marked up with ontologies, intelligent search is possible. Among the various answers, one referring to a site near Housesteads Fort catches her eye and by following various links through ArchWeb she eventually retrieves a text describing a part of the fort which has tentatively been identified as a hospital. The student (as apprentice archaeologist) is interested in (a) the argument structure for the possible interpretations, (b) the domain ontology used in the claims, (c) the interpretative strategies which result in the options. Since her browser is ontology-enabled she asks for an ontology-mark-up. This highlights (in different colours) the argument, domain and problem-solving ontologies.

Scenario 2 – Publication, ontologies and explicit argumentation
An archaeologist who has recently been working on a medieval monastery site in Scotland and who is also interested in Romano-British archaeology has come to the conclusion that the unidentified structure at Housesteads is indeed a military hospital. He bases this on (a) the similarity of layout between the monastic structures and the Housesteads building (he knows from documents that the monastic structure is a hospital), (b) the discovery at the two sites of artefacts of a similar shape, and (c) the discovery of ecofacts such as the seeds of medicinal plants. He decides to place a note on ArchWeb. In order to facilitate other researchers (and intelligent search agents) he marks up his text with various ontologies. He adds mark-up to his text for both the domain ontologies (items such as architectural structures, artefacts and ecofacts) and for the argument structure (by

identifying, for example, premises and conclusions). Since he finds that the standard set of problem solving methods for archaeological interpretation does not in fact include the particular form of analogical problem solving he wishes to use, he updates the list of PSMs associated with ArchWeb. The new PSM is a form of analogical reasoning derived from Hodder (1982) called Relational Analogical Reasoning (RAR). This PSM's ontology requires certain domain entities to be identified as base and target relations. Finally, the researcher publishes his Web page and notifies the ArchWeb server.

Scenario 3 – Querying ArchWeb, theory testing and collaborative knowledge modelling
Our student is alerted to the fact that a new interpretation has been added to ArchWeb. She finds that a new ontology has been created and that a new problem solving method has been added to ArchWeb. She is thus able to update her study of the social conditions of the Roman Imperial army with a new section on its medical practices and to gain insight into a new problem solving technique. She is able to grasp from the definitions available in the various ontologies what the researcher means by his use of new technical terms.

In addition (using the results of the IBROW3 project, Benjamins *et al.*, 1998) a PSM-aware browser is able to reason with interchangeable PSMs. The student can therefore simulate (or rehearse) the researcher's reasoning. This helps the student to understand how to apply the PSM to her own work. At the same time it allows her to test the researcher's reasoning by modifying it. Since PSMs are interchangeable the student can test not only facts but also the results of applying different PSMs in a variety of what-if scenarios. She decides to apply a more rigorous version of analogical interpretation (a PSM based on Hill's Tight Local Analogy method; Hill, 1994 and discovers that her PSM-aware browser no longer views the analogy between the Roman and medieval sites as sound (because the tightness between the two sets of buildings is insufficient).

Finally the student calls upon her colleagues to see if other refutations of the researcher's claim are possible. Since the various components that her browser uses to animate the knowledge model will normally be distributed throughout ArchWeb and the Web as a whole, she can call upon her colleagues (say, in a tutor group) to collaborate on the building of a new model (and a new argument). The student duly notes her results in ArchWeb which in turn leads the researcher to amend or abandon his theory.

Points from the scenario

As this example shows, the availability of knowledge modelling techniques can support knowledge sharing and learning by allowing a researcher to carry out the following tasks:

- publishing new material in readily comprehensible form;
- adding to the vocabulary of a domain;
- representing and adding novel forms of problem-solving.

For a student, a resource such as Arch Web provides the means for:

- searching for new material;
- understanding what she finds and extending her domain vocabulary;
- extending her problem-solving skills (in this case in site-interpretation),
- extending her intellectual skills (in arguing);
- extending her meta-cognitive skills (in problem-solving method and argumentation form selection);
- the simulation of interpretative reasoning;
- collaborative knowledge modelling.

Tools and initiatives for the Knowledge Web

While the scenario described above is still to some extent futuristic, a number of knowledge modelling tools exist on the Web, providing some of the functionalities required for building ArchWeb. We will briefly review some of the more interesting ones.

SHOE (Simple HTML Ontology Extensions) is a scheme by Luke *et al.* (1996) which allows authors of Web pages to add new tags to define the semantics of the contents of these pages. This is intended to be useful in searching the Web using agents which are aware of these tags. For instance a search for an individual who works on a particular project at a particular institution would be facilitated by having tags such as the following to express an ontology for personal names, organizations and employee relations:

<CATEGORY "our.person">

<RELATION "our.firstName" TO="George">

<RELATION "our.employee" FROM "http://www.cs.umd.edu">

ie, "George is the first name of a person employed at cs.umd".

With SHOE the representational primitives for instances, categories, relations and attributes are used to build and share ontologies. Each Web page which uses these primitives and ontologies is also a knowledge model. SHOE is thus a means of extending Web page authoring to include semantic information.

Ontobroker (Fensel *et al.*, 1998) is a tool which allows researchers in the knowledge engineering community to register and mark up their home pages with ontological information accessible by an inference engine which can deal with queries such as:

FORALL R <- EXISTS P R:Researcher[publication->>P] and

P:Publication[gen-topic->>"knowledge acquisition";

specific-topic->>"graphical knowledge"].

ie, 'Retrieve the home pages of all researchers who have published papers on the acquisition of graphical knowledge'.

This tool is going to be used in the (KA)2 initiative (Benjamins and Fensel, 1998), which aims to develop an ontology that models the knowledge acquisition community (its researchers, topics, products, etc). Consistently with the SHOE approach, this ontology will form the basis for annotating WWW documents produced by the KA community in order to enable intelligent access to these documents, by means of Ontobroker. The (KA)2 initiative combines several important research issues associated with the goal of constructing a Knowledge Web. Some of these issues are technical (developing an ontology annotation language and an intelligent broker), others have to do with the social construction of knowledge (producing a view of the knowledge acquisition community by group effort), yet others focus on the construction of a 'true' Knowledge Web, where the relatively poor dynamics associated with data retrieval are replaced by rich knowledge base access.

The aim of the IBROW3 project (Benjamins *et al.*, 1998) is to develop an intelligent brokering service that will enable third party knowledge-component reuse through the World Wide Web. The scenario is one in which suppliers provide libraries of knowledge components adhering to some standard, and customers can consult these libraries – through intelligent brokers – to configure a knowledge system suited to their needs. Thus, the idea of IBROW3 is to lower the costs associated with knowledge engineering technologies, making possible a rapid development of robust knowledge-based systems. IBROW3 is therefore a first step towards realizing the problem solving technology assumed by the ArchWeb scenario.

WebOnto is a tool developed at the Knowledge Media Institute (Chapter 14; Domingue, 1998). In common with the tools mentioned above it allows the browsing and creation of ontologies. Moreover it also supports the development and prototyping of complete application models, expressed in OCML (Operational Conceptual Modelling Language, Motta, 1998a). An important aspect of WebOnto is that it supports both synchronous and asynchronous collaborative model building. In particular, a WebOnto user can work in broadcast mode, which allows her to make changes or annotate parts of the model and transmit these to other users, without changing the underlying model. WebOnto thus provides the most complete knowledge modelling environment available on the Web. It supports both ontology and executable model development, provides support for collaborative model building by allowing users to share models (synchronously and asynchronously) and supports the specification of the argument structure used during collaborative model construction.

Conclusions: The case for knowledge modelling

In conclusion, we have three main arguments for the importance of knowledge modelling techniques in the context of developing the Knowledge Web.

- *Formalization argument.* This argument emphasizes the importance of formalized components, such as those produced by knowledge modelling techniques, in constructing the Knowledge Web. It is easier for the software agents populating the Web to understand, reason about and share formalized components. As Luke *et al.* (1996) point out, 'the Web is a disorganized place...World Wide Web users are finding it increasingly difficult to gather information relevant to their interests without considerable and often fruitless searching. Much of this is directly attributable to the lack of a coherent way to provide useful semantic knowledge on the Web in a machine-readable form.' Thus, future generations of search agents may need to understand the contents of a knowledge resource in order to support effective knowledge retrieval tasks. This goal can only be achieved if knowledge resources are associated with ontological specifications (including those for commonly performed tasks and their common solutions in particular domains), which describe their semantic contents.

- *Argument from education.* The Web already provides a wealth of educational resources. However, these are mostly static. New, dynamic resources are needed, which can provide inferential and discovery capabilities, thus transforming the Web from a passive repository of educational material to an active learning resource – see our earlier archaeological scenario for an example of how knowledge modelling technology can support education. Moreover, consistently with the constructivist view of knowledge (eg, Jonassen *et al.*, 1993), a number of researchers, such as Wideman and Owston (1993), have shown that involving students in constructing knowledge models improves their understanding of a discipline. Stutt (1997) builds on these results and argues that the application of knowledge modelling to education 'may provide the means for achieving some of the larger ambitions of constructivist researchers'.

- *Political argument.* Knowledge is being produced at an ever increasing rate. Moreover, globalization and concomitant technological advances mean that the traditional barriers to the diffusion of ideas have been removed. At the present time we can publish a paper on the Internet and it immediately becomes accessible to millions of potential readers. However, while we may all be publishers (and thereby knowledge producers in a traditional sense), only those communities which will be able to produce knowledge in a form which can be understood by the various semantic agents populating the cyber-world will become cyber-knowledge producers as well. Hence, we predict that, at least within the scientific community, the ability to (semi-) formalize ideas by means of the appropriate knowledge modelling languages will become a strong indicator of the influence of an individual or a group over a discipline.

The emerging Knowledge Age will be characterized by novel forms of knowledge production and sharing, novel loci of discussion, and heterogeneous agents. If such a prediction turns out to be correct, then it is crucial that not just the means of knowledge consumption (eg, enhanced Web browsers), but also the means of production (eg, knowledge modelling technology) are made available to knowledge users. Hence, the human-centred development of knowledge modelling and the introduction of this technology as part of a basic curriculum for the Knowledge Age will be – at some point in the future – essential, not just to ensure the success of the technology, but also to ensure democratic forms of knowledge production.

Chapter 14

The World Wide Design Lab: an environment for distributed collaborative design

Zdenek Zdrahal and John Domingue

Teams of engineers face major hurdles during collaborative design: they may not share the same vocabulary, concepts, or tools, let alone work in the same building, city, or even country. The World Wide Design Lab facilitates concept-sharing and knowledge reuse through a collection of novel representation and communication tools.

Introduction

The design of any complex artifact is necessarily a collaborative activity, dependent on the sharing and reuse of information and knowledge among the designers. Each designer receives the inputs needed for his or her work from the collaborating partners and in turn provides inputs to them. However, problem solving as a group activity is not necessarily straightforward and conflict free. Collaboration may lead to a variety of misunderstandings, for example: partners may misinterpret shared knowledge because they do not take the original context into account, their understanding of the same concepts may differ due to differences in their professional background and experience, or they may be pursuing different objectives.

If the collaborators are working in different geographical locations additional complications will arise: all the aforementioned collaboration and knowledge sharing problems must be resolved at a distance.

In this chapter we will describe how we solved three collaboration-at-a-distance problems using a real-life design scenario. Our scenario is centred on the preliminary design of a truck which was used to experimentally verify the knowledge models and field-test the support tools developed in the EU funded Encode project (Copernicus 94-0149). An overview of this application can be found in (Banecek *et al.*, 1997).

Imagine that a team of engineers is working on the design of a new truck. The first step in this type of project is the initial truck design consisting of a coarse-grained specification of all the major truck subsystems which are required to assess the basic vehicle properties. Examples of truck subsystems which are designed and evaluated at this stage include: the chassis, vehicle structure, axle kinematics, the brake system, vehicle stability, the suspension and the power train. Each of these design tasks requires different problem solving techniques, different support tools and above all, different skills and specialized knowledge. Initial vehicle design is therefore solved as a collaborative activity of a number of specialized problem solving agents – design engineers or computer programs. In the next section we will describe the three problems we address. We then describe the overall system architecture and the three support tools. In the final section we summarize our results.

The problems addressed

Problem 1: Collaborating of agents with differing domains of expertise

The first type of problem may occur when two or more design agents with different domains of expertise collaborate. Misunderstanding can occur if the experts do not share the same domain concepts or the shared concepts have differing interpretations. We resolve the communication difficulties by employing a formal representation of the shared knowledge for inter-agent communication. We will now outline how we used the formal representation within the truck domain.

The set of all objects existing in an agent's domain of expertise is called a universe of discourse. The universe of discourse specifies the portion of the world the agent works with. For example, the designer of a vehicle suspension makes use of the following concepts: sprung and unsprung vehicle masses, axle rigidity, shock absorber, spring, outer forces, spring constant, damping coefficients and oscillations. An explicit conceptualization of the universe of discourse is called an ontology (Gruber, 1993). An overview of the role that ontologies can play in sharing and reusing complex industrial design knowledge can be found in Borst and Akkermans (1997), and a brief introduction to related themes is provided in Chapter 13.

An ontology associates names with the objects in the universe of discourse and specifies their meaning by defining their relationship with other objects in the universe of discourse.

Obviously, design specialists work within a specialized domain of expertise and they therefore use a specialized domain ontology. When two designers collaborate they must resolve the communication problem arising from the use of different ontologies.

For example, the vehicle suspension is designed in two steps. First, from given vehicle parameters and required suspension characteristics, a designer calculates the suspension components and their ideal parameters. In the second phase an expert in dynamic systems simulation is brought in to model the vehicle behaviour for various road conditions, various tyre types and load values. If the results are not satisfactory the designer will change the parameters and characteristics considered for the calculation and the whole process starts again.

Computer simulation requires specialized knowledge to understand the underlying theory of simulation and technical skills to master all the simulation package features. The simulation expert will not usually be familiar with the vehicle suspension domain. From a simulation viewpoint vehicle suspension is just another type of dynamic system such as an electrical circuit or biological system. The simulation ontology describes 'the world of dynamic systems' without any commitment to a specific application. This ontology may include concepts such as linear and non-linear models, various types of non-linear functions, the order of a model, constant and variable coefficients, input, state and output variables and their derivatives, and sampling intervals.

The designer of the vehicle suspension and the expert in computer simulation can collaborate only if they construct a mapping between the relevant concepts of both ontologies. For example, they could agree to model the vehicle suspension as a second order piece-wise linear system and to associate the damping coefficient of the suspension with the coefficient of the first derivative in the model. Constructing shared ontologies is an important part of collaborative problem solving. On top of their specialized ontologies the collaborating agents need to construct a new ontology – in this instance an ontology for simulating vehicle suspensions. Empirical evidence for informal ontology construction within design teams was found by Sumner (1995) in the domain of telephone voice dialogue design.

To summarize, the first problem we wanted to address was that of supporting knowledge sharing in a group of collaborating problem solving agents, each with his or her own area of expertise, by constructing shared domain ontologies.

Problem 2: Recording and retrieving design discourse

Dialogue, for example to reach consensus or to disseminate information, is an important activity within communal design (Fischer, Lemke, McCall and Morch, 1991). As we saw in Chapter 8, even if the designers share the same domain of expertise and their communication is unambiguous, the record of their discussions will still be of great value. The discussion record captures the reasoning processes in a form which is usually more representative than experts attempting explicitly to articulate their knowledge.

Let us consider two designers solving two closely related problems. For example, in the vehicle design domain one designer is working on the layout of the dashboard controls while his or her partner is preparing the overall blueprint for the cabin interior. Both design tasks are interdependent: the dashboard layout affects the overall arrangement inside the cabin and vice versa, and solutions to the cabin interior constrain the possibilities for the dashboard layout. The designers need to be aware of the progress of each other's work because each of them requires updated inputs from the other partner to be able to proceed with his or her own work. Even if both partners work on the same project and share the same ontology, their objectives may conflict. For example, the most ergonomic dashboard layout does not necessarily produce the best overall cabin interior since additional criteria, such as the position of the driver's seat, contribute to the final outcome. The conflicts are usually resolved by negotiation. The designers will argue for and against design decisions before reaching a compromise. These discussions are traditionally supported by sketches and formal diagrams. Annotated records of these design reasoning processes, with the sketches and diagrams, are a valuable source of information. Indeed, these are often as important as the solution itself since the record can later be retrieved and the knowledge adapted and reused to solve similar problems in the future. Therefore, the second problem we address in this chapter is how to support, represent and archive complex discussions and negotiations including their graphical forms with minimum changes to the designer's style of work. Let us reiterate that recording designers' reasoning is equally important when constructing cross-domain ontologies as described in Problem 1.

Problem 3: Reusing previous solutions – case-based design

Designers often solve a problem by adapting previous solutions to similar problems. Reusing old solutions is a common design practice – this technique is called case-based design. A detailed treatment of this subject can be found in (Maher *et al.*, 1995). The best known example from the motor vehicle industry is the Ford Cosworth eight cylinder engine. This engine, which was used in Formula 1 winning racing cars, was designed by reusing and adapting the successful four cylinder Ford Cosworth engine. In the truck domain designers commonly adapt and reuse successful truck axle geometry design solutions. In our experience design institutions commonly maintain case libraries – archives of previous designs.

Case-based design is an example of knowledge sharing across time. Designers may reuse their own previous solutions or solutions published by other designers. In the latter case an interpretation problem arises as the previous solutions may be described using different concepts. Developing shared domain ontologies, as described in the previous paragraph, significantly contributes to case reusability. Organizing a case library also raises challenges. The library can be either centralized or distributed among the group members so that the designer who authored the case maintains all the relevant data. A distributed library has the benefit that the maintainer fully understands the cases and their organization, and is usually motivated to carry out any necessary maintenance work. Obviously, such an architecture makes case retrieval more difficult. There is a trade-off between reducing the time to find a previous solution and reducing the duplication of design solutions across collaborating groups. Organizing a case library distributed in the collaborating group is the third problem addressed in this chapter.

Collaborating at a distance

As we have already mentioned collaborating at a distance increases the complexity of the three aforementioned problems. Our solutions make use of the Internet and the World Wide Web (WWW) as a medium for sharing and reusing knowledge. The advantage of the WWW is the possibility to use a unified, widely available, platform independent interface. Obviously, all our conclusions also apply to intranets. Because of the similarities between the Internet and intranet technologies, the 'distance' factor in our approach becomes less important and the main

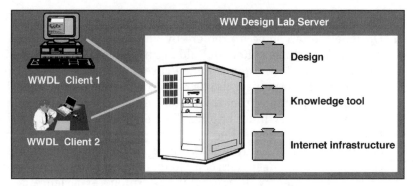

Figure 14.1. The general architecture of the World Wide Design Laboratory

novelty comes from the fact that the collaboration is carried out in a distributed environment.

Architecture

The architecture has two main components: a central WWW Design Lab Server and a WWDL client. The central server is composed of three layers: an Internet infrastructure layer, a knowledge tool layer and a design layer (Figure 14.1). The Internet infrastructure layer is responsible for interfacing to the Web and e-mail and allowing user interface actions to be broadcast. This layer is composed of a customized Web server, an e-mail handler and a broadcaster. The customized Web server is based on LispWeb (Chapter 12) a specialized HTTP server written in Common Lisp. In addition to implementing the standard HTTP protocol, the LispWeb server offers a library of high-level Lisp functions to dynamically generate HTML pages, a facility for dynamically creating image maps, and a server-to-server communication method.

The e-mail handler parses incoming e-mail and sends on the decomposed parts to interested knowledge tools. All WWDL clients have broadcast and receive modes. All the interface actions of broadcasting clients are copied to receiving clients. When broadcasting or receiving, a WWDL client maintains an open TCP/IP stream to the server. The broadcaster is responsible for distributing the incoming broadcast data to the receivers.

The knowledge tool layer enables reusable design ontologies to be constructed and partial solutions to be stored and retrieved. The layer is based on OCML, an operational knowledge modelling language (Motta, 1998a) and a Case Based Reasoning tool (Zdrahal and Motta, 1996).

The design layer currently contains a case library. Future work will expand the library of design problem solving methods (Motta and Zdrahal, 1996).

A designer interacts with WWDL using one of our WWDL design clients. There is a client for each of the knowledge support tools and a client for gaining an overview of a design.

Visualizing the discourse of design agents with Tadzebao

Tadzebao, which literally means 'Big Character Poster', is the Chinese word for the type of poster used to support political debate during the Cultural Revolution. During the Cultural Revolution a political argument or ideology would be expressed through the placement of a poster (a tadzebao). Rebuttals to or comments on the initial argument would be expressed by additional posters (tadzebaos) on top of or around the original poster.

WWDL uses an extension of this metaphor for guiding designers around ongoing design dialogues. Within Tadzebao, dialogues are centred around a notepad which contains a series of pages. Each notepad page can contain a mixture of text, GIF images, hand drawn sketches and design knowledge encoded in one of the knowledge tools. Dialogues can be browsed by clicking on the bottom right corner of a notepad.

Figure 14.2 shows six notepads each containing a design dialogue. We shall now briefly describe the top page of each of these notepads in turn, proceeding clockwise from the upper left.

Optimize PS Ontology – this page shows the top portion of a new design ontology and some textual comments. The designer added the ontology by clicking on the 'Add' button and choosing an ontology from a displayed list. The 'Add' button adds one of: a text area; GIF image; or ontology depending on the current choice (currently showing 'Ontology'). The text comments were added using a simple text editor provided within the environment. The text displayed in grey italics ('meeting on 3/2/97') is a hypertext link to the relevant page within the notepad.

Seat Positioning – this page contains a query on the distance between the driver's seat and the pedals within a truck cabin. The GIF image was added by specifying its Web address. The white (and black) sketched arrows specifying the distance were drawn

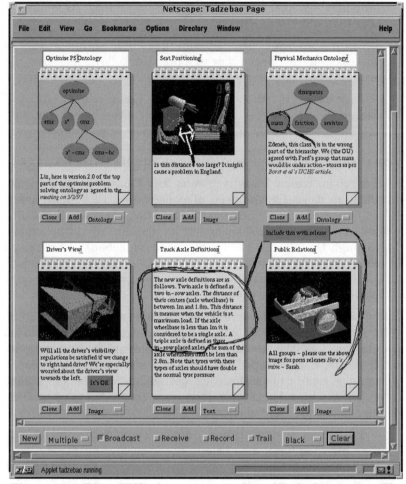

Figure 14.2 (Plate XVI). A screen snapshot of Tadzebao in use. The 'Broadcast' and 'Receive' buttons at the bottom are used for synchronous collaboration, as described in the text.

using the mouse after clicking on the 'Trail' button in the bottom control panel.

Physical Mechanics Ontology – this page shows a designer disagreeing with the structure of an ontology. The text displayed in grey italics ('Borst et al's IJCHS article') is a hypertext link to the article. Clicking on an ontology allows it to be edited within our ontology editor – see the next section.

Driver's View – the designer has added a reply to the visibility query by cloning the original page, using the 'Clone' button, and then sticking on a label (like a 'Post-It' sticky note) with the phrase 'It's OK'. It is possible to clone an entire notepad if a designer wishes to view two pages at once.

Truck Axle Definition – this plain text page was e-mailed to Tadzebao, using an address known to the e-mail handler, with the subject line 'Truck Axle Definitions' – the name of the notepad. The body of the message, describing new definitions of truck twin and triple axles, was then added to the top of the notepad. It should be noted that Tadzebao can also handle GIF image attachments to e-mail messages.

Public Relations – this text is a note delineating the use of a particular image for a press release. Clicking on an image creates a new window showing a full size version. The sketched circle around this page and the Truck Axle Definition page, and label 'include this with release' are part of a live broadcast. Selecting the 'Broadcast' button in the bottom control panel broadcasts all interface actions (including all sketching, page turning and adding of text, GIF images or ontologies) to receivers, ie, Tadzebaos with the 'Receive' button selected, in real time. The designer is using this to tell the public relations officer (Sarah) that it would be beneficial to have part of the axle definitions included with the press release. A broadcast can be recorded, if required, by selecting the 'Record' button. Recordings are stored in a 'movie' database and can be retrieved and replayed when convenient.

Collaboratively browsing and creating ontologies with WebOnto

WebOnto was designed to support the collaborative browsing, creation and editing of ontologies by providing a direct manipulation interface displaying ontological expressions using a rich medium. WebOnto was also aimed to be easy to use, yet have facilities for scaling up to large ontologies.

Figure 14.3 shows a scenario in which an ontology engineer is editing the truck-cabin ontology. As described earlier, the ontology is stored on a central server and the interface (shown in Figure 14.3) is provided by a set of Java clients. The engineer drew the class hierarchy, displayed in Figure 14.3, by clicking on the upper left hand (draw descendants) button. The class driver-angle was then selected and inspected by clicking on the 'eyeglasses' (inspect item) button. The detailed information for driver-angle is

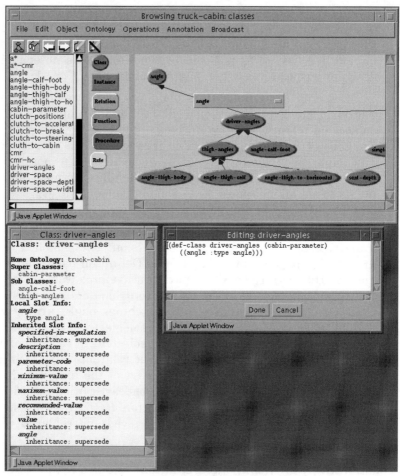

Figure 14.3. A screen snapshot of WebOnto in use

displayed in the bottom left window. The items in this window are
colour coded depending on their type, for example, class names
are displayed in green and relation names in turquoise. Ontology
components can be edited using a text editor (the window on the
bottom right of Figure 14.3), or by direct manipulation. In Figure
14.3 the ontology engineer is currently editing the driver-angles
class by:

- dragging a link from the driver-angles class to
  the angle class;

- clicking on the label; and

- choosing 'angle' from the selector button.

These gestures have the result of adding the expression '(angle :type angle)' – the value for the angle slot of the class must be of type angle – to the class definition. When the ontology definitions are altered using the client the corresponding code on the server is automatically updated.

It should be noted that WebOnto incorporates the sketching and synchronous communication tools described earlier for Tadzebao, enabling users to hold synchronous discussions about the details of an ontology. The synchronous communication tool relies on the fact that the architecture allows connections between a server and its clients to be left open. A more detailed overview of WebOnto and Tadzebao can be found in Domingue (1998).

The distributed case-based design tool

The generic case-based computational model consists of a case-library and a reasoning engine. The reasoning engine performs two major tasks: case retrieval and adaptation. The case retrieval task involves finding the case with the best match to the problem specification. This case then becomes the basis for the solution. In the adaptation step the case is evaluated and potential discrepancies are fixed. When this generic computation model is instantiated in a distributed collaborative environment, problems with case reusability and design efficiency arise.

When designers use different domain conceptualizations, it becomes impractical to share cases across the collaborating group. We solve this by using shared domain ontologies. We assume that the designers who want to offer their cases for sharing or those who want to use the cases of other designers have developed a shared domain ontology. This issue and our tools supporting the collaborative development of ontologies were described earlier.

The efficiency problem arises from the distributed organization of the case library and the use of the Internet as a medium for knowledge sharing. It is desirable that the number of Internet accesses is minimized since a high number of Internet accesses could make the tool too unresponsive to be of practical use.

Let us consider the retrieval algorithm in detail. For each case we calculate a similarity measure between it and the current requirements. The case with the highest score is selected and downloaded. As we have opted for a distributed case library we need to ensure that we do not invoke an Internet access for each

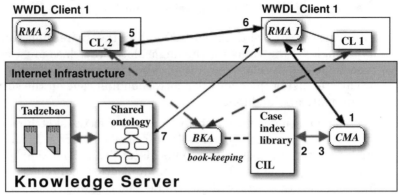

Figure 14.4. The agent based architecture of the case-based design tool. The abbreviations in the figure are: BKA – book-keeping agent; CMA – case-matching agent; RMA – request manager agent, CL – case library. The seven steps involved are: [1] ask for case index; [2] query CIL; [3] retrieve case index; [4] return case index; [5] ask for case; [6] return case; [7] query shared domain ontology.

similarity measure calculation, as this would notably degrade the performance of the tool.

Our solution uses the agent based architecture shown in Figure 14.4. The retrieval task is solved in a group of three collaborating software agents: a book-keeping agent (BKA), a case-matching agent (CMA) and a request manager agent (RMA). The book-keeping agent maintains a case index library (CIL) – a minimum collection of case data required for identifying the best case. The CIL subscribes to the shared domain ontology. Finding the best cases and presenting them to the designers is the responsibility of the clients' request manager agents and the case-matching agent.

Let's consider a small example using Figure 14.4. Imagine that Client 1 initiates a case retrieval. Client 1's RMA communicates this request to the case-matching agent – step number 1 in Figure 14.4. From the data in the case index library (CIL) the CMA selects the best case – steps 2 and 3. In Figure 14.4 we assume that this example resides in case library 2 (CL 2). The CMA returns the case index of the best case and the Internet address of CL 2 to client 1's RMA (step 4). Client 1's RMA then downloads the best case from CL 2 (steps 5 and 6). A potentially large number of Internet queries is reduced to 4 (RMA 1 -> CMA; CMA -> RMA 1; RMA 1 -> CL 2; CL 2 -> RMA 1). This number is independent of the size of the distributed case library. The client which retrieved the case may query the shared domain ontology, if this is required during the adaptation phase (step 7).

The book-keeping agent periodically updates the CIL by inspecting remote case libraries (CL 1 and CL 2 in Figure 14.4). The update interval is set to correspond to the collaborating design group's work schedule. If a designer produces a new result and immediately wants to make it available to the remote partners he or she can force an exceptional CIL update. In this instance the designer's RMA sends an update request to the book-keeping agent. This update strategy ensures that at any time the CIL contains up-to-date information. Designers can also send update requests to the book-keeping agent by e-mail.

Summary

In this chapter we have described how we solved three collaboration-at-a-distance problems using a real-life design scenario. Our work is based on the premise that in order to collaborate, designers must use a common shared conceptualization. Our approach uses a formal representation of the shared conceptualization – an ontology. We then described a set of tools which allow designers to share design knowledge across space and time. Using Tadzebao, designers can take part in synchronous and asynchronous design dialogues via a rich medium. Future versions of Tadzebao will incorporate audio annotations. The Web Ontology editor allows designers to collaboratively construct an explicit shared conceptualization which facilitates design reuse. The distributed case-based design tool allows designers to reuse previous results across large distances.

The distributed case-based design tool is currently being tested using a case library distributed over: Iowa University in the US, the Czech Technical University in Prague, the Technical University at Kosice and The Open University in the UK. Our architecture means that the number of Internet accesses for a case retrieval is a small constant, independent of both the number of collaborating partners and the number of cases within the distributed case library. We are also using the Web server/Java client architecture in a number of other contexts (eg software maintenance, Domingue and Mulholland, 1997b; see Chapter 11).

A distributed design approach, similar to the one described in this chapter, was successfully used in the Madefast project (Cutkosky et al., 1996). One of the recommendations from the project was that a tool which would enable multimedia discussions to be structured around varying viewpoints would be very useful. Tadzebao is a first step towards this as multimedia discussions can be organized in notepads.

It has long been known that engineering design is a complex time-consuming task. Our contribution has been to enable designers more easily to share the fruits of their labour.

Chapter 15

Psychological agents and the new Web media

Stuart Watt

Software agents can perform tasks on your behalf. At what point are you prepared to delegate authority to such agents? The problem of attributing intelligence and autonomy to software agents raises key issues at the core of psychology, philosophy, and artificial intelligence.

Introduction: Web media and heterogeneous groupware

As the previous chapters show, the Web is more than a medium through which people can get access to information. Because it is so easy to publish on the Web, it is also a medium through which people can communicate with each other. And increasingly, it is a medium for computer supported collaboration – or groupware – of different kinds. There is a gradual transition from Web servers which simply deliver files, to active Web servers (see Chapter 12) which provide access to all kinds of resources, resources people can change as well as browse, resources through which people can communicate and collaborate with one another.

Similarly, Web users are a diverse group. Most Web access is still by people using browsers, but even today approximately 2 per cent of all Web access is by 'robots' of one kind or another (often search engines such as Lycos and AltaVista) rummaging through the Web to provide better access or indexing of useful resources. And more is by 'proxies', programs which sometimes behave as a server and sometimes as a browser, and which can make a user's access much faster.

So the Web is more than a universe of information, it is a meeting place for people and robots, a mixed society of humans and computers each reading one another's texts and publications. It forms what can be called 'heterogeneous groupware' (Watt, 1993). Since the Web is a mixed society of people and software robots (or, as I'll call them, 'agents') how can we ensure that people can see agents as agents and use them to best effect, and that the social relationships within the system work smoothly?

But before continuing I should probably clarify this use of the word 'agent'. The term 'agent' originated with Oliver Selfridge, with much of the concept due to joint work with John McCarthy in the 1950s. What they had in mind was an assistant that could be given a task to carry out, and which would carry out that task both intelligently and autonomously. On the one hand, this idea led to artificial intelligence, and on the other, it led to the notion of agents in the human–computer interface (Kay, 1990; Maes, 1994). The difference between them is one of emphasis: in artificial intelligence, the emphasis is on how the agent works inside; in human-computer interaction, it is on how the agent is seen to behave by others. In this chapter, I'll be arguing for a synthesis of these positions – that for true agency agents must behave intelligently and be seen to behave intelligently. For this reason, we need an element of psychology, if only to find out what makes people believe that something is intelligent.

Technology, sociology and psychology

As the Web moves to become a mixed society of people and agents, issues other than the traditional technological ones come to the fore. To be sure, bandwidth, security and other technological issues do arise, but I would argue that more significant issues lie ahead. Put simply, we don't have much of a theory of agency; we don't know how these mixed societies work. We don't even really know how people see other people in societies, let alone how people see non-human systems like agents.

This is where psychology can begin to help. Recently there has been a growth of interest in 'theory of mind', in how people see one another as having minds rather than simply as physical bodies. Theory of mind is a complex and dynamic phenomenon, one which develops as we grow. However, there is evidence that it plays an important role in determining when we see things as agents rather than as objects. Theory of mind is too complicated to describe here in any detail, but see Baron-Cohen *et al.* (1993) or Whiten (1991) for a more complete description. For our purposes we don't need a complete analysis of theory of mind – we just need to bring psychology to bear in looking at how people see agents in psychological terms rather than in computational or mathematical terms from the culture of programming.

For now, the main lever for psychology and theory of mind in agency is anthropomorphism. By anthropomorphism I do not mean the 'jokey' kind of anthropomorphism of Lewis Carroll and Rev W D Awdry. It is not 'Thomas the Tank Engine' psychology.

Instead, a psychological theory of anthropomorphism is simply one way to look at how people tell the difference between an agent and an object (Caporael, 1986).

Generally speaking, we think of behaving systems in a number of different ways, what Dennett (1971) calls 'stances'. For example, we can think of the same system in physical terms, design (or functional) terms, intentional (or psychological) terms. Which stance we take depends on the way the system appears to us, what we know about how it works, how much we have used it in the past, and so on. In this sense, agents are just entities to which we take the psychological stance (what Dennett calls the 'intentional stance'), which we think about psychologically rather than physically or functionally. Anthropomorphism is the psychology of when we take the psychological stance.

Anthropomorphism is a subtle, complex and elusive phenomenon (Caporael, 1986), influenced by many possible factors (Watt, 1996). When dealing with agents, though, one factor is especially important. The more complicated the system physically or functionally, the greater the tendency to think about it casually in other terms, including psychological ones. If this principle is even vaguely correct (and for evidence that it is, see Watt, 1996) there will be an increasing tendency to see systems as agents as their technological complexity increases.

So the relationship between me and you – and between me and a computer – is a social and psychological one as well as a technological and physical one, and a set of social rules apply which help me to interpret the behaviour of those I interact with, whether they are people or computers. Of course, the social relationships between me and you and between me and a computer are superficially very different, reflecting different sets of social assumptions, but there are all sorts of interplay between them and in many ways they are closely tangled: 'people's expectations about human-computer interaction are often inherited from what they expect from human/*human* interaction' (Brennan, 1990, original emphasis). This very kinship opens up an immense possibility for conflict when there is a dissonance between these expectations and reality – when the expectations from human-human collaboration conflict with the reality of human-computer interaction.

People will readily attribute some kind of agency to many computer systems, but this is usually unwarranted anthropomorphism. People inevitably anthropomorphize their computer –

not because they are told to – but because it is part of the way people relate to each other, and they use this to 'read' the computer. Computers are after all, social objects, not merely physical ones – and people apply social and psychological principles when interacting with them (Nass *et al.*, 1994). 'At the grossest level, people simply attribute agency to the computer itself ('I did this, and then the computer did that'). They also attribute agency to application programs ('My word processor trashed my file')' (Laurel, 1991).

However, there is a lot of evidence that blatant anthropomorphism simply doesn't work. In Apple's 'Knowledge Navigator' video an agent, 'Phil', supported people as they used a kind of next generation DynaBook (Kay and Goldberg, 1977). In a concept video, acted by a human, agents like Phil can seem plausible, but the reality of computer agents today is a long way from this. For example, Microsoft's attempt to produce a 'social interface' product, Bob, didn't really succeed at all. Cute animations do not make an interface work. There is often an 'anthropomorphic dissonance' between the behaviour you'd expect from the agent, given its appearance, and its actual behaviour. The bigger the gap, the greater the dissatisfaction with the interface.

In many ways, the ideal agent would be invisible – not in the sense that it wouldn't be there, but in the sense that you would simply forget that you were using an agent. It would simply be the most natural way of dealing with a particular task. The worst case is when you have to 'negotiate with some little dip in a bow tie' (Laurel, 1990), when you know exactly how to achieve your goal quickly. This is where an understanding of Dennett's stances can help. When you are working at a relatively coarse scale, say manipulating words and letters in a word processor document, the physical stance is ideal, and manipulation is the best approach. When you are dealing with incomprehensibly complex functional and physical systems (like the World Wide Web) the physical and functional stances are just unworkable. This is where agents become necessary, and come into their own – but they have to be good agents, not just anthropomorphic characters that still leave their users with heavy functional and physical burdens.

Laurel (1990) suggests that agents should be more like characters than personalities – more like Wile E Coyote than Hamlet. And even Apple redesigned the video 'Phil' to be a cartoon character – a change that seemed to improve him (Laurel, 1991). There is sense in this. After all, it is relatively predictable that

Wile E Coyote will buy something from Acme Corporation and his latest attempt to eat Roadrunner will go disastrously wrong. This predictability is ideal for an agent. The problem of psychological agency is a different one; Wile E Coyote, as a cartoon character, is completely unable to 'read' Roadrunner's – or a user's – psychology. The proposal of psychological agency is simply this: that we should design agents to become more aware of their user's psychology, and to apply this awareness in carrying out their goals. The problem for agents is not just one of how they are seen by people, but is one of how they see people in their own right.

Psychological agents and the Web

So far, I've looked at the theory of psychological agents. Unfortunately, the practice is still a long way behind the theory. There are two reasons for this. First, true psychological agency requires a complete understanding of human psychology, and we simply don't have that yet, or anything even approaching it. Secondly, psychological agency is more a research programme, even an ideal, than a class of object. All I am suggesting is that for us to build proper agents, we need to look at how humans perceive things as agents, and learning from this, develop design principles that we can use. Although a complete understanding of these principles may be out of reach, some of those principles are already known. To that end, we can develop an approximate theory of agency which can be used to design agents today. I'll briefly mention a few psychologically influenced agent designs.

Luigi (Watt, 1997) is a Web- and e-mail-based meeting scheduling agent, designed to avoid role conflict. Role conflict (Watt, 1993) is the problem that arises when participants in collaboration are trying to do slightly different jobs; for example, a meeting organizer may need to hold a meeting, while some of the necessary participants may be trying to avoid meetings. Virtually all meeting scheduling systems exacerbate this conflict by 'taking sides', helping some participants while making life harder for others. Luigi avoids role conflict by using essentially unbiased media – e-mail and the Web – and by remaining neutral, ensuring that nobody has more work to do than they would without the system. Luigi helps to achieve this by interacting directly with people, so that they do not need to keep up a diary, or run any special software at all.

Virtual librarian (planned, but not yet implemented) is an agent that manages a virtual library automatically. This is intended to provide a context for a search engine, so that it is aware of a

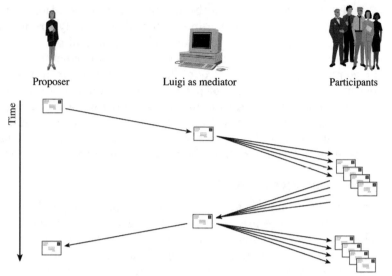

Figure 15.1. Luigi mediating messages between the proposer and the participants

domain (such as the psychology of memory) and a structure (such as academic papers). As a specific search agent which rejects material outside this domain and this structure, it does not pass a heavy filtering burden onto its user.

Virtual participant (Chapter 16) is an agent that lives in a computer-based conference, and records old discussions, ready to bring to people's attention later if these discussions again become relevant.

To illustrate these principles, we'll look at Luigi in a bit more detail. Figure 15.1 shows how Luigi acts as an intermediary managing the dialogue between a meeting's proposer and the invited participants. To ask Luigi to manage a meeting, a meeting organizer typically uses a Web form to book a meeting, consulting a diary and address book if required, as shown in Figure 15.2. Luigi then begins an e-mail dialogue with all the invited participants. When there is consensus on a date, it asks the proposer to confirm the meeting for that date. At any time, the organizer can monitor the progress of the meeting's planning process; Luigi shows all the participant's replies using a Web table. Luigi, then, acts for the proposer but interacts with all the potential participants. The organizer remains in charge at all times, and can confirm the meeting for any time; Luigi merely gives an

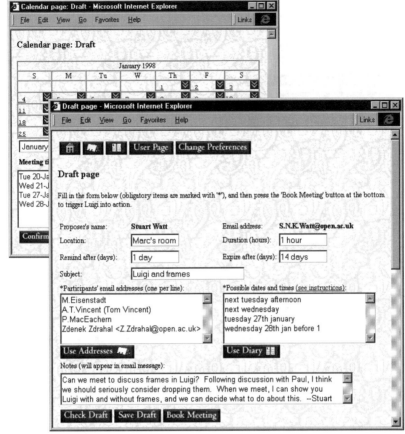

Figure 15.2. Asking Luigi to book a meeting, with Luigi's diary interface behind

appropriate recommendation (shown in Figure 15.3), while managing the e-mail dialogue for the organizer. Luigi takes away some of the administrative burden, but is careful to ensure that the proposer does not feel he or she has lost control of the meeting.

Luigi is a lot more than a naive scheduler. It has to accept real responsibility for a sensitive kind of discussion – that involved in planning a meeting. The texts that it uses for its messages have to be very carefully toned to avoid invoking feelings (such as those of alienation or frustration) in those it is bringing together. It is a system which must interact with people and with agents, and where it has to use well phrased natural language for communication and for negotiation. With this in place, we can work to

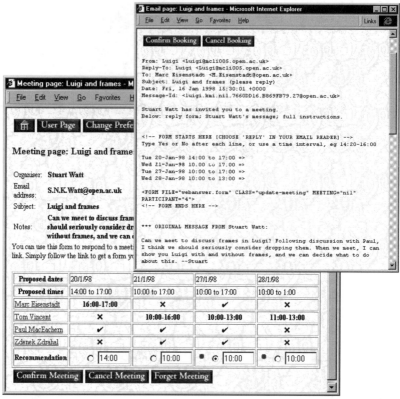

Figure 15.3. Monitoring a meeting with Luigi, with a sample of Luigi's e-mail

make Luigi gradually better at dealing with the human psychological processes which make real meeting planning and negotiation so hard. The important part of the approach for us is that we do not regard the successes and failures of Luigi as 'bugs' but as hints about how people, psychologically and socially, respond to agents. These hints can then be used in turn to refine the designs of future agents to work better with people.

Luigi shares some features with other agents for meeting scheduling, such as those of Kozierok and Maes (1993) and Sycara and Zeng (1994), but there are important differences. Maes' (1994) approach to agents stresses collaboration with an individual user in a single human-computer interface, where Luigi collaborates with a group rather than an individual. Secondly, Maes' agents operate within the user's work environment, but when Luigi takes on a task it passes partly outside that environment. Sycara and

Zeng's agent is primarily an artificial intelligence planning system; there is no strong connection to the user. On both scores, the fundamental difference between Luigi and similar agents is that Luigi is situated, in the sense of Suchman (1987), but situated in the human social world of collaborating to set up meetings.

Our approach, then, is to construct domain-specific rather than domain-general agents. For example, instead of building an agent which indexes the whole World Wide Web, we plan to build an agent that manages a small virtual library as part of it. Instead of organizing everybody's meetings, we want to help those who choose to use Luigi. Although these agents may be no help to many people, to a few they can help enormously. And there is no cost to the many. By sticking to domain-specific agents, we are building systems that are intelligent in small areas (which is possible with today's technology) rather than trying to build the ultimate intelligent machine (which is not). And with these domain specific agents, our implementation strategy is quite simple – as far as is humanly and technically possible, we develop them to work with whatever people throw at them. Luigi, for example, has an extremely rich set of heuristics which means that it can handle more or less any date and time representation people can think of.

Even though Luigi is far from being a true psychological agent, people can delegate a socially important goal (organizing a meeting) to it. In fact, I see Luigi in a different way – meeting schedulers are the laboratory rats of the groupware community, and we learn important lessons as we develop Luigi to be more acceptable socially. Already it seems that most of the problems people have accepting Luigi are social and psychological rather than technical. Luigi serves an important useful purpose as it makes these issues visible.

All of the above discussion seems very abstract and not at all relevant to the World Wide Web as it is today. To some extent this is true; we're in the realm of theories, not clear designs or specifications for the next generation of Web tools. But Rome wasn't built in a day, nor was the World Wide Web. And in many senses the Web cannot (and should not) be 'designed'.

Conclusions: beyond the Web?

What, then, makes the Web more than a next generation library? After all, some assert that the Web is 'the embodiment of human knowledge', and this certainly seems to follow in the path of libraries. And like a library, the Web is fundamentally a biased medium – information flow from users to suppliers is relatively scarce compared to the reverse. However, it is already clear that the Web will be more than a network of documents. What makes the Web different is that it is inhabited both by people and by agents. It is a social environment – a meeting place for real and virtual people. Already, on other parts of the Internet, the difference between people and agents is becoming more blurred.

In advocating psychological agents, I should not be read as suggesting that only artificial intelligence can save us from cyber-anarchy. People are psychological agents, too, and when faced with a new medium, they develop ways of dealing with the problems that it raises.

This approach to agency, then, is radical. Instead of building progressively more intelligent agents, we propose building progressively more human agents – or, rather, progressively more socialized agents. At first we will not succeed; the agents will both be and seem to be quite 'mechanical', but that must not put us off our long term goal. And we must accept our failure: it will only be through observing how people fail to grasp our agents that we will discover their shortcomings. That is the problem with social-ization: we've all got it, and we can't see it in each other. One might paraphrase John Culkin: 'we don't know who discovered water, but we are certain it wasn't a fish' – similarly, I don't know who will discover what it is to be human, but I am pretty sure it won't be a human.

The real issue of psychological agency is to change the relationship between the technology and the way we use it. Instead of being technocentric, we should become anthropocentric. Instead of learning to program, we need to teach computers our own languages. The danger is 'a trend towards computerizing socialization rather than socializing computing' (December, 1995). The only way to escape this trend is to learn how people socialize, and that is where theory of mind becomes necessary. Only through a good understanding of the processes of human social-ization (and, therefore, theory of mind) can we develop true agents.

For the Web to become the Knowledge Web, it needs the kind of understanding that only psychology – or at least psychological research – can offer. In one form or another, psychological agents are here to stay.

Chapter 16

The Virtual Participant: a tutor's assistant for electronic conferencing

Simon Masterton

Online discussion forums for large-population courses necessarily involve repeated discussion threads and potential duplication of effort. An automated assistant can spot common themes and bring relevant past discussions to everyone's attention.

Introduction

The development of the 'Virtual Participant' (VP) stemmed from two observations. First, we have observed that electronic conferencing interactions form a resource of problems and solutions. This resource can be reused. Second, electronic conferencing allows distance learning students to communicate more freely with each other and their tutors, resulting in an increasing pressure on staff time and resources (Nixon and Salmon, 1995). This chapter highlights how an agent can be used to support staff and assist students to the advantage of both.

Case-based teaching (Schank and Cleary, 1995) is founded on the reuse of the previous experiences of others. A case-base of student interactions provides the tutors with examples of common problems experienced by the students. Each individual case presents one problem experienced by past students and the key discussions around solving that problem.

To use these cases to the full we must provide them to the students in the right context and at the right time. If this task is automated, the burden on the tutors to answer common questions is reduced.

Other, structured, tasks carried out by the tutors can also be automated. It has been found that for students to benefit maximally from conferencing a structured approach must be taken (Salmon and Giles, 1997). Structuring conferencing involves welcoming students, introducing topics at relevant times and knowing when to intervene. The VP can be used for some of these tasks.

Electronic conferencing

At The Open University, many courses use an electronic conferencing system called FirstClass, from SoftArc. This system is currently provided to 20,000 (out of more than 100,000) students a year. As we saw in Chapter 6, the services available to the students include e-mail, asynchronous text-based discussion groups, and real-time text chat. Conferencing is a key tool for our students and provides for:

- a distributed student body (throughout Europe);
- an enhanced sense of learning community;
- contact for those who cannot attend tutorials;
- easier collaboration with peers.

Review of the problem

Motivating students to use electronic conferencing is a problematic task. Nixon and Salmon (1995) deal with these motivational aspects and introduce a four-stage student model describing how students access and become socially acclimatized to a conferencing environment. They note that the initial use of conferencing is an important time. To prevent students from dropping out they suggest that 'learner support is concentrated at the early stages'. To summarize our position:

- the number of students using electronic conferencing is growing; there may be no other contact for some students;
- the content of the discussions can be poor and not all topics relevant to the course may be discussed;
- the increased load on tutors may delay feedback.

Although we could make available the discussions of students from the previous year, their current form makes them difficult to utilize in teaching.

Our intention is to address these in a way that can enhance the students' experience of conferencing and helps them benefit from the discussions of previous students. For a more detailed discussion of these problems and the related work please see Masterton (1997).

Review of approach

We combine aspects of these systems (Masterton, 1997) to present students with relevant discussions from previous years. We use an 'interface agent' (Kay, 1990) to which we delegate the task of providing the students with contextually relevant cases. The VP approach has the core aims of:

- contextualizing cases from previous years by presenting them in current discussions about similar problems;
- eliminating the need for students to search for relevant cases;
- being non-intrusive, so that its messages can be easily ignored by those not interested;
- reducing the need for the tutor to repeatedly provide the same information;
- providing an immediate response to the student in an asynchronous environment.

As noted in Chapter 15, groupware fails when some users are required to do additional work without a clear benefit. This same effect has come to light again recently with work on recommender systems (Resnick and Varian, 1997).

In educational groupware situations it is necessary to demonstrate a clear benefit to all involved. The intention of the VP approach is that it should require no extra effort with its non-intrusive behaviour, and benefit all by providing extra materials at a relevant time.

Overview of the Virtual Participant

The Virtual Participant's case-based approach uses a simple pattern matching retrieval algorithm. Starting from a case-base of previous years' discussions, the VP interacts with the online conference, attempting to identify current conversations.

Step	Process	System
1	Group messages into threads	Threading program
2	Group threads into topics	Clustering program
3	Identify keywords & phrases for indexing	Concordance program
4	Generate stories	Manual editing using human judgement on output of above

Table 16.1. Process for generating the initial case-base

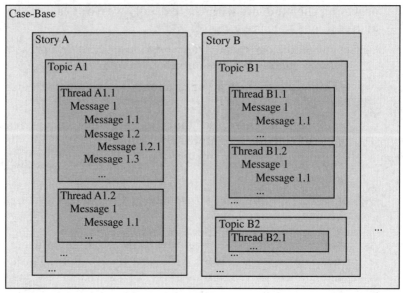

Figure 16.1. The VP's case-base contains stories which are made up of topics, which in turn are made up of threads, which in turn contain messages from previous years.

The case-base of past interactions is generated by a four-step process (Table 16.1). We feed into this process the messages from previous years and end up with our case-base.

The resulting case-base consists of four types of objects: the basic messages make up threads of conversation, threads which discuss the same thing make up topics and topics which discuss similar things make up stories (Figure 16.1). Stories are matched to current discussions by the retrieval algorithm, in a manner comparable to that of the Case Matching Agent described in Chapter 14.

As the system is interacting with the conferences, the retrieval algorithm is accumulating keywords from current conversations, and uses these to match cases from the case-base. When a case is retrieved an overview message is posted explaining that the VP has 'identified a thread of conversation from a previous year which may be of relevance to the current discussion'. The message gives the original context of the case and an overview of the problem it addresses. Students are then able to retrieve further information about the case by a number of fixed questions that can be asked by mailing them back to the conference.

The VP's aim is to effectively reuse knowledge in discussion conferences. We have created a multi-user system which gives access to contextually relevant discussions.

Design

The development plan for this system involves two prototypes. The first prototype, a proof of concept system, was given the user name 'Uncle Bulgaria' (Beresford, 1968) and served as a virtual participant in the electronic conferences of The Open University Business School's 'Creative Management' course. Assessment of this prototype identified some important lessons which are reported in the evaluation section below. The second prototype is being developed with these in mind and is described in the current work section.

The first of four assignments in the course encourages the students to explore their creativity through the use of psycho-metric tests. The students ask many questions about the tests and how to interpret them. In the second assignment students learn various brain-storming techniques and discuss their experiences with these techniques and their application to common problems. As we mentioned earlier, students need the maximum amount of support in the early stages of using electronic conferencing (Nixon and Salmon, 1995). In fact, in the opening stages of the course the problems experienced and the terms used to describe them are quite constrained, which is good news for VP: its retrieval algorithm uses pattern matching, relying on the use of these simple terms in the discussions taking place. But over time, the terms used and the problems experienced become more diverse, making the application of the VP approach inappropriate. Therefore, we have concentrated our efforts on the first two assignments.

Before the first trial, the tutors expressed some technical and pedagogical worries: 'it might go haywire' and 'it might put the students off'. To counter the former, the VP was run only manually, rather than autonomously. To counter the latter, the VP was designed only to volunteer the overview message of a story; any others require questions to be asked.

Example interaction

To illustrate the functioning of the VP, we have selected an example from this year's first assignment conference.

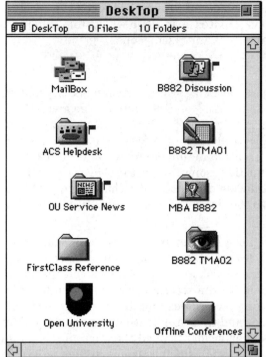

Figure 16.2. Students' desktop in FirstClass. The folders represent conferences. Flags indicate unread messages.

When students initially log into FirstClass, they are presented with their 'Desktop' showing their personal mailbox and the conferences to which they are subscribed (Figure 16.2).

When they then open a conference, in this example 'B882 TMA01', they are presented with a list of the current messages, most recent first (Figure 16.3). A number of the messages are 'greyed out,' meaning that they are open. These messages are an

	B882 TMA01			
☐ Folder 62 Files 0 Folders				
✉ B. Tutor	2K Re(5): Psychometric Tests	9/3/97	10:14 pm	
✉ B. Tutor	2K Re(4): Psychometric Tests	9/3/97	10:10 pm	
✉ B. Tutor	1K Empowerment	9/3/97	10:02 pm	
✉ B. Tutor	2K Re(2): Psychometric Tests	9/3/97	10:00 pm	
✉ D. Student	2K Fwd: Thomas Long Internationa	9/3/97	8:54 pm	
✉ Uncle Bulgaria	3K Re(4): Psychometric Tests	9/3/97	11:51 am	
✉ C. Student	1K Re(3): Psychometric Tests	9/3/97	10:37 am	
✉ B. Student	3K Re(3): Psychometric Tests	9/3/97	8:47 am	
✉ A. Student	2K Re(2): Psychometric Tests	8/3/97	12:55 pm	
✉ A. Tutor	1K Re(3): Case Study	7/3/97	9:55 pm	
✉ A. Tutor	2K Re(3): Welcome to B882 Discus	7/3/97	9:42 pm	
✉ A. Tutor	2K Re(2): Welcome to B882 Discus	7/3/97	9:28 pm	
✉ Uncle Bulgaria	5K Re(2): Psychometric Tests	7/3/97	11:35 am	

Figure 16.3. The contents of conference 'B882 TMA01'. The names of the contributors have been changed but the distinction between tutor and student has been maintained.

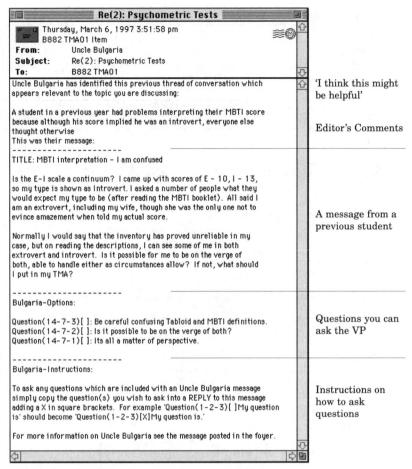

'I think this might be helpful'

Editor's Comments

A message from a previous student

Questions you can ask the VP

Instructions on how to ask questions

Figure 16.4. This is the first, overview, message from Uncle Bulgaria

example of one interaction by the VP. The next four figures are the messages from this interaction.

Figure 16.4 shows a typical overview from the VP (triggered by a message not shown in this diagram). The messages from the VP are in four sections. The first section comprises VP's introduction implying 'I think this might be useful', and an initial editorial. The second section is a selected message from a former student. The third section is questions one may ask the VP about this message. The final section is instructions on how to ask the questions in section three.

In the second message (Figure 16.5) a student has followed the instructions to ask the VP the first choice question. To do this the

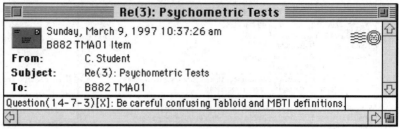

Figure 16.5. A student asks the VP a question

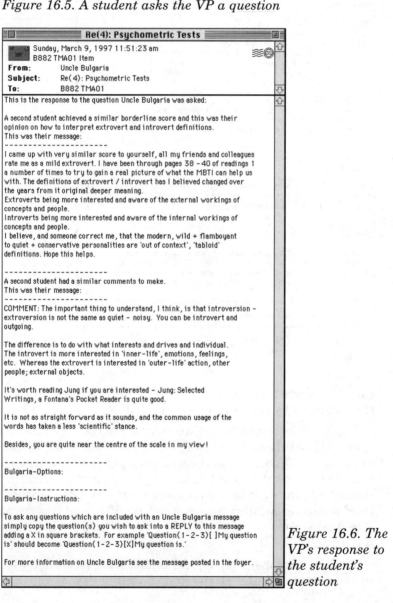

Figure 16.6. The VP's response to the student's question

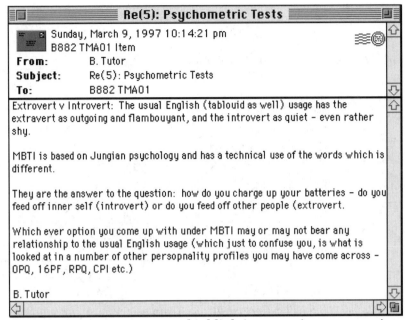

Figure 16.7. A tutor message highlighting some important points

student first creates a reply to the VP's message, which is automatically addressed to the conference, not the VP. The student then copies the question he or she wants to ask, placing an X in the box. This message is then posted to the conference.

The VP, reading all messages in this conference, picks up on this question and retrieves and posts a reply to the conference (Figure 16.6). In this case the reply contains two messages from previous years, with a short editorial for each. There are no questions available to ask about this message.

In the fourth message (Figure 16.7) a tutor has picked up on an important point from the VP's reply (Figure 16.6). This message from the tutor serves to highlight some important points from the VP's message.

This is the typical form of a VP interaction. In others, the students often ask more questions, and/or more than one student asks questions.

Application

Using the four-step process outlined in Table 16.1, we generated a case-base of interactions from the three previous years' conference discussions. For the first and second assignments this gave

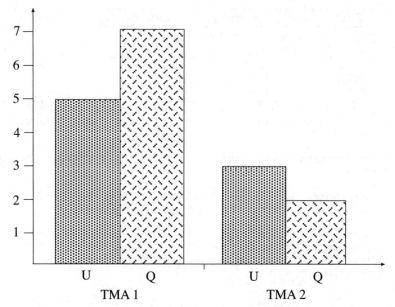

Figure 16.8. The Contributions from the VP in the conferences broken down by Tutor-Marked Assignment (TMA) numbers and unsolicited messages (U) vs. questions answered (Q)

us 9 and 16 unique stories consisting of a total of 40 and 51 messages respectively. The VP then used this case-base to match with the current year's discussions.

During the first two assignments the VP made 17 contributions to the discussions. As the experiment progressed some questions received by the VP were via private e-mail; the tutors agreed to let the VP place responses to these in the discussion conference. The breakdown of the VP's contributions is shown in Figure 16.8. There were eight unsolicited messages and nine responses to questions. Of the eight unsolicited messages six had between two and four fixed questions for further information. In total there were 132 messages on assignment 1 and 98 messages on assignment 2. The 'history' information stored by the VP allows us to study the number of students who have read these messages and thereby may have received some benefit from them. Of the 618 registered users 556 have logged in at least once, and of those 363 (65.3 per cent) have read one or more VP messages.

We were disappointed in the total number of messages sent by the VP. The retrieval algorithm was weaker than expected, and visual inspection of the conferences revealed discussions for which

VP failed to retrieve relevant stories. The same visual inspection confirmed that all retrieved cases were relevant to the context.

Evaluation

We surveyed students from the group of 363 who read at least nine VP messages. Of 120 who fit this criterion, we were forced to eliminate 16 (leaving 104) because they had already been surveyed by the university this year.

Of those surveyed we have had 40 returned questionaires, of which two claimed to have never read any VP messages. We asked questions about many of the aspects of the conferencing they had experienced. For the VP we asked them to rate the following statements as 'strongly agree', 'agree', 'disagree', and 'strongly disagree':

Uncle Bulgaria's messages...

1. contained useful information
2. were relevant to the discussion
3. answered questions I wanted to ask

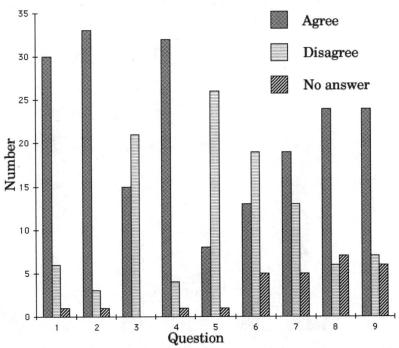

Figure 16.9. Number of students agreeing and disagreeing with statements about Uncle Bulgaria

4. provided a different viewpoint

5. put me off sending my own messages

6. I would prefer to ask UB questions directly by private e-mail, rather than through the conference.

7. The name Uncle Bulgaria is a good choice

8. Uncle Bulgaria should continue to be used on this course

9. I would like access to all the information UB has

These statements, except statement 5, were all positive and we were looking for agreement from the students (disagreement for statement 5). When we look at the results (Figure 16.9) we see large positive agreement with statements 1, 2, 4, 8, 9 and also 5 (because they disagreed with a negative statement).

When we look more closely at questions 3, 6 and 7 (Figure 16.10) a clearer picture emerges. In the case of question 3 there is a pretty even split between agree/disagree. We think that some respondents may have been slightly confused by this question taking it to mean 'answered questions that I asked' rather than 'answered questions that I wanted to ask'. Given the strong agreement with statements 1 and 2 we feel that the responses to this question are not a bad indication.

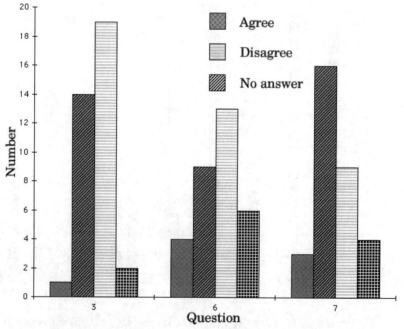

Figure 16.10. Distribution of answers for questions 3, 6 and 7

Question 6 however, is a different matter, because here a higher proportion of students tended to the extremes of 'strongly agree' or 'strongly disagree'. Some of the comments we received on the questionnaires indicated indifference amongst many of those on the agree/disagree boundary. From the answers to this question and the other feedback we have decided that asking questions directly by private e-mail is preferable, since asking questions in the conference is a distraction and generates unnecessary excess traffic.

Question 7 asks for an explicit opinion on the name of the VP. The majority of the opinons were favourable or indifferent, eg 'No feelings either way its just a name to recognize. Made me think of parrots!' However, there was some extreme negative reaction from some users, discussed in the following section.

In addition to the ranked statements we have some student comments and some anecdotal feedback from the conference discussions. These comments fall into four categories: VP name, presentation of the messages, content and context in which they were presented, and finally user confusion.

Name

Some users did not like the name 'Uncle Bulgaria' (UB). They felt that messages from that user implied 'you silly people, this topic was discussed and sorted out ages ago' [quote from a B882 student] and that 'the name had an adverse affect on what the objectives of UB were' [questionnaire comment]. Given the separate feedback we received and the specific dislike expressed we believe this is due not to the contents of the messages, but to the 'avuncular' presentation of the name. Students who were not native speakers did not make any comments on the name.

Presentation

The communication protocol available to the VP was limited to the use of plain text. The normal interface to the conferencing system provides much richer formatting. Users like to skim messages and plain text does not easily emphasize important information. One questionnaire comment was 'useful at times: continue with it, more "white space" on some please'. The conferencing system does not support threading so when more than one question was asked all replies would appear together.

Content and context

A B882 student said that 'Some of the contributions are appropriate, others are a tad on the side, but this may be useful as it may be providing a view from another angle.' A surveyed student commented that 'I felt UB helped structure/ensure good quality information in the conference. One of my criticisms of conferencing is that tutors (as they would in a real tutor group) do not control poor quality student input.' A B882 tutor noted 'I don't get the impression from the chat that people are very strongly negative about it, and a few people have responded to it over the weeks'. We feel these comments accurately summarize the tutor's and student's feelings about the VP's contributions.

User confusion

Finally we received comments to our survey of the form 'Did not find of any great use, and did not fully understand the concept – where was it explained?', and 'Was a bit confused what it was all about and had difficulty following the thread of discussion' [questionnaire comments]. In addition to our other motivations this has encouraged us to make the role and behaviour of the system much more clearly defined, and we feel these reasons are summarized by this final comment: 'It needs an unusual name so it is clear that it is not a student or a tutor. Unfortunately there are always some who do not read the messages explaining what UB is and then post a message asking "who is Uncle Bulgaria?"' [surveyed student].

We also received some feedback from the tutors who felt that they would like to know more about what information the VP had, and its current state of operation. We feel that the lack of this information led to a certain 'fear of the unknown' from the tutors.

Summary of evaluation

Our introductory work has raised a number of points that need to be considered.

- Even something as simple as the user name can provoke negative reactions.

- The format of messages should conform to the expectations of the users. Confusing formats reduce the impact of the information.

- Stories provide 'a view from another angle' that can be useful to the students.

The direct messages the VP has received have caused us to rethink our interaction model. Although we felt that having students ask questions in the conference helped others observe the interactions we feel that this has put off some students from asking questions and benefiting from the information available.

Current work

The second prototype of the VP is designed to enhance the existing system and extend its abilities to other areas. From our initial work and the feedback we have received we made a number of design choices to change the functioning of our system. These choices have been affected by our opinions on how the system benefits and can be controlled by its users.

We believe that the major stumbling blocks to the acceptance and use of this system are not technical but social. We need to address the social acceptance of the system by providing clear benefits to the tutors and the students. We believe that for the tutors to accept and make use of this system they need to be able to control it directly. In this way they will be in a better position to exploit the potential benefits of the system. For the students we currently only make available the information that the VP reveals during its interactions. However, in keeping with the idea of FAQs, we intend to make all the information available to those who wish to browse it in the future. We will still maintain the VP's presence within the conference, but with the added benefit of a digest.

To best understand how the VP compares with other systems and the changes being made to it, we return to Table 17.1 and consider the VP in terms of: interaction, format of cases, retrieval and maintenance.

Interaction with users

The design supports active interaction with the users. The VP identifies current topics and joins in opportunistically with suggestions. The users then ask questions to retrieve more information. For the next presentation, we intend to make the whole case-base available in a read only conference. This will take the form of a conventional FAQ and be called 'keypoints-digest'. There are three reasons for this: the course team would like an FAQ available for the students, it permits passive access to all information, and it will spread the maintenance load (see maintenance subsection below). We hope that in addition to these reasons the change in presentation to that of FAQs from previous tutors and students will address the earlier student comment that 'it must be made clear that it is not a student or a tutor' but rather a tool for presenting the experiences of their predecessors. To address this the VP will be known as 'keypoints', functioning as before, but allowing tutor intervention.

Format of cases

The format of the case-base was hidden in the initial implementation. When the VP identified a match, relevant cases were linked to current discussions. With the advent of 'keypoints-digest' the case-base will be open to those who are interested. However, the VP will continue to link cases from this with relevant discussions (see retrieval subsection below).

Retrieval

The retrieval algorithm is automatic. In addition the case-base will be opened to manual searching by the students, and the tutors will have control over the automatic retrieval algorithm. We are also thinking of introducing a refractory period – a time of waiting between the triggering of a message and its actually being sent. The intention here is to allow other development of the discussion to occur before the VP joins in – this would also permit the use of an 'approval' mechanism whereby the tutors are notified of the pending message and have the choice of interceding.

Manual retrieval through questioning is to be changed to direct e-mail to the VP rather than in-conference messages. The reply will go directly to the student, and if enough students are interested in specific questions, follow-up messages will be posted by the VP to the conference.

In addition to these changes we also aim to develop better retrieval algorithms, perhaps by using a case-based natural language system.

Maintenance

Maintenance is in the hands of the VP's administrator. With the case-base being open to the public it is intended to allow students and tutors to submit additions to be considered. This is the most important area where there needs to be a clear benefit to the students and tutors so that maintenance is actually carried out. To make sure that the submissions are suitable it will be necessary for a tutor to edit and approve them. There are two reasons for this: firstly, this helps keep the information current; secondly, everyone benefits in the following year because these answers will already be present. For the students, and tutors, we rely on a certain amount of altruism to make anonymous submissions (students in future could be rewarded, and attribution given for specific FAQs). Additionally the system can be used to identify possible additions to its case-base. The users are then asked if they would mind their message being added to the FAQ list and whether they would like to contribute anything else. This offers them the chance to make a permanent contribution to the course.

Tutors' assistant

The VP has always been intended to serve as a tutors' assistant. As we mentioned earlier, there are a number of tasks that tutors do that could be augmented or even automated by such a system. Our aim for doing this is to increase benefit to and motivation of the students. Experiences with asynchronous conferencing have highlighted two areas where the VP can help:

- welcoming students the moment they get on-line;
- structuring discussions by introducing topics at a preset time.

It has been found that greeting students and offering words of encouragement, even if initially automatic, helps improve their motivation and the likelihood that they continue to use conferencing (Salmon and Giles, 1997). We also believe, from our survey and other experience, that it is necessary to impose a structure on conferencing. There needs to be an obvious additional benefit over and above the ability to contact a wider range of people and leave messages. As we've seen in Chapters 4 and 6, the content must be of high quality and appropriate to the students, as this low bandwidth medium has to compete with the telephone and face-to-face contact.

With the second prototype we have taken into account the importance of showing a clear benefit to the users of the system. With the changes we have made, we hope to observe an increase in the use of the VP by the students, and in the use of the VP's assistant capabilities by the tutors. We hope that our next trial will prove successful enough for the VP to be fully adopted by B882 and other courses.

References

Ackerman, M and Malone, T (1990) 'Answer Garden: a tool for growing organisational memory', *Proceedings of the Conference on Office Information Systems,* ACM Press, New York.

Adamson-Macedo, C (1996) 'PCs, the bandwidth revolution and engineering curricula,' *IEEE Computing and Control Engineering Journal,* **7**, 3, pp 129–35.

Adkins, L and Adkins, R (1983) *The Handbook of British Archaeology,* Papermac – Macmillan, London.

Bailey, D, Brown, J and Kelly, P (1997) 'Academic advice, personal counselling and on-programme guidance in the Open University,' in *Personal tutoring and Advice in Focus,* Higher Education Quality Council, London.

Baker, J E, Cruz, I F, Liotta, G and Tamassia, R (1996) 'Algorithm animation over the World Wide Web', in *Proceedings of the International Workshop on Advanced Visual Interfaces,* ACM Press, New York.

Banecek, J, Drvota, J and Valasek, M (1997) TR-Encode-DccS-3-97, *Project Encode,* DccS Engineering, Prague.

Baron-Cohen, S, Tager-Flusberg, H and Cohen, D J (eds) (1993) *Understanding Other Minds: Perspectives From Autism,* Oxford University Press, Oxford.

Benjamins, V R (1993) *Problem Solving Methods for Diagnosis,* PhD Thesis, University of Amsterdam, Amsterdam.

Benjamins, V R and Fensel, D (1998) *Community is Knowledge! in (KA)2,* Paper submitted to Knowledge Acquisition Workshop 1998, WWW document, URL http://ksi.cpsc.ucalgary.ca/KAW98S/benjamins1

Benjamins, V R *et al.,* (1998) *IBROW3: An Intelligent Brokering Service for Knowledge-Component Reuse on the World Wide Web,* paper submitted to Knowledge Acquisition Workshop 1998. WWW document, URL http://ksi.cpsc.ucalgary.ca/KAW98S/benjamins3

Beresford, E (1968) *'The Wombles',* Benn, London.

Bieber, M *et al.,*(1997) 'Fourth Generation Hypermedia: Some Missing Links for the World Wide Web', in *World Wide Web Usability, Special Issue, Int. J. Human-Computer Studies,* Buckingham Shum, S and McKnight, C (eds), **47**, 1, pp 31–65.

Bing Software PhonePro (1998), WWW document, URL http://www.bingsoftware.com

Borst, P and Akkermans, H (1997) 'Engineering ontologies', *Int. Journal of Human–Computer Studies,* **46**, 2/3, pp 365-406.

Bradshaw, J M (ed) (1997) *Software Agents,* AAAIPress/MIT Press, Menlo Park, CA.

Brayshaw, M (1993) 'Intelligent Inference for debugging concurrent programs', in Marik, V (ed.) *Conference on Expert Systems and Database Applications (DEXA-93),* Springer-Verlag, Berlin.

Brayshaw, M and Eisenstadt, M (1991) 'A Practical Tracer for Prolog', *International Journal of Man-Machine Studies,* **42**, pp 597–631.

Brennan, S E (1990) 'Conversation as Direct Manipulation: An Iconoclastic View', in Laurel, B and Mountford, S J (eds), *The Art of Human-Computer Interface Design,* Addison-Wesley, Reading, MA.

Brown, J S and Duguid, P (1994) 'Borderline Issues: Social and Material Aspects of Design', *Human-Computer Interaction,* **9**, pp 3–36.

Brown, J S and Duguid, P (1996) 'The Social Life of Documents,' *First Monday,* 1, WWW document, URL http://www.firstmonday.dk/issues/issue1/documents

Brown, J S, Collins, A and Duguid, P (1989) 'Situated Cognition and the Culture of Learning', *Educational Researcher,* **18**, 1, pp 32–42.

Brown, M H (1988) *Algorithm Animation,* ACM Distinguished Dissertations, MIT Press, New York.

Brown, M H and Najork, M A (1996) 'Collaborative Active Textbooks: A web based algorithm animation system for an electronic classroom', in *Proceedings of IEEE Symposium on Visual Languages,* VL.

Brown, M H, Najork, M A and Raismo, R (1997) 'A Java-based implementation of collaborative active textbooks,' in *Proceedings of IEEE Symposium on Visual Languages,* VL '97, Capri, Italy.

Buckingham Shum, S (1996a) 'Analyzing the Usability of a Design Rationale Notation', in Moran, T P and Carroll, J M, *Design Rationale: Concepts, Techniques, and Use,* pp 185–215, Lawrence Erlbaum Associates, Hillsdale, NJ.

Buckingham Shum, S (1996b) 'Design Argumentation as Design Rationale,' *The Encyclopedia of Computer Science and Technology,* **35**, 20, pp 95–128, Marcel Dekker Inc, NY.

Buckingham Shum, S (1998) 'Negotiating the Construction of Organisational Memories', in Borghoff, U M and Pareschi, R (eds), *Information Technology for Knowledge Management,* pp 55-78, Springer, Berlin (Reprinted from: Journal of Universal Computer Science, Special Issue on Information Technology for Knowledge Management), **3**, 8, pp 899–928, WWW document URL http://www.iicm.edu/jucs_3_8

Buckingham Shum, S and Hammond, N (1994) 'Argumentation-Based Design Rationale: What Use at What Cost?', *International Journal of Human-Computer Studies,* **40**, 4, pp 603–52.

Buckingham Shum, S and McKnight, C (1997) (eds.) 'World Wide Web Usability: Special Issue', *Int. J. Human-Computer Studies,* **47**, 1, pp 1–222, WWW document, URL http://www.hbuk.co.uk/ap/ijhcs/webusability

Buckingham Shum, S and Sumner, T (1997) *Publishing, Interpreting and Negotiating Scholarly Hypertexts: Evolution of an Approach and Toolkit,* Technical Report KMi-TR-57, Knowledge Media Institute, Open University, Milton Keynes.

Buckingham Shum, S, MacLean, A, Bellotti, V and Hammond, N (1997) 'Graphical Argumentation and Design Cognition', *Human-Computer Interaction,* **12**, 3, pp 267–300.

Buñuel, L (1985) *My Last Breath,* Fontana, London.

Buxton, W (1997) 'Living in augmented reality: ubiquitous media and reactive environments', in Finn, K, Sellen, A and Wilber, S (eds) *Video Mediated Communication,* Erlbaum, Hillsdale, NJ. Also available as Web document, URL http://www.dgp.toronto.edu/OTP/papers/bill.buxton/augmentedReality.html

Byme, M D, Catramono, R and Staske, J T (1996) 'Do algorithm animations assist learning?' Graphics, Visulization and Usability Center, Georgia Institute of Technology, Technical Report GIT-GVLL-96-18.

Caporael, L R (1986) 'Anthropomorphism and Mechanomorphism: Two Faces of the Human Machine', *Computers in Human Behavior,* **2**, 3, pp 215–34.

Carr, L, Roure, D D, Hall, W and Hill, G (1995) 'The Distributed Link Service: A Tool for Publishers, Authors and Readers', in *Proceedings of WWW4: Fourth International World Wide Web*

Conference, Boston, MA (Dec. 11–14), WWW document , URL http://www.w3.org/Conferences/WWW4/Papers/178

Carswell, L (1997) 'Teaching via the Internet: the impact of the Internet as a communication medium on distance learning introductory Computing students', *ACM SIGCSE Bulletin* (Special Issue: *Proceedings of ITiCSE '97 – SIGCSE / SIGCUE Conference on Introducing Technology into Computer Science Education*), pp 1–5.

Chen, C (1997) 'Structuring and Visualising the WWW by Generalised Similarity Analysis,' in *Proceedings of The Eighth ACM Conference on Hypertext,* Southampton, pp 177–86, WWW document , URL http://journals.ecs.soton.ac.uk/~lac/ht97 /pdfs/chen.pdf

Chesnais, P R, Mucklo, M J and Sheena, J A (1998) 'The Fishwrap Personalized News System', WWW document, URL http://fishwrap-docs.www.media.mit.edu/docs/dev/CNGlue/ cnglue.html

Chi, M T H, Bassok, M Lewis, M, Reimam, P and Glaser, R (1989) 'Self-Explanations: How Students Study and Use Examples in Learning to Solve Problems', *Cognitive Science,* **13**, 2: pp 145–82.

Cimino, J J, Socratous, S A and Clayton, P D, (1995) 'Internet as a clinical information system: application development using the World-Wide Web', *Journal of the American Medical Informatics Association,* **2**, pp 273–84.

Coats, M, Leach, A, Lentell, H, Phillips, M and Scott, E (1992) *Open Teaching Toolkit: Effective Tutorials,* The Open University, Milton Keynes.

Collins, H M (1990) *Artificial Experts: Social Knowledge and Intelligent Machines,* MIT Press, Cambridge, MA.

Conklin, J and Begeman, M L (1988) *gIBIS: A Hypertext Tool for Exploratory Policy Discussion.* ACM Transactions on Office Information Systems, **6**, 4, pp 303–31.

Conway, M and Kahney, H (1987) *Transfer of learning in inference problems,* John Wiley, Chichester.

Crawley, R M (1997) *JISC Report, WWW document, URL* http:// spica.bton.ac.uk/cscl/jtap/paper2.htm

Crow, J G (1989) *Housesteads Roman Fort,* English Heritage, London.

Cutkosky, M R, Tenenbaum, J M and Glicksman, J (1996) 'Madefast: Collaborative Engineering over the Internet', *Communications of the ACM*, **39**, 9, pp 78–87.

Daniel, J S (1997) *Mega-universities and Knowledge Media: Technology Strategies for Higher Education,* Kogan Page, London.

Day, A (1996) *Romanticism,* Routledge, London.

Davis, R (1979) 'Interactive Transfer of Expertise: Acquisition of New Inference Rules', *Artificial Intelligence,* **12**, pp 121–58.

Dearing (1997) *'Higher Education in the Learning Society,'* National Committee of Inquiry into Higher Education, United Kingdom, WWW document, URL http://www.leeds.ac.uk/educol/ncihe

Dearing Report Discussion Website (1997) Knowledge Media Institute, The Open University, Milton Keynes, UK, WWW document, URL http://kmi.open.ac.uk/Dearing

December, J (1995) 'Editorial: Searching for Bob', *Computer-Mediated Communication Magazine,* **2**, 2, February 1995.

De Kerckhove, D (1997) *Connected Intelligence: the Arrival of the Web Society,* Rowland, W (ed.), Patrick Crean–Somerville House, Toronto.

Dennett, D C (1971) 'Intentional Systems,' *Journal of Philosophy,* **68**, pp 87–106.

DeRose, S J (1989) 'Expanding the Notion of Links', in *Proceedings of the Hypertext'89 Conference,* Pittsburgh, PA (Nov.), ACM Press, New York, pp 249–57.

DiGiano, C and Eisenberg, M (1995) 'Self-Disclosing Design Tools: A gentle introduction to end-user programming', *Symposium on Designing Interactive Systems (DIS '95),* Ann Arbor, MI (August 23–26), ACM Press, New York.

Domingue, J (1994) *The VITAL Visualization Tool Report [VITAL Report DD3.4.2],* The Knowledge Media Institute, The Open University, Milton Keynes.

Domingue, J (1998) *Tadzebao and WebOnto: Discussing, Browsing, and Editing Ontologies on the Web,* paper submitted to Knowledge Acquisition Workshop 1998, Banff, Canada. WWW document, URL http://ksi.cpsc.ucalgary.ca/KAW98S/domingue

Domingue, J, and Mulholland, P (1997a) 'Fostering Debugging Communities on the Web', *Communications of the ACM,* **40**, 4, pp 65–71, April, 1997.

Domingue, J and Mulholland, P (1997b) 'Teaching Programming at a Distance: The Internet Software Visualization Laboratory', *Journal of Interactive Media in Education,* **97**, 1, WWW document, URL http://www-jime.open.ac.uk/97/1

Domingue, J, Price, B and Eisenstadt, M (1992) 'Viz: a framework for describing and implementing software visualization systems', in Gilmore D and Winder R (eds) *User-Centred Requirements for Software Engineering Environments,* Springer-Verlag, pp 197–12.

Dossick, S E and Kaiser, G E (1996) 'WWW access to legacy client/server applications', *Computer Networks and ISDN Systems,* **28**, pp 931–40.

Duffy, T M and Jonassen, D H (1991) 'Constructivism: New Implications for Instructional Technology?', *Educational Technology,* **31**, 5, pp 7–12.

ECCTIS (1998) WWW document, URL http://www.ecctis.co.uk

Eisenstadt, M and Brayshaw, M (1988) 'The Transparent Prolog Machine (TPM): an execution model and graphical debugger for logic programming', *Journal of Logic Programming,* **5**, 4, pp 277–342.

Eisenstadt, M and Breuker, J (1992) 'Naive iteration: an account of the conceptualizations underlying buggy looping programs', in Eisenstadt, M, Keane, M T and Rajan, T (eds), *Novice Programming Environments: Explorations in Human-Computer Interaction and Artificial Intelligence,* LEA, Hove, UK.

Eisenstadt, M, Dixon, M and Kriwaczek, F (1988) *Intensive Prolog,* The Open University Press, Milton Keynes, UK.

Eisenstadt, M *et al.* (1996) 'Teaching, learning, and collaborating at a virtual summer school,' in Dix, A and Beale, R (eds) *Remote cooperation: CSCW issues for mobile and tele-workers,* Springer-Verlag, London.

Falasconi, S and Stefanelli, M (1994) 'A library of medical ontologies', in Mars, N (ed.), *Proceedings of the ECAI-94 Workshop on Comparison of Implemented Ontologies,* Amsterdam, August 1994, pp 81–91.

Feigenbaum, E A and McCorduck, P (1984) *The Fifth Generation: AI and Japan's Computer Challenge to the World,* Pan Books, London.

Fensel, D *et al.* (1998). *Ontobroker: transforming the WWW into a Knowledge Base,* Paper submitted to Knowledge Acquisition Workshop 1998. WWW document, URL http://ksi.cpsc.ucalgary. ca/KAW98S/fensel1

Fischer, G *et al.* (1991) 'Making Argumentation Serve Design', *Human-Computer Interaction,* **6**, 3/4, pp 393–419 [Reprinted in: Moran, T P and Carroll, J M (eds.) *Design Rationale: Concepts, Techniques, and Use,* (pp 267–93), Lawrence Erlbaum Associates, Hillsdale, NJ, 1996].

Fischer, G *et al.* (1991) *The Role of Critiquing in Cooperative Problem Solving* ACM Transactions on Information Systems, **9**, 2, pp 123–51.

Fischer, G *et al.* (1994) 'Seeding, Evolutionary Growth and Reseeding: Supporting the Incremental Development of Design Environments', in *Proceedings CHI 94: Conference on Human Factors in Computing Systems,* ACM Press, New York.

Ford, K *et al.* (1990) 'ICONKAT: An Integrated Constructivist Knowledge Acquisition Tool', *in Proceedings of the 5th Banff Knowledge Acquisition for Knowledge-Based Systems Workshop,* November 1990, pp 7.1–7.20.

Fung, P, Calder, J and Monteiro, B (1994) 'MOSS (Monitoring of Student Satisfaction): A report on completion of pilot research', *OU Student Research Centre Report 90,* IET, The Open University, Milton Keynes, UK.

Gaines, B R and Shaw, M L S (1995) 'Concept Maps as Hypermedia Components', *International Journal of Human-Computer Studies,* **43**, pp 323–61.

GDSS (1996) *QuestMap.* Group Decision Support Systems, Inc., 1000 Thomas Jefferson Street, NW, Suite 100, Washington, DC 20007, U.S.A, WWW document, URL http://www.gdss.com/OM. htm

Genesereth, M R and Ketchpel, S P (1994) Software Agents, *Communications of the ACM,* **37**, pp 48–53.

Goldberg, A, Abell, S and Leibs, D (1997) 'The LearningWorks Development and Delivery Frameworks', *Communications of the ACM,* **40**, 10, pp 78–81.

Gonzalez, A J and Dankel, D J (1993) *The Engineering of Knowledge-based Systems: Theory and Practice.* Prentice-Hall International, Englewood Cliffs, NJ.

Gruber, T R (1993) 'A Translation Approach to Portable Ontology Specifications', *Knowledge Acquisition,* **5**, pp 199–220.

Grudin, J (1996) 'Evaluating Opportunities for Design Capture', in Moran, T P and Carroll J M, *Design Rationale: Concepts, Techniques, and Use,* pp 453–70, Lawrence Erlbaum Associates, Hillsdale, NJ.

Haajanen, J *et al.* (1997) 'Animation of user algorithms on the web', in *Proceedings of IEEE Symposium on Visual Languages,* VL '97, Capri, Italy.

Harvey, D (1990) *The Condition of Postmodernity: an Enquiry into the Origins of Cultural Change,* Blackwells, Cambridge, MA.

Hassan, I (1986) 'Pluralism in Postmodern Perspective', *Critical Inquiry,* **12**, pp 503–20.

Hayes-Roth, F, Waterman, D A and Lenat, D (1983) *Building Expert Systems,* Addison-Wesley, Reading, MA.

Headliner (1998) WWW document, URL http://www.headliner. com

Hill, J N (1994) 'Prehistoric cognition and the science of archaeology', in Renfrew, C and Zubrow, E B W (eds), *The Ancient Mind,* Cambridge UP, Cambridge.

Hodder, I (1982) *The Present Past: An Introduction to Anthropology for Archaeologists,* Batsford Ltd, London.

HyperNews NCSA: *National Center for Supercomputing Applications,* Univ. Illinois, Urbana-Champaign, WWW document, URL http://union.ncsa.uiuc.edu/HyperNews/get/ hypernews.html

Jameson, F (1993) 'Postmodernism, or the Cultural Logic of Late Capitalism', in Docherty, T (ed), *Postmodernism: A Reader,* pp62–92, Harvester Wheatsheaf, Hemel Hempstead.

Jennison, K (1996) *CoSy takes the distance out of distance learning; the computer-mediated campus,* Open University, London Papers, January.

JIIG-CAL (1997) Careers Research Centre, University of Edinburgh, 5 Buccleuch Place, Edinburgh, UK.

JIME: *Journal of Interactive Media in Education*. Knowledge Media Institute, Open University, WWW document, URL http://www-jime.open.ac.uk

Joiner, R, Messer, D, Light, P and Littleton, K (1995) 'Peer interaction and peer presence in computer-based problem-solving', *Cognition and Instruction*, Vol **13**, 4, pp 583–84.

Joiner, R, Messer, D, Light, P and Littleton, K (1996) 'Gender, computer experience and computer-based problem-solving', *Computers and Education*, **26**, 1-3, pp 179–87.

Jonassen, D H *et al.* (1993) 'Constructivist Uses of Expert Systems to Support Learning', *Journal of Computer-Based Instruction*, **20**, 3, pp 86–94.

Joukowsky, M (1980) *A Complete Manual of Field Archaeology: Tools and Techniques of Field Work for Archaeologists*, Prentice-Hall, Englewood Cliffs, NJ.

Kamba *et al.* (1997) 'Anatagonomy: a personalised newspaper on the world wide web', *International Journal of Human-Computer Studies*, **46**, 789–803.

Kay, A (1972) *Personal Communication*.

Kay, A (1990) 'User Interface: A Personal View', in Laurel, B and Mountford, S G (eds), *The Art of Human-Computer Interface Design*, pp 191–207, Addison-Wesley, Reading, MA.

Kay, A and Goldberg, A (1977) 'Personal Dynamic Media', *Computer*, **10**, 3, pp 31–41.

Kemppainen, E, Gjoderum, J and Martin, M (1995) Legislation as a Support for Telecommunications Availability and Accessibility, in Roe, P W R (ed.) *Telecommunications for All*, Commission of the European Communities, COST 219.

Kolb, D (1997) 'Scholarly Hypertext: Self-Represented Complexity', in *Proceedings of The Eighth ACM Conference on Hypertext*, Southampton, pp 29–37, WWW document, URL http://journals.ecs.soton.ac.uk/~lac/ht97/pdfs/kolb.pdf

Kozierok, R and Maes, P (1993) *A Learning Interface Agent for Scheduling Meetings*, Paper presented at the ACM SIGCHI International Workshop on Intelligent User Interfaces, Orlando, Florida.

LaLiberte, D and Stegall, N (1998) *Web Mastery*. WWW document URL http://www.hypernews.org/HyperNews/get/www/html/guides.html

Landow, G P (1992) *Hypertext: The Convergence of Contemporary Critical Theory and Technology*, John Hopkins University Press, Baltimore/London.

Large, A *et al.* (1995) 'Multimedia and comprehension – the relationship among text, animation and captions', *Journal of the American Society for Information*, **46**, 5, pp 340–47.

Laurel, B (1990) 'Interface Agents: Metaphors With Character', in Laurel, B and Mountford, S J (eds), *The Art of Human-Computer Interface Design*, pp 355–65, Addison-Wesley.

Laurel, B (1991) *Computers as Theatre*, Addison-Wesley, Reading, Massachusetts.

Laurel, B, Oren, T and Don, A (1990) 'Issues in Multimedia Interface Design: Media Integration and Interface Agents', *Human Factors in Computing Systems (CHI '90)*, Seattle, WA (April 1–5), ACM Press.

Laurillard, D (1993) *Rethinking University Teaching: A Framework for the Effective Use of Educational Technology*, Routledge, London.

Laurillard, D (1995) 'Multimedia and the changing experience of the learner', *British Journal of Educational Technology*, **26**, 3, pp 179–89.

Lawrence, A W, Badre, A M and Stasko, J T (1994) 'Empirically evaluating the use of animations to teach algorithms', in *Proceedings of IEEE Symposium on Visual Languages*, VL 94, St Louis.

Luke, S, Spector, L and Rager, D (1996) 'Ontology-Based Knowledge Discovery on the World-Wide Web', in *Proceedings of the Workshop on Internet-Based Information Systems*, AAAI-96, Portland, Oregon.

Lyotard, J F (1984) *The Postmodern Condition: A Report on Knowledge*, Manchester UP, Manchester.

Machin, D and Sheppard, P (1997) 'A computer vision system for natural communication', *British Telecommunications Engineering*, **16**, 1, pp 45–8.

McKerlie, D and MacLean, A (1994) 'Reasoning with Design Rationale: Practical Experience with Design Space Analysis', *Design Studies*, **15**, 2, pp 214–26.

McKillop, C (1997) *On-line study guides for distance education students: can 'advisor' agents help?*, School of Cognitive and

Computing Science, University of Sussex (also available as a Knowledge Media Institute Technical Report, KMI-TR-55).

Maes, P (1994) 'Agents that Reduce Work and Information Overload', *Communications of the ACM,* **37**, 7, July.

Maher, M L, Balachandran, M B and Zhang, D M (1995) *Case-Based Reasoning in Design,* Lawrence Erlbaum Associates, Mahwah, NJ.

Mandinach, E B and Cline, H F (1996). 'Classroom dynamics: the impact of a technology-based curriculum innovation on teaching and learning', *Journal of Educational Computing Research,* Vol **14**, 1, pp 83–102.

Marcus S (ed) (1988) *Automatic Knowledge Acquisition for Expert Systems,* Kluwer Academic, Boston, MA.

Mason, R (1994) *Using Communications Media in Open and Flexible Learning,* Kogan Page, London.

Mason, R (1998) *Globalizing Education: Trends and Applications,* Routledge, London.

Masterton, S J (1997) 'The Virtual Participant: Lessons to be learned from a case-based tutors assistant', *Proceedings of Computer Supported Collaborative Learning,* Toronto 10–14 December.

Milewski, A E and Lewis, S H (1997) 'Delegating to software agents', *International Journal of Human-Computer Studies,* **46**, pp 485–500.

Motta, E (1997) 'Trends in Knowledge Modelling: Report on the 7th KEML Workshop', *The Knowledge Engineering Review,* **12**, 2, June.

Motta, E (1998a) 'An Overview of the OCML Modelling Language', *8th Workshop on Knowledge Engineering: Methods and Languages (KEML'98),* pp 21–2, Karlsruhe, Germany, January.

Motta, E (1998b) *Reusable Components for Knowledge Models,* PhD Thesis, Knowledge Media Institute, The Open University, UK. WWW document, URL http://kmi.open.ac.uk/people/motta/thesis.html

Motta, E and Zdrahal, Z (1996) 'Parametric Design Problem Solving', *Proceedings of the 10th KAW* (Gaines, B and Musen, M, eds), Banff, Canada.

Motta, E and Zdrahal, Z (1997) 'An Approach to the Organization of a Library of Problem Solving Methods which Integrates the Search Paradigm with Task and Method Ontologies', to appear in *International Journal of Human-Computer Studies*. WWW document, URL http://kmi.open.ac.uk/~enrico/papers/ijhcs_psm.ps.gz

Mulholland, P (1997) 'Using a Fine-Grained Comparative Evaluation Technique to Understand and Design Software Visualization Tools', *Empirical Studies of Programmers*, ACM Press, Washington DC, USA.

Mulholland, P (1998) 'A principled approach to the evaluation of Software Visualization: a case-study in Prolog', in Brown, M, Domingue, J, Price, B and Stasko, J (eds), *Software Visualization: Programming as a mutli-media experience*, MIT Press, Cambridge, MA.

Mulholland, P and Eisenstadt, M (1998) 'Using Software to Teach Computer Programming: Past, Present and Future,' in Brown, M, Domingue, J, Price, B and Stasko, J (eds), *Software Visualization: Programming as a mutli-media experience*, MIT Press, Cambridge, MA.

Multicosm Ltd: *Webcosm*. WWW document, URL http://www.webcosm.com

Nass, C, Steuer, J, and Tauber, E R (1994) *Computers are Social Actors*, paper presented at the CHI'94.

Newell, A (1982) 'The Knowledge Level', *Artificial Intelligence*, **18**, pp 87–127.

Nicaise, M and Barnes, D (1996) 'The Union of Technology, Constructivism, and Teacher Education', *Journal of Teacher Education*, **47**, pp 205–12.

Nixon, T and Salmon, G (1995) 'Spinning your web: Interactive computer-mediated conferencing - its potential for learning and teaching in higher education', in *Proceedings of the Society for Research into Higher Education annual conference*, Edinburgh 12–14 December.

Nixon, T and Salmon, G (1996) 'Computer mediated learning and its potential', in Mills, R and Tait, A (eds) *Supporting Open Learners*, Pitman, London.

Nonaka, I and Takeuchi, H (1995) *The Knowledge Creating Company: How Japanese Companies Create the Dynamics of Innovation*, Oxford UP, Oxford.

Norman, D A (1993) *Things That Make Us Smart*, Addison-Wesley, Reading, MA.

Nunberg, G (ed) (1996) *The Future of the Book*, University of California Press, Berkeley.

Okerson, A and O'Donnell, J (eds) (1995) *Scholarly Journals at the Crossroads: A Subversive Proposal for Electronic Publishing (An Internet Discussion About Scientific and Scholarly Journals and Their Future),* Washington, DC: Association of Research Libraries, WWW document, URL http://cogsci.ecs.soton.ac.uk/~harnad/subvert.html

Pain, H and Bundy, A (1987) 'What stories should we tell novice PROLOG programmers?' in Hawley, R (ed), *Artificial Intelligence Programming Environments,* Ellis Horwood, Chichester, UK.

Parsons, J J and Oja, D (1996) *New Perspectives in Computer Concepts – Comprehensive Edition,* 2nd edition, International Thompson Publishing, Albany.

Pask, G (1975) *Conversation, Cognition and Learning,* Elsevier, London.

Peek, R and Newby, G (eds) (1996) *Scholarly Publication: The Electronic Frontier,* MIT Press, Cambridge MA.

Perkins, D N (1991) Technology meets Constructivism: Do they make a marriage? *Educational Technology,* **31**, 5, pp 18–23.

Petre, M and Price, B (1997) 'Teaching programming though paperless assignments: an empirical evaluation of instructor feedback,' *ACM SIGCSE Bulletin (Special Issue: Proceedings of ITiCSE '97 – SIGCSE / SIGCUE Conference on Introducing Technology into Computer Science Education)* pp 94–9.

Phillips, M and Harrington, S (1998) 'Educational Counselling through E-mail and Computer Conferencing – A Toolkit for Tutors', *Canadian Conference for Distance Education,* Banff, May.

Phillips M, Scott P and Fage, J (1988) 'Towards a strategy for the use of new technology in student guidance and support', *Open Learning,* May.

Pilgrim, C J, and Leung, Y K (1996) 'Appropriate use of the Internet in Computer Science courses', *ACM SIGCSE Bulletin, 28 (Special Issue: Proceedings of ITiCSE '96 – SIGCSE / SIGCUE Conference on Introducing Technology into Computer Science Education),* pp 81–6.

PlainTalk (1998) WWW document, URL http://www.speech.apple.com/speech/ptk

Plowman, L (1996) 'Narrative, interactivity and the secret world of multimedia', *The English and Media Magazine,* (Autumn), **35**, pp 44–8.

PointCast (1998) WWW document, URL http://www.pointcast.com

Postman, N (1993) *Technopoly: The Surrender of Culture to Technology,* Vintage Random House, New York.

Prawat, R S and Floden, R E (1994) 'Philosophical Perspectives on Constructivist Views of Learning', *Educational Psychology,* **29**, 1, pp 37–48.

Price, B and Petre, M (1997) 'Large-scale interactive teaching via the Internet: experience with problem sessions and practical work in university courses', *Proceedings of ED-MEDIA / ED-TELECOM '97 Conference,* Calgary, Canada.

Rabinow, P (1986) *The Foucault Reader,* Penguin, London.

Ramoni, M and Riva, A (1993) 'Belief maintenance with probabilistic logic', in *Proceedings of the AAAI Fall Symposium on Automated Deduction in Non Standard Logics,* AAAI, Raleigh, NC.

Reinhardt, A (1995) 'New ways to learn,' *Byte,* **20**, 3, 50.

Resnick, P and Varian, H R (1997) 'Recommender Systems', guest editors 'special section: recommendation systems' in *CACM,* March, **40**, 3, pp 56–8.

Rice, J *et al.* (1995) 'Lessons learned using the Web as an application interface', *Knowledge Systems Laboratory Technical Report KSL-95-69,* Department of Computer Science, Stanford University.

Rieber, L P (1990) 'Animation in computer-based instruction', *Educational Technology, Research and Development,* **38**, 1, pp 77–86.

Rieber, L P (1991) 'Animation, incidental learning and continuing motivation', *Journal of Educational Psychology,* **83**, 3, pp 318–28.

Riva, A and Bellazzi, R (1996) 'Current AI Technologies for Distributed Patient Management', in *Proceedings of the AAAI Spring Symposium on Artificial Intelligence in Medicine,* Stanford, CA.

Riva, A and Ramoni, M (1996) 'LispWeb: a Specialized HTTP Server for Distributed AI Applications', *Computer Networks and ISDN Systems,* **28**, 7–11, pp 953–61. (Also available at WWW document, URL http://kmi.open.ac.uk/~marco/papers/www96/www96.html).

Riva, A, Bellazzi, R and Stefanelli, M (1997) 'A Web-based system for the intelligent management of diabetic patients', *M. D. Computing*, **14**, 5, pp 360–64, Nov.

Rowntree, D (1992) *Exploring Open and Distance Learning*, Kogan Page, London.

Salmon, G and Giles, K (1997) *'Moderating On Line.'* Online Educa Conference, Berlin, 29–31 October.

Scaife, M and Rogers,Y (1996) 'How do graphical representations work?', *Int. J. Human-Computer Studies*, **45**, pp 185–213.

Schank, R C and Cleary C (1995) *Engines for Education*, Lawrence Erlbaum Associates.

Schreiber, G, Wielinga, B, Hoog, de R, Akkermans, H and Van de Velde, W (1994) 'CommonKADS: A comprehensive methodology for KBS development', *IEEE Expert*, **9**, 6, December, pp 28–37.

Scott, P *et al.* (1996) 'A computer based student welfare information support and help system', in Carlson, P and Makedon, F (eds) *Proceedings of Educational Multimedia and Hypermedia 96*, AACE, Charlottesville, VA.

Shipman, F M and McCall, R (1994) 'Supporting Knowledge-Base Evolution with Incremental Formalization', Proc. CHI'94: *Human Factors in Computing Systems, Boston, Mass*, pp 285–91, ACM Press, New York.

Shipman, F M and Marshall, C C (1994) *Formality Considered Harmful: Experiences, Emerging Themes, and Directions.* Technical Report ISTL-CSA-94-08-02, Xerox Palo Alto Research Center, CA. WWW document, URL http://bush.cs.tamu.edu:80/~shipman/formality-paper/harmful.html

Skillicorn, D B (1996) 'Using distributed hypermedia for collaborative learning in universities', *Computer Journal*, **39**, 6, pp 471–82.

Smith, R B (1987) 'The alternate reality kit: an example of the tension between literalism and magic', in *Proceedings of CHI + GI, Toronto*, April 5–9.

Soper, J (1997) 'Integrating Interactive Media in Courses: The WinEcon Software with Workbook Approach', in *Journal of Interactive Media in Education*, **97**, 2, WWW document, URL http://www-jime.open.ac.uk/97/2

Star, S L and Griesemer, J R (1989) 'Institutional Ecology, 'Translations' and Boundary Objects: Amateurs and

Professionals in Berkeley's Museum of Vertebrate Zoology, 1907–39', *Social Studies of Science,* **19**, pp 387–420.

Stasko, J T (1996) *Using student-built algorithm animations as learning aids,* Graphics, Visualization and Usability Center, Georgia Institute of Technology, Technical Report GIT-GVU-96-19.

Stasko, J T and Kraemer, E (1993) 'A Methodology for Building Application-Specific Visualizations of Parallel Programs', *Journal of Parallel and Distributed Computing,* **18**, 2, pp 258–64.

Stasko, J, Badre, A and Lewis, C (1993) 'Do algorithm animations assist learning? An empirical study and analysis', in *Proceedings of INTERCHI '93,* Addison-Wesley, Reading, MA.

Steeples, C *et al.* (1996) 'Technological support for teaching and learning: computer-mediated communications in higher education (CMC in HE)', *Computers and Education,* **26**, 1–3, pp 71–80.

Stefik, M (1986) 'The Next Knowledge Medium', *AI Magazine,* **7**, 1, pp 34–46.

Stefik, M (1995) *Introduction to Knowledge Systems,* Morgan Kaufmann, San Francisco.

Stefik, M, Foster, G, Bobrow, D G, Kahn, K, Lanning, S and Suchman, L (1987) 'Beyond the chalkboard: computer support for collaboration and problem solving in meetings', in *Communications of the ACM,* **30**, 1, pp 32–47.

Stratfold, M (1997) *Editing text in a MIAW,* WWW document, URL http://www.mcli.dist.maricopa.edu/director/tips/miaw/edit-text. html part of the Director Web site WWW document, URL http://www.mcli.dist.maricopa.edu/director

Stutt, A (1987) *Second Generation Expert Systems, Explanations, Arguments and Archaeology,* Technical Report No. 25, HCRL, The Open University, Milton Keynes.

Stutt, A (1997) 'Knowledge Engineering Ontologies, Constructivist Epistemology, Computer Rhetoric: A Trivium for the Knowledge Age,' in *Proceedings of Ed-Media'97,* Calgary, Canada, June.

Suchman, L A (1987) *Plans and Situated Actions: The Problem of Human-Machine Communication,* Cambridge University Press, Cambridge.

Sumner, T (1995) 'The High-Tech Toolbelt: A Study of Designers in the Workplace', *Human Factors in Computing Systems (CHI '95)*, Denver, CO (May 7–11), ACM Press, New York.

Sumner, T and Buckingham Shum, S (1998) 'From Documents to Discourse: Shifting Conceptions of Scholarly Publishing', in *Proceedings CHI 98: Human Factors in Computing Systems*, Los Angeles, CA, ACM Press, New York.

Sumner, T and Taylor, J (1998) 'New Media, New Practices: Experiences in Open Learning Course Design', *Human Factors in Computing Systems (CHI '98)*, Los Angeles (April 18–23), ACM Press, New York.

Sumner, T R, Bonnardel, N and Kallak Harstad, B (1997) 'The Cognitive Ergonomics of Knowledge-Based Design Support Systems', in *Proceedings CHI'97: Conference on Human Factors in Computing Systems*, Atlanta, Georgia (March 22–27), pp 83–90. ACM Press, New York.

Sumner, T, Taylor, J and McKillop, C (1997) *Developmental Testing of the M206 Interactive Course Map*, Knowledge Media Institute, Technical Report KMI-TR-49, The Open University, Milton Keynes.

Sycara, K and Zeng, D (1994) *Visitor-Hoster: Towards an Intelligent Electronic Secretary*, paper presented at the CIKM-94 (International Conference on Information and Knowledge Management) workshop on Intelligent Information Agents.

Tait, K (1994) 'Discourse: the design and production of simulation-based learning environments', in Jong, T de and Sarti, L, *Design and production of multimedia and simulation-based learning material*, Kluwer, Dordrecht.

Taylor, J, Sumner, T and Law, A (1997) 'Talking about Multimedia: A Layered Design Framework', *The Journal of Educational Media*, **23**, 2 and 3, 215–41, (also available as a Knowledge Media Institute Technical Report, KMI-TR-53).

Terveen, L G, Selfridge, P G and Long, M D (1993) 'From "Folklore" to "Living Design Memory"', in *Proceedings of InterCHI 93: Conference on Human Factors in Computing Systems*, pp 15–22, ACM Press, New York.

Thagard, P (1997) *Collaborative Knowledge, Noûs*, **31**, 2, pp 242–61.

Thomas, P et al. (1996) 'Distance education over the Internet', *ACM SIGCSE Bulletin, 28 (Special Issue: Proceedings of*

ITiCSE '96 – SIGCSE/SIGCUE Conference on Introducing Technology into Computer Science Education), pp 147–49.

Trigg, R H (1983) *A Network Based Approach to Text Handling for the Online Scientific Community,* Doctoral Thesis (University Microfilms #8429934), University of Maryland.

Turoff, M, Rao, U and Hiltz, S R (1991) 'Collaborative Hypertext in Computer-Mediated Communications', in *Proceedings of the 24th Hawaii International Conference on System Sciences,* Volume IV, pp 357–66, IEEE Computer Society.

US Department of Justice (1990) Americans with Disabilities Act, WWW document, URL http://www.usdoj.gov/crt/ada/adahom1.htm

Valente, A and Breuker, J A (1996) 'Towards Principled Core Ontologies,' in *Proceedings of the 10th Banff Knowledge Acquisition for Knowledge-Based Systems Workshop.*

van de Velde, W (1994) 'Issues in Knowledge Level Modelling,' in *Proceedings of the 8th Banff Knowledge Acquisition for Knowledge-Based Systems Workshop,* **2**, 38, pp 1–38.11.

Vincent, T (1994) Distance Teaching and Visually Impaired Students: An Electronic Environment for Learning, *in All Our Learning Futures: The Role of Technology in Education,* SCET, Glasgow.

Vincent, T and Taylor, M (1995) Access to Books for Visually Impaired Learners, in Heap, N W et al (eds) *Information Technology and Society,* Sage, London.

W3C *World Wide Web Consortium (1997) Metadata and Resource Description.* WWW document, URL http://www.w3.org/Metadata

Watt, S N K (1993) *Role Conflict in Groupware,* Paper presented at the First International Conference on Intelligent Cooperative Information Systems, Rotterdam, Netherlands.

Watt, S N K (1996) Naive Psychology and the Inverse Turing Test, *Psycoloquy,* **14**, 7.

Watt, S N K (1997) Artificial Societies and Psychological Agents, *British Telecom Technology Journal,* **14**, 4.

WebCast (1998) *Astound Incorporated,* WWW document, URL http://www.astoundinc.com/products/webcast/webcast.html

Whalley, P (1998) WWW document, URL http://met.open.ac.uk/

Whalley, P (1994) Control Technology, in *Computer Based Learning: Potential and Practice*, David Fulton Publishers, London.

Whalley, P (1995) 'Imagining with Multimedia', *British Journal of Educational Technology*, **26**, 3, pp 190–204.

Whiten, A (ed) (1991) *Natural Theories of Mind: Evolution, Development and Simulation of Everyday Mindreading*. Basil Blackwell, Oxford.

Wideman, H H and Owston, R D (1993) 'Knowledge Base Construction as a Pedagogical Activity', *J. Educational Computing Research*, **9**, 2, pp 165–96.

Wielinga B J and Breuker, J (1986) 'Models of Expertise', in *Proceedings of the 7th European Conf*, on AI, Vol 1, Brighton, July, pp 306–18.

Wild, G and Hinton, R (1992) *Requirements of Tactile Diagrams for Visually Impaired Students in Higher Education*, Educare (Skill), No.42.

Winer, D (1998) Dave Winer's scripting page, WWW document, URL http://www.scripting.com/dwiner

Winograd, T and Flores, F (1986) *Understanding Computers and Cognition: A New Foundation for Design*, Addison-Wesley, Reading, MA.

Woodman, M and Holland, S (1996) *From Software User To Software Author: An Initial Pedagogy For Introductory Object-Oriented Computing*, First ACM SIGCSE/SIGCUE Conference on Integrating Technology into Computer Science Education, Barcelona (June).

Woolley, D (1998) *Conferencing on the World Wide Web, WWW document*, URL http://thinkofit.com/webconf

Zdrahal, Z and Motta, E (1996) 'Case-Based Problem Solving Methods for Parametric Design Tasks', in *Advances in Case-Based Reasoning*, Smith, I and Faltings, B (eds), Springer, pp 473–86.

Index

(software titles are shown in italics)

140

direct manipulation authoring environment 184
Director 53, 59, 82, 83
DirectX 53
disability 31
Disability Discrimination Act 44
disabled 3, 41
  learner 45
  people 45
  students 33, 36
discussion 258
  groups 250
  leader 131
  lists 141
  space 143
  threads 249
distance
  education 25, 63, 67, 81, 97, 98, 130, 186
  learning 23, 65, 135
  learning environment 98
  teaching 100
  training 42
distributed learning 25
document 137
  annotations 141
domain
  expert 6
  ontology 219
  specific agents 247
  vocabulary 220
DynaBook 242
dynamic
  resources 223
  systems simulation 227
  thumb-nails 42

e-journal 135, 137, 141
e-mail 14, 26, 54, 67, 68, 82, 92, 103, 104, 106, 110, 132, 137, 141, 154, 185, 188, 230, 250, 258
  dialogue 244
  lists 138, 174
earth sciences 38
EBBS 126
editor 139, 147
educational resources 223

electronic
  assignment handling 13, 97, 98, 101, 112, 115
  communication 65, 100, 105, 113
  conferencing 249, 250, 253
  examination 101
  journals 137
  mail; *see* email
  marking 98, 112
  presentation 110
  problem sessions 113
  troubleshooting 52
  tuition 111
  workbook 130
Electronic Environment for Learning 31
email; *see* e-mail
empirical studies 187
enabling technologies 32, 43
encoding 151, 195
epistemic engineering 213
epistemification 211
evaluation 108, 131, 187, 253, 259
examination 98, 101, 162
experiential 69
experiment mode 58
expert systems 211, 214
explicador 72, 75, 76
Extended Bulletin Board System (EBBS) 123

face-to-face
  teaching 124
  tuition 81
  tutorial 110, 112, 113
FAQ (frequently asked question) 104, 121, 133, 263
feedback 67, 99, 100, 112, 115, 132, 188
Fight Sail 53
firewalls 171
First Flight 41
FirstClass 36, 91, 92, 128, 156, 250
follow-up messages 264
forms 102, 103
FORMSCORE 81
forum 10, 14, 136
frameset 143
front page 176, 181

journalists 175, 179
Jsamba 196

(KA)2 218, 221
keyboard 32
  emulator 32
keypoints 263
KMi Planet 202, 209
KMi Stadium 28, 29, 76
knowledge 5, 66, 136, 225
  acquisition 214
  acquisition community 221
  age 211, 213, 223
  -based economies 63
  bases 208
  capture 6
  communities 213
  contextualized 10
  -creating company 212
  directors 212
  discovery 212
  economy 212
  engineer 6
  engineering 211, 214
  media 1, 3, 4, 17, 24, 211
  models 215
  level 214, 216, 217
  management 16, 150, 211, 212
  Media Institute 2, 3, 4, 27, 179
  mining 211
  model 219
  modelling 3, 16, 184, 211, 214,
    215, 222
  navigator 242
  production 223
  representation 3, 16, 202
  resources 212, 215
  sharing 217, 220, 235
  society 7
  source 215
  systems 9, 15, 16, 211, 212, 214
  workers 16, 211
  web 151, 222, 248
Knowledge Media 1, 3, 4, 17, 24,
  211
Knowledge Media Institute 2, 3, 4,
  27, 179
Knowledge Navigator 242
Knowledge Web 151, 222, 248

Law of the Telecosm 28
learner(s) 49, 122, 128, 132
  dialogues 14
learning 2, 217, 220
  conversations 60
  environments 6, 63
  lifelong 63
  resources 65, 74
  skills 80
LearningBook 72, 74
Learning.Org 165
library 247
link 143, 151
Lisp 15, 173, 193
  ANSI standard Common
    Lisp 205
  Common Lisp 202
  Common Lisp HTTP protocol 230
LispView 205
LispWeb 15, 173, 193, 202, 209, 230
Logic-based BMS (LBMS) 205
longitudinal testing 69
Luigi 10, 209, 243, 244
lurk(ers) 113, 134
Lyceum 169, 171
Lycos 239
Lynx 45

MA in Open and Distance Education
  130
Mac OS 59
Macintosh 120, 169
mailing list 174, 181 (see e-mail)
management systems 137
mapping 195, 227
mark-up 140
marking 164, 188
marking tool 101
Mars Buggy 39
Marscape 39
master classes 14
Maven of the Month 157
MBA 162
media 63, 65, 75, 81, 211, 239; *see
  also* knowledge; intelligent
meeting
  management/planning/schedul-
  ing 243, 244, 246